The Democratic Virtues of the Christian Right

The Democratic Virtues
of the Christian Right

Jon A. Shields

PRINCETON UNIVERSITY PRESS

PRINCETON AND OXFORD

Published by Princeton University Press, 41 William Street,
Princeton, New Jersey 08540
In the United Kingdom: Princeton University Press, 6 Oxford Street,
Woodstock, Oxfordshire OX20 1TW
Library of Congress Cataloging-in-Publication Data

Shields, Jon A.
The democratic virtues of the Christian right / by Jon A. Shields.
p.   cm.
Includes bibliographical references and index.
ISBN 978-0-691-13740-7 (hardcover : alk. paper)
1. Christian conservatism—United States. 2. Religious right—United States.
3. Christianity and politics—United States. 4. United States—
Politics and government—21st century. I. Title.
BR516.S485 2009
322.4′40973—dc22
2008027808

British Library Cataloging-in-Publication Data is available.

This book has been composed in Sabon

Printed on acid-free paper. ∞

press.princeton.edu

Printed in the United States of America

10 9 8 7 6 5 4 3 2 1

IN MEMORY OF MY FATHER

John R. Shields, who taught me to approach strangers with charity and an open mind.

Contents

List of Tables and Figures   ix

Acknowledgments   xi

INTRODUCTION   1

CHAPTER ONE
Democratic Education in the Christian Right   19

CHAPTER TWO
Christian Radicalism   46

CHAPTER THREE
The Varieties of Pro-Life Activism   68

CHAPTER FOUR
Deliberation and Abortion Politics   100

CHAPTER FIVE
Reviving Participatory Democracy   '115

CHAPTER SIX
Participation, Deliberation, and Values Voters   147

Notes   161

Index   189

Tables and Figures

TABLES

TABLE 2.1 Property Violence at Abortion Clinics in the
United States and Canada, 1977–2004   56
TABLE 2.2 Disruption and Harassment at Abortion Clinics in the
United States and Canada, 1977–2004   58
TABLE 2.3 Coverage of Pro-Life Organizations in
Elite Newspapers, 1989–2006   63
TABLE 2.4 Coverage of Pro-Life Organizations in Elite Magazines,
1989–2006   63
TABLE 2.5 Trends in Coverage of Pro-Life Organizations in
Elite Newspapers and Magazines, 1989–2006 (percents
are in parentheses)   64
TABLE 5.1 Participation in the 1972 Election   119
TABLE 5.2 Turnout, Various Groups, 1972–1988   120
TABLE 5.3 Measures of Partisanship, 1972–1988   122
TABLE 5.4 Turnout, Various Groups, 1972–2004   123
TABLE 5.5 Other Forms of Participation, 1972–2004   126
TABLE 5.6 Measures of Political Knowledge, 1972–2004   127
TABLE 5.7 Measures of Partisanship, 1972–2004   128
TABLE 5.8 Effects of Religious Mobilization on Voter Turnout,
1996, 1998, and 2000   134
TABLE 5.9 Effects of Religious Mobilization on
Influencing Others to Vote, 1996, 1998, and 2000   136
TABLE 5.10 Effects of Religious Mobilization on Political
Discussions, 1996, 1998, and 2000   137
TABLE 5.11 Effects of Religious Mobilization on Displaying
Campaign Buttons or Stickers, 1996, 1998, and 2000   138
TABLE 5.12 Effects of Religious Mobilization on
Vote Decision, 1996 (percentages)   139
TABLE 5.13 Effects of Religious Mobilization on Identifying
Party Differences, 1996, 1998, and 2000   141
TABLE 5.14 Effects of Religious Mobilization on Identifying
as a Strong Partisan, 1996, 1998, and 2000   142

FIGURES

FIGURE 5.1 Turnout Gap between Conservative Evangelicals
and Non-Evangelicals, 1972–2004   124
FIGURE 5.2 Voter Guide Distribution by Interest Group   131

Acknowledgments

THIS BOOK BEGAN at a chapter meeting of the NAACP. I attended because I was interested in what citizens learned in political organizations and I was searching for something to write a Master's thesis on. I began to have second thoughts, however, when I discovered just how sparsely the meeting was attended, and I further wondered whether I could say anything new about the NAACP.

And so I went looking for another movement, one that was not as well studied and that had some real grassroots vitality. I found it in the Christian Right. And although my liberal Protestant upbringing initially made me feel out of place hanging out with conservative Christians, I found them disarming, gracious, and more misunderstood than I ever imagined. So it is with special gratitude that I thank the many Christian activists who shared their lives with me. I hope they will find that I have returned the favor by taking their movement with the seriousness and fairness it deserves.

I have also been blessed by great mentors. Sidney Milkis impressed upon me the importance of a vigorous public life to any healthy democracy. His enthusiasm for a contentious politics informs this book from cover to cover. I am equally indebted to Brian Balogh. Brian is simply the most gracious academic I know. As someone of a strong secular bent, he approached my findings with an open-mindedness that few of us achieve. It is to Peter Skerry, however, that I owe the greatest intellectual debt. It is unlikely that I would have even become an academic without his persistent and timely intercessions. Peter also taught me the indispensible value and joys of fieldwork, as well as the need to challenge academic orthodoxies.

Many others gave generously of their time and wisdom. At the University of Virginia, I am indebted to Gerard Alexander, James Ceaser, Zach Courser, Joseph Davis, Martha Derthick, Daniel Disalvo, James Davison Hunter, Steven Finkel, Lynn Sanders, Herman Schwartz, Brad Wilcox, Stephen White, and Joshua Yates. Richard Bensel, Jason Frank, Mary Katzenstein, Isaac Kramnick, Jeremy Rabkin, Nick Salvatore, Elizabeth Sanders, and Martin Shefter made Cornell University an ideal place to finish my manuscript. At the University of Colorado in Colorado Springs I owe a special thanks to Josh Dunn, James Null, and Paul Sondrol. Others were a tremendous help from afar, including Garrett Brown, Jeffrey

Friedman, James Gimpel, Jennifer Hochschild, Jonathan Imber, Steve Lagerfeld, Paul Quirk, Clyde Wilcox, John Wilson, and James Q. Wilson.

Fred Appel, my editor at Princeton University Press, skillfully and patiently guided this book through the peer-review process. He also improved it immeasurably, as did two excellent reviewers. My copyeditor, Linda Truilo, cheerfully and expertly polished my clunky prose. This book would also not be possible without the generous funding of the Center on Religion and Democracy and the Miller Center of Public Affairs at the University of Virginia.

My greatest debt is to my family, especially my wife, Stephanie Muravchik. Without her I would not have survived the hardships of graduate school and the challenges of starting an academic career. I also thank my in-laws and my mother and father for their love. To my father, who suffered an untimely death while I was in the midst of doing fieldwork, I dedicate this book.

The Democratic Virtues of the Christian Right

REPUBLICAN VICTORIES IN THE 2004 elections unleashed yet another wave of reporting that pummeled the Christian Right for compromising democratic values. In an election postmortem, Thomas Friedman of the *New York Times* accused the Right of violating the sacred line between church and state, so much so that it was in effect "rewriting the constitution."[1] Following his lead, Robert Kuttner, editor of the *American Prospect*, opined that Christians have become even more aggressive in their efforts to undermine the American Constitution, which was a "triumph of reason over absolutism."[2] A more tempered and otherwise iconoclastic *New Republic* soon followed with some conventional wisdom. According to its editor, religious conservatives routinely fail to "find nonreligious justifications for their views."[3]

The claim that theologically conservative Christians threaten democratic values is not new. In fact, it would be hard to find a more well-entrenched and enduring belief among elite journalists and academics alike.[4] Yet it is also one of the least-examined beliefs. Despite all of the interest in the Right and culture wars more broadly, we know surprisingly little about the Christian Right. For instance, we do not know very much about what goes on inside Christian Right organizations. This neglect reflects a larger shortcoming in the study of interest groups, since few social scientists have bothered to investigate the internal lives of political organizations. As Lawrence Rothenberg observed in 1992, "Curiously, life inside political organizations has rarely received much attention from contemporary social scientists."[5] Even less attention has been devoted to the study of how religious activists actually behave in the public square.[6] And certainly no systematic attention has been spared to study the central subject of this book, which is how Christian Right leaders shape the public behavior of ordinary Christians.

Careful attention to this subject offers some good news. Drawing on interviews, participant observation, survey data, and movement sources, I argue that scholars and political observers need to reconsider the Christian Right's contribution to American democracy, regardless of where they align themselves in the larger culture wars.

First, many Christian Right organizations have helped create a more participatory democracy by successfully mobilizing conservative evangelicals, one of the most politically alienated constituencies in twentieth-century America. This has been a startling development. After all, it was the New Left that emphasized the importance of opening up American democracy to alienated citizens. What is more remarkable, this participatory revival took place in an era in which social scientists have been increasingly anxious about the erosion of civic life. Yet as the ink dried on Robert Putnam's now-famous "bowling alone" thesis, conservative Christians were turning out to vote in record numbers.[7]

In mobilizing Christian conservatives, the Right achieved another important New Left goal. It realigned American parties and public debate around contentious moral questions that animate citizens rather than bureaucratic, technical, or economic issues that tend to bewilder and subdue them. The Christian Right has therefore helped to reinvigorate American democracy and eliminate the end-of-ideology politics that the New Left held in such contempt.

Second, I argue that the vast majority of Christian Right leaders have long labored to inculcate deliberative norms in their rank-and-file activists—especially the practice of civility and respect; the cultivation of real dialogue by listening and asking questions; the rejection of appeals to theology; and the practice of careful moral reasoning. Movement leaders teach these norms because they have strong pragmatic incentives to do so. Public appeals, after all, are most persuasive when they are civil and reasonable. Movement leaders further ground these norms in scripture. For instance, activists are regularly instructed to practice civility because the Gospels command Christians to love their neighbors, and they are encouraged to be honest because God forbids believers from bearing false witness. Likewise, Christian apologetic organizations teach thousands of citizens every year to make philosophical arguments rather than scriptural ones because Paul instructs Christians to give reasons for their beliefs. From this perspective, then, Jesus Christ was not a belligerent moralist. Thus, ignoring deliberative norms is not merely impolitic; it is also unfaithful.

While I argue that Christian activists follow many deliberative norms, I do *not* argue that they are deliberative democrats. Indeed, even if these norms were practiced perfectly (which they are not), the behavior of Christian activists would still fall short of deliberation in the sense that political theorists use the term. This is because some norms are not practiced or taught at all. Most critically, activists are not moral skeptics who hold truths provisionally and quickly abandon beliefs when challenged with counter-evidence; nor are they encouraged to become such skeptics by their leaders. In fact, when activists are educated in the larger debates surrounding their objectives, they become even more confident in their political opinions because this training supplements scriptural truths with philosophical and social scientific evidence.

Therefore, politics pushes Christian activists even further from the moral skepticism that deliberative democrats champion. But this fact may be less a limitation of the Christian Right than of democratic politics itself. After all, there is no evidence that citizens with a Socratic-like moral skepticism, however desirable in theory, ever maintained any real-world social movement. Social movements, whether celebrated or not, all have been driven by strong convictions rather than provisionally held truths. Put simply, a dogmatic resistance to opposing ethical views may be the price of a more participatory democracy. But if Christian activists' democratic education does not bring them any closer to moral skepticism, it still sharpens and expands their thinking. It also raises the level of public debate for the benefit of the vast majority of more ambivalent Americans.

Deliberation is often compromised in another critical respect. While Christian leaders teach new activists how to engage the wider public, they also must mobilize and sustain their moral commitments through passionate and strident exhortations. In fact, some of the harshest rhetoric identified by critics of the culture war has been communicated in the context of mobilization. Like the absence of moral skepticism in the Christian Right, however, the polemical nature of mobilization tactics is more a function of the exigencies of democratic politics than a flaw of any particular movement. It highlights a much deeper tension between the competing ideals of participation and deliberation. Political theorists, especially proponents of deliberation, need to appreciate better the fundamental tension between these two democratic goods.

More troubling to advocates of deliberation are the militant fundamentalists who swelled the ranks of the Operation Rescue and the Moral Majority as well as contemporary fringe groups, such as God Hates Fags, Operation Save America, and Operation Rescue West. Christians in many of these groups do not understand their obligation to love their neighbor in a way that encompasses a political ideal of civility. Instead, they root their activities in a bellicose interpretation of Christianity and embrace tactics consistent with their theology. Many of the most militant activists are extreme Calvinists who believe that because they are the chosen instruments of God's justice, they should break human laws. Such beliefs were especially common among those who bombed abortion clinics and murdered physicians.

Militant Christian activists also tend to regard moderate strategies as politically inefficacious. Thus, radicalism is often self-consciously a reaction against the very deliberative moderation that dominates the Christian Right. Such moderation has often bred uncompromising and violent radicalism at the fringes of social movements. There were "Garrisonians" in the abolitionist movement, axe-wielding temperance crusaders, disciples of Black Power in the civil rights movements, the Weatherman in the New

Left, and eco-terrorists in the environmental movement. Yet radicalism also tends to encourage further moderation within social movements. This has been especially true in the Christian Right, where movement leaders are trying to escape the long shadow of fundamentalists like Randall Terry and Jerry Falwell.

The good news is that fundamentalists are not very good at building political organizations and are broadly unpopular in the Christian Right. Indeed, one reason the Moral Majority never became a broad-based, grassroots organization is that Falwell's brand of politicized fundamentalism was so unappealing to most conservative evangelicals. Today, the few remaining radical organizations are practically without members.

Mistaking such marginal fundamentalists as representative of the Christian Right as a whole prevents us from undertaking a thoughtful assessment of the right or understanding the complex relationship between Christianity and deliberation. Because we have regarded fringe fundamentalists as paradigmatic representatives of the Christian Right, we have assumed falsely that orthodox believers more broadly are a grave threat to a democratic culture that depends on civil and reasonable citizens. The reality is far more complicated: some orthodox faiths shore up deliberative ideals, while others compromise them.

This book's findings should further prompt us to reevaluate the claims of critics who hope to cure American democracy of bitter contentiousness by either marginalizing or transcending moral conflict in the public realm. These views do not account for how the democratic ideals of participation and deliberation play out in political practice. On the one hand, we should not marginalize the very moral questions that engage and connect citizens to larger public causes in our vast commercial and administrative republic. We also need to be more tolerant of the excesses of moral conflict if we value participation. On the other hand, we can also take some comfort in the promise of deliberation in public life. Social movements, whether of Christian origin or not, will never cultivate the kind of moral skepticism political theorists champion, because they are ultimately driven by deep convictions. But such movements are also interested in promoting other deliberative norms far more than most critics have appreciated.

Evaluating Social Movements

Assessing a movement's commitment to deliberative norms is irrelevant, some observers might object, if its goals are unjust. We should therefore consider the main criteria by which political movements can be evaluated. First, they can be judged in terms of their success at mobilizing and politicizing citizens, especially disaffected, marginalized, or disenfranchised ones. That is, how effective are they at increasing democratic participation? Second, we can base our evaluation of social movements on how their participants conduct themselves in the public sphere. For instance, are they civil or hostile? Do they appeal to public reason or make theological declarations? In sum, do they abide by deliberative norms and invigorate political debate? And, third, do the goals of a given movement enhance freedom, justice, equality, or other key political goods? On this basis, most of us laud some movements, such as abolitionism, and condemn others, such as nativism.

The assessment of social movements can shift as the criteria used to evaluate them change. The temperance movement is a good example. Much like the contemporary Christian Right, scholars initially regarded it negatively because its goal was to restrict coercively one feature of America's cultural pluralism. As the historian Jed Dannenbaum noted in his study of the temperance movement, until "very recently" most historians shared the popular stereotype of temperance reformers as "humorless, censorious, arch-conservative Protestants; overbearing fanatical women with hatchets; and as narrow-minded, hypocritical farmers with an intense hatred of cities and their inhabitants."[8] And, of course, the movement's aims were indeed part of a broader campaign to create a homogenous Protestant civilization in the face of increasing social heterogeneity. More recently, however, this evaluation has changed radically as feminist scholars have shifted our focus from the movement's goals to its success at increasing women's participation in public life.[9]

Like previous feminist scholarship on the temperance movement, this project shifts our focus away from the Christian Right's policy ends. I inquire instead into its effects on participation and public debate. Focusing the book in this way reveals fresh insights into one of the most significant social movements in American history. It is also a more prudent approach for social scientists to take when evaluating contentious contemporary movements. When moral consensus is lacking on contestable ethical questions, they are perhaps better left to other quarters of the academy, especially philosophy, law, theology, and religion departments. In the abortion debate, for instance, thoughtful intellectuals and ethicists on both sides offer compelling arguments, and it remains an issue that reasonable people disagree about. Meanwhile, there is a broad and enduring public and academic consensus on the first two criteria—almost all of us believe that more participation is good for democracy and that citizens should make civil and reasonable arguments in the public square. Moreover, these virtues become especially important precisely when there is broad social disagreement over the public interest.

In time, of course, it is likely that we will achieve something approaching moral consensus on such issues as abortion, pornography, and gay marriage; and when we do, the Christian Right will be evaluated accordingly. Even if the Christian Right follows the fate of the temperance movement, and we eventually conclude that its goals were misguided or worse, this fact will have to be weighed against the movement's effects on public life.

PASSIONS, INTERESTS, AND THE CHRISTIAN RIGHT

If this analysis is correct, why have scholars and political observers misunderstood the Christian Right? A partial explanation can be found in one of the most enduring, though largely untraced, theories in the history of social science. The general theory I am referring to sharply divides the world of political factions or interest groups between those with narrowly economic concerns and those with noneconomic ones. According to this hard distinction, individuals and groups that seek material goods do so in a calculating, tempered, and instrumental manner, while all other citizens seek merely symbolic or cultural goods and do so in a rash and strident manner. Such zealotry follows from the basic assumption that citizens must be somehow deranged if they actively promote causes over and above their own material self-interest. Thus, various pathological motives have been ascribed to noneconomic interests, including irrational bigotries, religious fervor, and anxiety over ones' challenged status, personal lifestyle, or worldview.

Throughout the twentieth century scholars have developed this theory with religious conservatives in mind. In fact, it is doubtful that the sharp theoretical distinction between noneconomic and economic interests would have developed and survived as it has without the enduring influence of Christianity on American politics. This tradition is obscured by the fact that scholars from a wide array of backgrounds have routinely recast the distinction. Noneconomic factions, for instance, have been described as symbolic, status, expressive, or cultural groups. Meanwhile, nearly all thinkers in this broad tradition, including those as varied as James Madison, Seymour Martin Lipset, Kristen Luker, Morris Fiorina, and Thomas Frank, have found that groups preoccupied by moral rather than economic causes undermine deliberative democracy due to their unrestrained zealotry.

The theoretical division between rational economic interests on the one hand and irrational noneconomic ones on the other has deep historical roots. By the end of the seventeenth century, in fact, the calculated pursuit of political goals was thought to apply to economic interests alone, because they were regarded as universal, predictable, orderly, and capable of taming the other more unruly passions. As Albert Hirschman has argued, those who were guided by economic interests were "expected or assumed to be steadfast, single-minded, and methodical, in total contrast to the stereotyped behavior of men who are buffeted and blinded by their passions."[10]

These ideas influenced the American founders. According to Thomas Pangle, James Madison regarded economic interests as natural and far more rational than those based on religious or political grounds. In a letter to Thomas Jefferson, Madison wrote, "In addition to these *natural* [economic] distinctions, *artificial* ones will be founded, on accidental differences in political, religious, or other opinions." Such factions, moreover, will be incapable of seeing the "*erroneous* or *ridiculous*" grounds of their claims.[11] Accordingly, they did not enjoy any real place in Madison's deliberative republic since he regarded the regulation of economic interests as the "principal task of modern legislation."[12]

Meanwhile, there was a similar impulse to marginalize moral issues and passions in some of the earliest work by political scientists. Because of the zealous and uncompromising behavior of some political activists, Harold Lasswell suggested in 1920 that they should be marginalized from politics. According to Lasswell, social movements routinely create "fictitious values" and demonstrate that the citizen is a "poor judge of his own interest." Furthermore, political actors, according to Lasswell, "are notoriously contentious and undisciplined" and glorify those who "stir the public conscience by exhortation, reiteration, and vituperation." Lasswell concluded, "The time has come to abandon the assumption that the problem of politics is the problem of promoting discussion among all the interests concerned with a given problem."[13]

It was midcentury sociologists, however, who really stressed the political virtues of economic interests. Not unlike today's intellectuals, these thinkers looked with great alarm at the moral passions that fueled conservative and religious movements. With the rise of anticommunism in the postwar years, sociologists articulated various versions of what Joseph Gusfield has called "psychological expressivism" and applied them almost exclusively to social conservatives.[14] Seymour Martin Lipset, for instance, routinely drew on a status-movement theory to make sense of McCarthyism. Distinguishing class-based movements from status movements, Lipset argued that the latter "refers to political movements whose appeal is to the not uncommon resentments of individuals or groups who desire to maintain or improve their social status." McCarthyism, in Lipset's view, appealed to "common men" and especially low-status fundamentalists and Catholics who felt they had been "victimized by members of the upper classes, by the prosperous, by the wealthy, by the well-educated." Conservatism, therefore, allowed such groups "to gain a feeling of superiority over the traditionally privileged groups" and purge their "frustrations."[15]

By 1960 Daniel Bell was equally puzzled by the "new American right wing" and turned to status-movement theory for help. In Bell's view, traditional conceptions of interest groups as rational and instrumental could not make sense of these new radicals. As he explained, the American right could not be explained by "what had traditionally been called 'interest-group' politics." Only "status politics" could make intelligible the "ugly excesses" and "rancors of McCarthyism."[16]

Even though the theory of status politics did not preclude liberal or secular citizens, it developed with religious conservatives in mind. Lipset explained McCarthyism in terms of a "puritanical morality" that believes in "a fundamental difference between right and wrong." This morality, Lipset believed, contributed to the "political intolerance" of religious conservatives.[17] Bell also stressed the importance of religion, especially American evangelicalism. As Bell explained, McCarthyism was driven by a "moralism" rooted in "the peculiar evangelicalism of Methodism and Baptism, with its high emotionalism, its fervor, enthusiasm, and excitement, its revivalism, its excesses of sinning and of high-voltage confessing."[18]

Following the lead of sociologists, the historian Richard Hofstadter concluded that in order to understand the crusading zeal of religious citizens, scholars needed to turn to psychology. Only the psychological sciences could explain why citizens "would expend so much emotional energy and crusading idealism upon causes that bring them no material reward," as well as account for their "emotional intensity" and "massive irrationality." Like Lipset and Bell, Hofstadter was drawn to status-movement theory. As he explained, "Political life is not simply an arena in which the conflicting interests of various groups in concrete material gains are fought out; it is also an arena in which status aspirations and frustrations are, as the psychologists would say, projected." Hofstadter further saw the rise of status politics as seriously compromising deliberative ideals. According to Hofstadter, the Right "psychologically stands outside the frame of normal democratic politics" because it "accepts no compromises" and "accepts no half measures." He further feared an alliance "between Protestant and Catholic fundamentalists, who share a common Puritanism," a "mindless militancy," and an "ecumenicism of hatred."[19]

There was a tendency in all this scholarship to believe that elites purposely deranged ordinary citizens by distracting them from their fundamental economic interests. In fact, as early as 1949 intellectuals criticized conservatives for luring citizens away from their true economic interests, a critique that has found new life more contemporarily in Thomas Frank's *What's the Matter with Kansas?* Leo Lowenthal and Norbert Guterman's

1949 *Prophets of Deceit* accused right-wing leaders of avoiding the "material needs" of citizens by focusing on their "emotional frustrations."[20] John Bunzel's critique of the emerging new Right especially lamented the abandonment of economic concerns for moral issues among America's working class. In *Anti-Politics in America* Bunzel scolded the Religious Right for not directing its attention "to the area of material needs" and for having "nothing concrete to say about how to confront such urgent problems as unemployment, automation, discrimination, or a host of other society-wide ills." Like other intellectuals, Bunzel thought the anticommunist preoccupations of the Right were partly the product of disturbed minds. As he put it, the "politics of the right rests on frustration and fear" and speaks "in tones of moral certainties, patriotic pieties, and emotional satisfactions."[21]

These two diametrically opposite behavioral paradigms—one based on rational interests and the other on irrational motives—emerged again, surprisingly enough, in Mancur Olson's classic *The Logic of Collective Action*, which more than any other work laid the theoretical ground for contemporary interest-group theory. Olson observed that in stark contrast to economic lobbies such as unions and professional lobbies, a "fanatical devotion to an ideology or leader is common in mass movements." Olson therefore doubted the ability of rational-choice theory to tell us anything "where philanthropic lobbies, that is, lobbies that voice concern about some group other than the group that supports the lobby, or religious lobbies, are concerned." When "nonrational or irrational behavior is the basis for a lobby," Olson explained, social scientists should draw on psychology rather than economics.[22]

Following his lead, political scientists sought help from sociologists, who had emphasized the irrational nature of noneconomic groups for years. But instead of rejecting economic theory, as Olson suggested, they adapted sociological insights to rational-choice theory.[23] Political scientists such as Robert Salisbury argued that citizens participated in noneconomic groups only because doing so allowed them to *express* their values and moral convictions. Like the sociologists before him, then, Salisbury argued that while economic interests are preoccupied with acquiring concrete benefits, noneconomic groups are interested in expressing their own values and convictions instead of creating policy change. Salisbury in 1969 defined expressive group action as follows: "Expressive actions are those where the action involved gives expression to the interests or values of a person or group rather than instrumentally pursuing interests or values."[24]

Although today's rational-choice thinkers only occasionally invoke this distinction in an explicit way, they nonetheless tend to regard noneconomic groups as primarily interested in expressing outrage. According to

Morris Fiorina, for example, contemporary culture-war activists are "self-righteous and intolerant, their rhetoric emotional and excessive" and that their rising influence in party politics reveals the "dark side of civic engagement."[25]

In large part, this distinction between instrumental and expressive interests reflects the theoretical perversities of rational-choice theory. A core tenet of rational-choice theory, of course, is that citizens will never work for collective benefits unless selective incentives are provided; otherwise political activism is wholly irrational. Selective incentives are any direct benefit to the individual that can be acquired only through political participation. In this case, what would otherwise appear to be irrational behavior is revealed to be rational by the assumption that activists receive "expressive" benefits. Therefore, citizens do not participate in politics because they seek public goods since doing so is irrational; rather, they participate because activism itself is its own end and reward. As Salisbury put it, citizens participate in noneconomic interest groups because they "provide mechanisms for the public expression" of individual values.[26]

The development of a theory of expressive action represented a rejection of Peter Clark and James Q. Wilson's more sensible understanding of "purposive" incentives. Clark and Wilson argued that purposive incentives are the intangible rewards that are acquired through contributing to the realization of an important goal.[27] The implications of their theory for rational-choice theory were evident. As David King and Jack Walker put it, "[D]esires for purposive benefits are desires for collective goods."[28] But in a rational-choice world, "desires for collective goods" cannot stimulate public action. The dangerous notion of purposive incentives to rational-choice theory was clearly realized by Salisbury. He rejected "purposive benefits or incentives" because they "consist in the realization of supra-personal goals, goals of the organization or group."[29]

The parallels between theories of status and expressive politics are interesting. Both schools actually began with the same question—namely, why would anyone act against his or her own self-interest. But whereas status politics allowed sociologists and historians to understand movements that struck them as patently irrational, it allowed political scientists to assimilate irrational movements into a rational-choice framework. Yet all camps denied instrumental rationality since changes in public policy were not the point of political action.

The Christian Right and Its Critics

As the modern Christian Right mobilized, political observers continued to understand religious activists through the troubled social-scientific assumptions and categories developed by midcentury sociology. Some drew explicitly on theories of status politics, while many more argued that Christian politics was shaped by symbolic fights over worldviews. Whatever strand of sociology they drew on, however, all agreed that unlike fights over economic policy, culture-war politics was especially immune to compromise and deliberation. Such politics seemed to serve only as a means of purging passions and airing beliefs, rather than as an arena in which actors strategically labored toward concrete goals.

Perhaps the most important work to draw upon midcentury sociology is Kristin Luker's canonical work, *Abortion and the Politics of Motherhood*. Both because of its remarkable influence and because it argues that politics is symbolic even in the case of abortion, Luker's book demonstrates the enduring appeal of the social science first pioneered by the likes of Lasswell, Lipset, Bell, and Hofstadter. Luker dismisses pro-life activists' own explanation that they were spurred to action by concern over the fetus itself. As she explains, "While on the surface it is the embryo's fate that seems to be at stake, the abortion debate is actually about the meaning of *women's* lives." Luker continues, "[T]he abortion debate is so passionate and hard-fought" because "two opposing visions of motherhood are at war." Abortion is, therefore, only the "tip of the iceberg."[30] This perspective is reflected in the very term *culture* wars and is accepted by other important students of contemporary moral conflict, especially in studies of the Religious Right.[31]

Meanwhile, other scholars have again emphasized that a focus on moral or cultural questions distracts us from the really important economic issues. For instance, political scientists Sidney Verba, Kay Schlozman, and Henry Brady lament that American religious institutions have tended to "distort citizen activity" by mobilizing around social issues rather than around "an economic agenda focused on the less advantaged."[32] More recently, Thomas Frank's best-selling *What's the Matter with Kansas?* repackaged the theory that economic interests are somehow rational and "fundamental" while noneconomic ones lead to political "derangement." According to Frank, working-class, Bible-belt Americans have been seduced by the Republican Party trough "explosive social issues," such as abortion and gay marriage, at the expense of their own economic interests. Frank calls this manipulation the "Great Backlash" since it depended on the mobilization of anger and resentment rather than real, fundamental interests. In Frank's view, then, the newly politicized Christian Right is little more than a "plague of bitterness," a scourge of "public outrage," "cultural anger," and "zealotry." Or, as Frank describes his home state of Kansas even more polemically, "[R]age is a bumper crop here, and Kansas has produced enough fury to give every man, woman, and child in the country apoplexy."[33]

A variant of the thesis that conservatives are fighting a symbolic and irrational defense of their own worldview has been given greater force recently by the concept of fundamentalism. Although it is often not well defined, fundamentalism is usually described as a kind of illiberal, anti-modern, dogmatic militancy that cuts across all of the world religions. The sociologist Marsha Jones offers a typical definition: "Fundamentalism . . . is born out of the clash between modernity and traditional cultures."[34]

The most serious effort to study fundamentalism, however, is the Fundamentalism Project—a major interdisciplinary undertaking of the American Academy of Arts and Sciences at the University of Chicago. Two of its principal investigators, historians R. Scott Appelby and Martin E. Marty, offer a definition much like that of Jones: "[F]undamentalists . . . are likely to spring up anywhere people perceive the need to fight a godless, secular culture—even if they have to depart from the orthodoxy of their traditions to do it."[35] In the culminating work of this ambitious project, *Strong Religion: The Rise of Fundamentalisms Around the World*, political scientist Gabriel Almond and his colleagues offer a somewhat more developed understanding of fundamentalism as "a discernable pattern of religious militancy by which self-styled 'true believers' attempt to arrest the erosion of religious identity, fortify the borders of religious community, and create viable alternatives to secular institutions and behaviors."[36]

Partly because the entire project depends on identifying "family resemblances" between remarkably diverse faiths and traditions, important differences are muted or ignored altogether. The result is that theologically orthodox Christians in America appear to have more in common with Islamic terrorists than they do with other Christians. According to Martin Marty, for example, Christian conservatives and Islamic terrorists embrace similar political strategies: "Al Qaeda and the New Christian Right in America . . . mimic, adapt to, absorb, and exploit many of the strategies, tactics, hardware, lifestyles, and even the rational arguments of the secular forces."[37]

Yet *Strong Religion* does open some room for important political departures between Christian and Islamic fundamentalism. Although it argues that "extremist violence" and "intolerance" are "a strong tendency of fundamentalist movements," they are not "inevitable." It nonetheless describes the Christian Right as a fundamentalist movement that is primarily composed of uncompromising and even violent xenophobes who operate from an enclave culture. Far from embracing the norms of a pluralistic democracy, conclude the authors of *Strong Religion*, the Christian Right emerged from and is sustained by fear of the disintegrating effects of pluralism itself on a Christian America.[38]

The theoretical nuance offered by the authors of *Strong Religion* has, in general, been entirely lost on academics and journalists. One common formulation revised Samuel Huntington's clash of civilizations' thesis such that all worldwide fundamentalisms are in fact a unified culture or civilization. According to Ellen Willis, the director of the Cultural Reporting and Criticism program at New York University, "[T]he 'clash of civilizations' thesis [is] half right. There is such a clash, but it is not between East and West. The struggle of democratic secularism, religious tolerance, individual freedom and feminism against authoritarian patriarchal religion, culture and morality is going on all over the world."[39] The freelance author Barbara Ehrenreich made a similar revision: "There is no 'clash of civilizations,'" but "throughout history" there has been "a clash of alternative cultures." Ehrenreich describes one culture as "represented by the Islamic and Christian fundamentalists" who are "crabbed and punitive in outlook, committed to collectivist discipline, and dogmatically opposed to spontaneity and pleasure," while the other "is more open, liberatory, and trusting of human impulses." We are confronted, then, with a stark choice "between freedom, on the one hand, and religious totalitarianism on the other."[40]

Such views are well entrenched among academics and the media elite. Don Corrigan, a professor of communications, recently called the Christian Right the "taliban wing" of the GOP, while the Cornell University political scientist Sydney Tarrow placed the Christian Right among the "ugly movements" along with Islamic fundamentalism and skinhead groups.[41] Likewise, the *American Prospect* continued a well-established tradition of treating orthodox believers as subhuman: "[T]he Bush administration is plainly eager to construct a Fundamentalist International where part of its base—the overtly Neanderthal wing of the Christian right—mixes with like-minded primitives from reactionary Islam."[42]

While many liberals have found the temptation to draw parallels between the Christian Right and radical Islam hard to resist, especially in light of the Right's strong support for a preemptive war on terrorism, others argue that Christian conservatives have more in common with secular fascists. The Pulitzer-prize winning journalist Chris Hedges of the *New York Times* is currently on a mission to expose the Christian Right as "totalitarian" and "anti-democratic." In fact, Hedges taught a course one semester on the subject at New York University, where he darkly warned his students, "Right now, we're living in the equivalent of 1910 Germany."[43] Meanwhile, John Swomley, a professor emeritus of social ethics at St. Paul School of Theology, called the Promise Keepers "storm troopers." Like Hedges, he emphasizes the importance of exposing the Right: "Any disciplined religious movement can exercise control over government and social organizations if people do not expose it, organize counter movements, and educate their fellow citizens about the importance of separation of church and state."[44]

Scholars and the media elite also routinely argue that the political views and actions of the Christian Right are built on a foundation of hatred. Orthodox Christians, in this view, oppose gay marriage and abortion because they hate homosexuals and women. Sara Diamond, a sociologist who has written numerous books and articles on the Christian Right, argues that its campaign against more expansive extensions of gay rights is "aroused by fear and loathing of homosexuals."[45] The editor of *Home-Grown Hate*, Abby Ferber, assumes dark motives as well. Ferber introduced the volume by arguing that "women's bodies and control over reproduction are central to white supremacy."[46] Likewise, an article in *Harpers* claimed that the Christian Right was driven "by the gospels of fear and hate,"[47] while an editorial in the *Washington Post* compared the right to the KKK because it criticized judges for disrespecting Christian ethics.[48] After George W. Bush's presidential victory in 2004, yet another *Washington Post* editorial opined that the election went to the Republicans because "fundamentalist preachers" had "viciously" stirred up fear and hatred of homosexuals, leaving "men and women in communities across this country at personal and professional risk."[49]

Those critics who do not believe Christian Right activists are violent bigots nonetheless assert that they refuse to compromise and moderate their own theocratic designs. The philosopher Fritz Detwiler, for instance, concludes that the Christian Right "intends to bring every aspect of the culture into conformity with its divinely revealed beliefs, values, and strictures."[50] Consistent with Detwiler's view, religious studies professor Jason Bivins argues that the Christian Right is founded on an "antiliberalism" that has "antidemocratic" and "intolerant tendencies."[51] From an even more critical perspective, political theorist Mark E. Warren finds that the Christian Right does not even enjoy the capacity to "negotiate conflicts with other groups," and law professor William Simon warns that religious fundamentalism is "explicitly hostile to deliberation."[52]

Many of these criticisms have been echoed in a much more general way by prominent and thoughtful intellectuals who charge that the culture wars corrupt American democracy. For instance, James Hunter writes that "the traditions of moral logic" have been distorted by activists' "rhetorical hyperbole whose main use is to appeal to the emotional predispositions of the listener."[53] Similarly, E. J. Dionne exhorts, "If we are to end the cultural civil war over what has so distorted our politics, we need to begin to practice a certain charity and understanding."[54] Furthermore, Morris Fiorina laments that culture warriors are responsible for "hijacking" American democracy because they allow "[a]ngry attacks [to] substitute for reasoned debate."[55]

Amidst all this criticism, a group of even-handed and empirically oriented scholars whose work, though rarely consulted by most of the authors just described, casts doubt on the reigning view of the Christian
Right. The research of scholars such as Clyde Wilcox, Mathew Moen,
and Mark Rozell suggests that at least some Christian Right organizations
try to moderate their rhetoric and policy objectives.[56] Especially with the
rise of the Christian Coalition, these scholars saw a new generation of
Christian leaders who were more willing to compromise, work with others, and tone down their rhetoric. As Rozell describes the political matura-
tion of the right in the 1990s, "The rhetorical appeals are more moderate
sounding; the issue-appeals are more broad based; leading organizations
express a sincere desire to reach out to as broad and ecumenical a base
as possible."[57]

Interests and Deliberative Democracy

For all the hyperbole in most assessments of the Right, this survey
highlights a common social-scientific logic: noneconomic interests compromise deliberative ideals because they are engaged in an inherently
irrational, even pathological, defense of symbols, status, cultures, and
worldviews.

Of course, there are good theoretical reasons to suspect that Christian
leaders might have little interest in deliberative norms. Less appreciated
by many social commentators are the very rational incentives that encourage Christian leaders to compromise these norms. After all, movement
leaders must excite and sustain the moral passions of activists to build
their organizations. To this end, they have a strong incentive to make
strident appeals that compromise deliberative ideals, especially in the context of mobilization. Michael Walzer has emphasized a similar point in
his critique of deliberative democracy. According to Walzer, however valuable reasoned debate is to a healthy democracy, "[i]ndividual men and
women have to be stimulated, provoked, energized, excited, called to
arms" if political mobilization is to succeed.[58] Decades earlier, Reinhold
Niehbuhr made a similar critique of John Dewey's rationalistic view of
democratic life: "Contending factions in social struggle require morale;
and morale is created by the right dogmas, symbols, and emotionally po-
tent oversimplifications."[59] They also have little incentive to advocate an
open-mindedness to alternative moral views lest they compromise the
very conviction that sustains their organizations. Morris Fiorina suggested just this point when he observed that those who become highly
active in politics tend to have "*intensely held*, extreme views."[60]

On the other hand, movement leaders have powerful incentives to discipline and educate the passions of mobilized activists before they practice public advocacy. To be sure, some political activism, such as militant varieties of direct action, actually provides group leaders with a disincentive to encourage deliberation. However, political activities that aim to *persuade* public officials or citizens, such as contacting representatives, writing letters to the editor, participating in school-board meetings, and engaging in informal moral suasion are generally far more efficacious when undertaken by citizens who practice deliberative norms. Therefore, "the passions and the interests," to borrow Albert Hirschman's term, is less useful for identifying divisions *between* political groups as it is for highlighting tensions *within* them.

The possible tension between successful organization maintenance and successful activism has gone virtually unnoticed by scholars. One exception is James Q. Wilson, who observed that leaders of voluntary associations are confronted with the difficult task of "motivating indifferent members and controlling militant ones."[61] Much of this book develops and explores Wilson's pregnant observation.

METHOD AND OVERVIEW

This book is not a work of political science as that term now tends to be understood in the discipline. That is, it is not a work of normal science in which discrete causal relationships are tested with quantitative data or an experimental design. In such studies, normative questions are often something of an afterthought and approached with caution, if at all. In this book, however, normative questions frame the discussion. From the outset, I am interested in whether or not a particular social movement has undermined or advanced democratic values. Because of the nature of this question, I am less interested in discovering laws of social science and more interested in understanding and describing the Christian Right.

This does not mean that I am uninterested in social science theory. In fact, I engage the social-scientific distinction between economic and non-economic groups as well as consider some of the conditions that shape social movements' interest in deliberative norms. In addition, I further develop interest-group theory by highlighting the organizational tension between mobilization and advocacy. To what extent this tension holds outside of the Christian Right is a question this study cannot definitively answer. This is the limitation of a case study.

Discovering genuine laws of social science, however, will never succeed unless we know more about politics. In the case of social movements, political scientists know shockingly little about them because they are not easily studied with the preferred tools of a rigorous methodologist. For example, by using such methods it is difficult to discover how movement elites try and shape the behavior of rank-and-file activists. And we certainly cannot know what activists do and say in the public square with surveys, experimental designs, or formal mathematical models. To answer these kinds of questions, we need to make room for the kind of political anthropology pioneered by the likes of James Q. Wilson, Edward Banfield, and Richard Fenno. The alternative is to abandon such questions altogether as beyond the scope of political science, which was suggested to me by one scholar during my graduate education.

The kind of social science developed by the likes of Wilson and Fenno promises not only to improve social science theory in time. It will also help political theorists hone and revise their theories in response to what we know about the empirical realities of political life. A good example is the literature on deliberative democracy, which this book engages directly. It has elaborated principles that ideally should govern public debate without taking into account the constraints of political life or considering how in real life the democratic ideals of participation and deliberation cannot both be endlessly maximized. That this scholarship has not been attentive to such problems is at least partly because social scientists have done such a poor job of illuminating public life and conducting research that has relevance to political theorists.

The remainder of this book proceeds as follows: In chapter 1, "Democratic Education in the Christian Right," I examine how Christian Right leaders try to shape the public behavior of rank-and-file activists. Drawing primarily upon interviews with leaders in thirty different Christian Right organizations and organizational materials, I show that most Christian citizens are taught deliberative norms. However, in Chapter 2, "Christian Radicalism," I also demonstrate the vitality of Christian radicalism especially in the rescue movement where the removal of abortion policy from the legislative to the judicial realm and the militancy of evangelical fundamentalism combined to send waves of violence crashing down on abortion clinics. Although today such violence has greatly abated, a handful of Christian rescuers continue systematically to harass abortion providers. Meanwhile, I also show that strident and belligerent rhetoric is commonly found within mainstream groups as well, especially in the context of mobilization where elites attempt to stir the passions of uninvolved citizens or maintain the morale and energies of committed ones. Finally, this chapter also focuses on the role the media has played in magnifying the most radical and sensational elements of the Christian Right.

But do leaders' efforts influence the behavior of rank-and-file activists? Chapter 3, "The Varieties of Pro-Life Activism," sheds empirical light on how Christian activists conduct themselves in public forums, largely by observing them in their own environments—city streets, abortion clinics, university campuses, and other public places. In addition to observation of hundreds of activists in six American cities, I also draw upon sixty personal interviews, video footage, and over 100 written personal testimonies.

One of the most surprising findings is the relative disinterest in creating spaces for civil dialogue in the pro-choice camp. In chapter 4, "Deliberation and Abortion Politics," I explore the causes of this discrepancy, and especially highlight how very different strategic incentives in both movements shape their respective investments in deliberative norms.

In chapter 5, "Reviving Participatory Democracy," I further argue that Christian elites have also had a powerful effect on participation. It is often forgotten that conservative evangelicals have been among the most alienated constituencies in twentieth-century America. This is partly because they feared that political engagement compromised an authentically Christian life. Indeed, while secular critics feared that religion corrupts politics, evangelicals have long held the opposite concern: it is politics that contaminates religion. Drawing upon National Election Studies, this book is the first to trace the gradual assimilation of Christian conservatives into American politics over a broad sweep of time. Using a wide variety of indicators, this method demonstrates that over the course of only a handful of election cycles, evangelical citizens have emerged as among the most engaged, knowledgeable, and sophisticated American citizens. The Right has achieved this success because Christian Right organizations have labored to change evangelicals' view of politics. Of greatest importance, though, Christian Right organizations departed from the example set by New Left public interest groups and the Moral Majority. Instead, the right returned to a much older tradition established by many religious movements, including the abolitionist, temperance, and civil rights campaigns, by mobilizing through churches.

In chapter 6, "Participation, Deliberation, and Values Voters," I conclude by criticizing the scholarly and popular view that moral conflict needs either to be marginalized or transcended. Such a view fails to account for the much deeper tension between the democratic ideals of participation and deliberation.

CHAPTER ONE

Democratic Education in the Christian Right

POLITICAL OBSERVERS HAVE TENDED to see organized interests, especially those driven by religious convictions, as chronically failing schools of American democracy. For this reason, many scholars champion the creation of entirely new civic and political institutions to transform citizens into good deliberative democrats.[1] A central problem with this view, however, is that few social scientists have bothered to investigate the internal lives of political organizations.[2] Far less—and certainly no systematic—attention has been spared to study the central subject of this chapter, which is how Christian Right leaders try to shape the public behavior of their rank-and-file activists.

This chapter shows that within the very movement singled out by critics as uniquely destructive to deliberative democracy, some of the most passionate American citizens are taught many but not all deliberative norms. But what do I mean by *deliberative norms*? I have in mind the norms of behavior that collectively make public deliberation possible. They include the following: (1) the practice of civility and respect; (2) the cultivation of real dialogue by listening and asking questions; (3) the rejection of appeals to theology; (4) the practice of careful moral reasoning; and (5) openness to alternative points of view. These norms have never been catalogued in this way, but individually they have all been emphasized by a variety of political theorists and social scientists.

Most Christian leaders teach all of these norms with the exception of the fifth one. That is, they do not encourage activists to question their own convictions. Advocating such skepticism would undermine the very moral passions that sustain the Christian Right. Movement leaders do, however, encourage the first four norms because these do not compromise the maintenance of their organizations and because they have strong pragmatic incentives to do so. That is, such norms are taught because public appeals are most persuasive when they are civil and reasonable. Perhaps more surprising, movement leaders further ground these norms in scripture.

In making this case, this chapter examines communications from movement leaders that tell activists how to behave in the public square in a wide variety of Christian Right organizations.[3] Included in this survey are some of the movement's largest political organizations, such as the Christian Coalition, Concerned Women for America, and National Right to Life Committee, as well as many state and local organizations. I also canvassed organizations that devote themselves exclusively to moral suasion rather than electoral politics or grassroots lobbying. Such organizations include Justice for All, the Center for Bioethical Reform, and Care Net, which combined have reached millions of ordinary Americans. I also investigated Stand to Reason, which is currently the most important activist training organization in the Christian Right. These groups differ widely in terms of their tactics, the issues they advocate, and their influence. For example, some groups train tens of thousands of Christians every year, while others train only a small handful. In every case I was interested in whether elites promoted or discouraged deliberative norms.

The communications that I collected were found in newsletters, magazines, web-based documents, pamphlets, radio broadcasts, and especially activist training seminars. Training seminars are the most significant way in which Christian elites try to shape the public behavior of rank-and-file activists. I acquired information on these seminars by interviewing leaders in thirty different Christian Right organizations. In most of these organizations I was further able to acquire internal training documents that corroborated the accounts of Christian leaders. In other cases, I acquired internal documents but was not able to conduct an interview.

Of course, the evidence I collected does not represent a scientifically representative sample of all behavioral instructions from elites to activists. As with so much social-scientific inquiry, it was impossible to attain such a sample because the population of communications is not known. The instructions that I surveyed, however, were remarkably consistent.

CIVILITY

Critics of the culture wars tend to argue that the practice of civility and respect is what is most wanting in public life.[4] Perhaps this is because civility is arguably the most fundamental of all deliberative norms. After all, discussions quickly descend into heated shouting matches without some modicum of goodwill. Yet the most universally taught deliberative norm in the Christian Right is the practice of civility. Christian Right leaders preach the virtues of civility because they want to persuade, not alienate, other citizens. Just as often, movement elites ground this norm in Christ's command to love one's neighbor.

Rank-and-file citizens are encouraged by their leaders to develop into truly *Christian* activists. The "mantra" that the president of New York State Right to Life, Lori Kehoe, repeats to her activists is "Love your neighbors as yourself." Such Christian love, according to Kehoe, is necessary to build relationships and open others up to the movement's message.[5]

Kehoe's counterpart at Right to Life of Michigan, Barbara Listing, elaborates a similar Christian ethic to her rank and file: "Let us work together spreading the message of life in ways that recognize the dignity of all those created in the image of God. . . . May we not spread hatred and bitterness. May we not tear down others to advance ourselves."[6] The state chairman of the Colorado Christian Coalition, Chuck Gosnell, also promotes public civility with the Gospels: "As we strive to present an authentic Christian witness in the public square, it is vital that we speak in a manner that is honoring to God. . . . As a ministry in the sphere of public policy, we must remember to relate to our adversaries and friends alike in a godly humility, for we never know when today's adversary will become tomorrow's ally. Therefore, I believe that our mission should be to maintain open and respectful dialogue with any person or group who is interested in doing likewise."[7] Likewise, the Christian Coalition of New Jersey tells its activists to approach other citizens "in a spirit of love."[8] Beverly LaHaye, the president of Concerned Women for America (CWA), reports a similar emphasis. According to LaHaye, staffers at CWA "urge [activists] to share their convictions with graciousness, in a Christian spirit."[9]

Wedding public civility to the Gospels is not unique to large, highly professionalized Christian Right organizations. It is also prevalent in small, upstart organizations like the Central Virginia Family Forum (CVFF). Over one hundred of its members recently gathered at a County Board of Supervisors meeting to protest a large Planned Parenthood building that was being constructed near a public high school in a residential neighborhood of Charlottesville. Before the meeting these members were gathered together by the forum's leadership for prayer and instruction. Mike Sharman, who is a board member of the forum, then instructed activists always to behave in a way that "honors God" when talking to Board of Supervisor members, the press, or their neighbors.[10] Once the activities of the Central Virginia Family Forum caught the attention of Planned Parenthood weeks later, the leadership of CVFF prepared for a confrontation at a subsequent Board of Supervisors meeting. CVFF's founder, Marnie Deaton, directed her activists to "Please pray in advance for this meeting that Christ's love for these women [pro-choice activists] and their families will be evident through our actions."[11]

Christian Right organizations of all sizes often hire organizations to train their members. These activist training organizations stress the importance of Christian love as well. Stand to Reason, a Christian apologetic organization that trains some 40,000 activists every year and reaches millions more through mass media appearances, targets college students, churches, and a wide variety of pro-life organizations. Stand to Reason seeks to build what it calls "Christian Ambassadors." In the broadest sense, a Christian diplomat is someone who in public life behaves in ways that model Christ's example. Scriptural support for such Christian diplomacy is found in 2 Corinthians 5:20, which reads, "We are ambassadors for Christ, as though God were entering through us."

But what does it mean to be a vessel for Christ in the public square? Among other criteria, Stand to Reason defines a Christian ambassador as someone who practices "grace," "kindness," and is always "sympathetic and understanding towards the opposition." Anything short of this high standard, according to Stand to Reason, "dishonors Christ."[12]

This view of Christian activism was on display at a Stand to Reason seminar where Justice for All volunteers were trained to engage college students in moral and philosophical discussions about abortion. Justice for All, which routinely hires Stand to Reason to train its volunteers, is an organization that travels to many university campuses, where it sets up large displays that feature images of aborted fetuses at various levels of gestation. Like those who pioneered this method of moral suasion at the Center for Bio-Ethical Reform, Justice for All staffers labor to provoke discussion and moral sentiments with the aid of graphic images.

At the seminar I attended at Arvada Covenant Church in the Denver suburbs, students were trained to engage other students at the local Auraria campus, which is home to the Colorado University at Denver, Metropolitan State College of Denver, and Community College of Denver. It is a task that routinely draws emotional and even hostile reactions from at least some students and professors. Because Stand to Reason and Justice for All want to foster deliberative discussions even as they provoke emotional responses through graphic images, volunteers must be very disciplined if they are to succeed in calming public passions and tolerating angry reactions. To this end, Steve Wagner, a Stand to Reason instructor, continually reminded his students that they were "representatives of Christ" and that they should therefore always treat others with respect, even when it is not reciprocated. Wagner also did a series of role-playing games in which he acted the part of an angry pro-choice student to test volunteers and prepare them for the hostility to come.[13] When the training session ended, volunteers were then required to sign Justice for All's volunteer agreement form, part of which reads as follows: "I will always treat people with respect, even if they are verbally angry and/or abusive. I will not shout at people."[14]

Stand to Reason staffers do not tend to see a tension between political expedience and Christian virtues. Its staffers, in fact, often point out that Christian ambassadors are far more effective than militant radicals. Scott Klusendorf, the former director of bioethics at Stand to Reason, described the radicalism of Jerry Falwell and Pat Robertson as nothing less than a "disaster" for the pro-life movement.[15] Consistent with this charge, Klusendorf routinely tells large evangelical audiences that they can either make a "loving, persuasive case" or be marginalized from public life.[16]

Indeed, Stand to Reason's belief in the perfect compatibility between Christian love and political success sometimes appears more like an organizational dogma than a strategic application of faith to political life. When I asked one instructor about the success some Christian Right organizations enjoy closing abortion clinics by harassing abortion providers, he responded sharply, "I hope that is not what you think of Christianity!" In his view, it is simply unchristian to harass others.[17]

Even in organizations that are not especially interested in engaging other citizens in conversation, there is a similar commitment to Christian love. Life Chain, for example, coordinates peaceful prayer vigils across the country on the first Sunday of October. Christians pray and hold signs as they form human chains that wind busy city streets. The activity began in Yuba City, California, in 1987 and spread to over 1000 cities by 2003. Local pastors, who are instructed by leaders at Life Chain to inform all volunteers that they must abide by its code of conduct, often coordinate the chains. As an additional precaution, moreover, this code is printed on the back of each Life Chain sign. The code reads in part, "In the spirit of Christian love, commit to being peaceful, prayerful, and polite, in word and deed. Any misconduct from passersby should be met with silence, which will convey your inner peace."[18]

The Christian media also promotes the deliberative norm of civility to even wider audiences. Hosted by James Dobson, the "undisputed king of Christian radio," Focus on the Family's radio broadcasts reach about four million listeners every week.[19] A recent broadcast featured Tom Minnery, the director of a social action center at Focus on the Family and author of numerous books on Christian politics. Minnery exhorted Dobson's largely evangelical audience to "bless those who persecute you" (Romans 12:14). Dobson agreed and added that "ridiculing" or "marginalizing" other citizens was a recipe for failure.[20]

In books and magazines, Minnery has articulated this vision of Christian activism for many years now. More than a decade prior to his appearance on Dobson's radio program, Minnery cautioned evangelicals in *Citizen* magazine that "[i]n the heat of Christian activism, it is easy to lose the self-discipline and compassion that mark the disciple of Christ."[21] Charles Colson, who converted to Christianity while facing prison charges related to Watergate, complements Minnery's efforts. In the pages of *Christianity Today* Colson put the choice before fellow evangelicals in stark terms: "A broken world will see either our faces twisted in hate and anger or the face of Christ, listening, serving, speaking the truth in love."[22]

James D. Kennedy, who commands an evangelical media empire, echoes Minnery and Colson. Kennedy joined the 45-member Coral Ridge

Presbyterian Church, in Fort Lauderdale, Fla., in 1959 and built it into one of the largest in the country, with nearly 10,000 members. In addition, Kennedy's TV broadcasts reach a remarkable 40,000 towns and cities in America as well as 200 other countries. Included in his media empire is the Center for Reclaiming America, which emphasizes the biblical basis of political action. For instance, it instructs Christian activists to "always be courteous" when contacting elected officials because "the Bible tells us" that "all men are made in the image of God."[23]

When all Christian Right organizations are considered, however, devotion to Christian love is probably greatest in the roughly 2,300 crisis pregnancy centers across the country. These centers discourage women from having an abortion through moral suasion and by providing resources, such as furniture, baby items, medical services, and housing. Often they have informal ties with local Christian doctors who agree to provide prenatal services to their clients without charge.

Volunteers at crisis pregnancy centers are also probably the best-trained Christian activists. Julie Parton, who founded a pregnancy center in Dallas and currently directs the Pregnancy Resource Ministry at Focus on the Family, informed me that most volunteers receive an initial training that runs approximately twenty hours, which is followed by in-service trainings to keep volunteers current with new information and protocols.[24] A dominant theme in these extensive trainings is that the behavior of volunteers must reflect the love and compassion of Christ. For example, training seminars provided by Care Net, which is an affiliate that oversees more than 750 pregnancy centers and among the largest in the country, inform volunteers that the "goal of pregnancy center ministry is to reach out and offer hurting people the love of Christ." Citing Colossians 3:12, Care Net trainings describe how the "love of Christ" should be shared: "[C]lothe yourselves with compassion, kindness, humility, gentleness, and patience." Such love even requires volunteers in a Christ-like manner to "love those who oppose what we believe" and to speak in ways "that reflect an attitude of respect for all people, including those who do not agree with us."[25]

To be sure, not all Christian Right leaders look primarily to biblical foundations to promote public civility. Many others stress pragmatic considerations. There has been no greater pragmatist in the Christian Right than Ralph Reed. As the director of the Christian Coalition, Reed cautioned rank-and-file members in the pages of the Coalition's magazine, *Christian American*: "We can never win until we learn to communicate effectively." Efficacious communicators, Reed continued, "avoid hostile and intemperate language," "acknowledge the opinion of others and sincerity of their beliefs," and remain "tolerant of diverse views and respectful of those who espouse them."[26]

Reed's pragmatic orientation shaped training seminars in the 1990s when the Christian Coalition was still a thriving organization. One seminar, for instance, offered this consideration: "Even if they [political leaders] are on the other side of an issue, a sincere and not-threatening visit from faith-based activists can do much to move them toward an understanding of your concerns. You may not change their minds at first, but civil behavior always leaves the door open to future visits." This instruction concluded categorically with these words: "Never, ever burn a bridge."[27]

Other institutional safeguards at CWA and the Christian Coalition, which were the largest grassroots organizations in the Christian Right in the 1990s, helped ensure that the rank and file adopted the more pragmatic orientation of movement leaders. The state leaders whom I interviewed within the Christian Coalition overwhelmingly reported that they selected chapter chairs to ensure that chapters will follow the pragmatic direction of the state organization. They also seek leaders who are politically savvy and experienced.[28] Some of the more vital state organizations, such as the Florida Christian Coalition, conduct formal interviews and require letters of recommendation from the prospective chair's pastor and others in the community. The Florida organization even requires the selection of a board of directors for each chapter. As the development director of the state organization explained, these boards serve as a "check and balance" on the leadership of the chapter chair.[29] CWA spells out similar qualifications clearly in its *Opportunities for Leadership*, which is distributed at its annual conventions and must be read by all chapter-chair applicants. Specifically, chapter leaders must agree to be "directly responsible to the state leader" and "must be willing to work under the counsel of her state representative."[30]

The selection of effective chapter chairs is complicated, however, by the need to select passionate chairs who can inspire others to participate, a fact that reveals the deeper organizational tension between successful mobilization and public advocacy. As the Christian Coalition's training manual explains, a large part of the chapter chairman's role is to "motivate and encourage others to get involved."[31] Or, as one state leader candidly put it in an interview, "I want a zealot!" Concerned Women for America also requires its chapter leaders to be diligent in recruiting and motivating other members.[32]

Leaders within the Christian Coalition and CWA are certainly not alone in emphasizing the strategic pragmatism of political civility. The National Right to Life Committee (NRLC), a nonsectarian organization by charter, stresses the strategic importance of civil behavior over and above theological considerations. The NRLC's lobbying guidelines, for instance, encourage pro-life activists to do the following: "Be calm, reasonable, and respectful. . . . Threats or open antagonism are seldom if ever helpful and often counterproductive; they can even turn an apathetic pro-abortion legislator into a committed pro-abortion activist."[33]

State affiliates of the NRLC offer similar advice. Arkansas Right to Life encourages its members to "[a]lways be courteous, reasonable, and respectful in all contact with the elected official and staff."[34] Meanwhile, Ohio Right to Life Society—an especially active state affiliate with nearly 70 chapters—directly challenges the prejudices of its rank-and-file activists: "Do not assume that he or she is a proabort, feminazi, anti-religious bigot; a liberal know-nothing; just plain evil or other negative stereotype. We must start by respecting our listener's humanity. . . . We must be models of what we are trying to teach, which is respect for the dignity of others."[35] Similarly, Massachusetts Citizens for Life regards "tolerance" and "compassion" as some of its foundational values.[36]

A major objective of many Christian Right organizations is defusing the many negative stereotypes that have been fueled by a hostile media, elite cultural prejudices, and militant radicals. This mission is especially evident in the pro-life movement. At Arizona Right to Life, the director of volunteers described the challenges and opportunities of pro-life activism for her membership: "We are portrayed as angry, intolerant, extremists with one agenda—to impose our self-righteous views on the rest of the world. . . . You have the opportunity to let the world see who the pro-life movement really is—a compassionate, intelligent, self-sacrificing group of people who are interested in helping others see what they see— that human life is precious, regardless of its quality or location."[37] The leadership of Human Life of Washington betrayed similar concerns when it offered advice on crafting letters to editors: "Never NEVER use your letters as a tool to attempt to impose guilt on them. NEVER MUD SLING. Let the other side do all the foaming at the mouth. Nothing does more to dispel the slur of 'fanatic' than sticking to rational discourse."[38] And Jane Grimm, the president of the Ohio Right to Life Society, did not mince words when she recently described the right-to-life movement's image problems: "We are perceived . . . as violen[ce]-prone, religious bigots, and uncaring people who are only concerned about the baby." Changing this distorted public image, Grimm continued, requires activists to "communicate the love that we have for [all] life."[39]

Even Randall Terry, who is the founder of Operation Rescue and bears much of the responsibility for the Right's negative public image, now seems to share the concerns of more moderate pro-life organizations. Before activists in his recently founded Society for Truth and Justice protested at the March for Women's Lives and 2004 Democratic National Convention, for example, they had to agree to these terms: "I commit to be peaceful in word and deed . . . I recognize that abortionists and their supporters in the press would love to portray us as angry or 'hate-filled.' Hence, I will maintain a gracious demeanor toward our adversaries."[40]

Meanwhile, even many clinic activists—who are still the most radical and least-organized activists within the pro-life movement—have found much reason to embrace the norms of civil discourse as they have been forced to abandon the tactic of blockading clinics for sidewalk counseling. While the former tactic required physical boldness, the latter practice demands good interpersonal skills if women are to be persuaded to walk away from abortion clinics. Accordingly, the mostly Catholic volunteers at Operation Rescue Boston are instructed to "[c]onvey love/empathy to the woman in sidewalk counseling. If you can't, you don't belong on the street. People have *no ears for the truth* if they *don't detect love* in the speaker."[41] Similarly, Operation Rescue West provides this instruction: "Love should be the motivation for confrontation. . . . If the sidewalk counselor is acting out of anger, frustration, or ambivalence, the woman will realize this and terminate the contact." Operation Rescue West further provides guidance to activists who encounter angry responses as sidewalk counselors inevitably do. Citing Proverbs 15:1, "a soft answer turns away wrath," activists are encouraged to disarm others through a humble and peaceful demeanor.[42] In Virginia, the sidewalk counseling-group Life and Liberty Ministries gives the same advice for defusing anger. According to its leadership, activists who confront angry citizens should "immediately lower their voice and speak softly and gently."[43]

The evangelical media emphasizes these pragmatic concerns as well. *Citizen*, which is published by Focus on the Family, routinely highlights the pitfalls of public belligerence. One article by Charles Colson provided this warning: "Rather than piercing anyone's conscience, I wonder if we are stabbing both our neighbors and our own cause." Colson continued, "[W]e must woo people's hearts toward righteousness. But we cannot woo unless we love."[44] *Christianity Today*'s campaign against Christian militancy has been even more aggressive.[45] In just one such article, John D. Woodbridge, a professor of Church History at Trinity Evangelical Divinity School, opined, "[C]ulture-war rhetoric leads us to distort others' positions, to see enmity in the place of mere disagreement. It leaves no room for nuanced positions, or for middle ground."[46] Guy M. Condon, the president of Americans United for Life, struck a similar note in another issue. Condon insisted that if Christian activists are sincerely interested in persuasion, they must be "caring, sensitive, and inclusive" and use "reasonable and compassionate" language.[47]

A lack of civility can be so poisonous to the objectives of Christian conservatives that even missionary groups, such as the National Association of Evangelicals, concern themselves with the international effects of domestic radicalism. But unlike most Christian Right groups, which have been preoccupied with rank-and-file radicalism, the leaders of the National Association of Evangelicals and other missionary groups are far more concerned with the behavior of prominent elites. This concern peaked after the attacks on the World Trade Center and Pentagon prompted radicals such as Jerry Falwell and Pat Robertson to denounce Islam as an evil and violent religion. Concerned with the damaged image of American evangelicalism in the Islamic world, the National Association of Evangelicals called a meeting of evangelical leaders who are active in Muslim countries to strategize. At the meeting, association members agreed to draft guidelines on dialogue with Islamic leaders and censured the invective of prominent evangelicals. Susan Michaels, the U.S. director of the International Christian Embassy in Jerusalem, summed up the views of others at the conference when she reported to the *Washington Post* that evangelicals "need to learn to speak the truth in love and friendship."[48]

This pervasive emphasis on Christian love, however, does not mean that leaders want activists to be passive in public forums. Although some Christian activists are certainly too zealous and need disciplining, others are too fearful of hostility from other citizens. It is a concern that gets repeatedly expressed by Christian leaders. For example, Sandy Rios, the director of Concerned Women for America, exhorted Christians on her daily radio broadcast not to disengage from public life because they fear being accused of intolerance. Rios pleaded, "Please be bold and courageous."[49] At the Ohio Right to Life Society this concern is even more salient as it organized a "Coming Out of the Closet" campaign, which encouraged pro-life activists to be assertive and open about their views in their daily lives and work places. One tactic, for instance, was to wear buttons that read "Ask Me About Abortion" and "Ask Me How Old I Am."[50] Of course, this does not mean that Ohio leaders want overbearing activists. Instead they advocate "humble assertiveness."[51]

Where these concerns are most common, however, is in organizations that devote themselves to moral suasion, such as those that engage students at university campuses, sidewalk counseling-groups, and pregnancy centers. On the morning of the first Justice for All exhibit at the Auraria campus, for example, the staff huddled together and, in addition to humility, prayed for courage and boldness.[52] Some even confessed that despite having visited many campuses, their heart still begins to pound as they approach other citizens. Furthermore, the training seminar hosted by Stand to Reason on the previous day asked volunteers to pray for "boldness" so that they might "create conversations" and "ask tough questions."[53] Leaders in the sidewalk counseling movement also stress the importance of social courage. Operation Rescue West, for instance, makes this plea to sidewalk counselors: "You must be aggressive. . . . Your popularity is not worth a child's life."[54] Likewise, Life and Liberty Ministries in Virginia counsels its activists to be "fearless."[55]

Within crisis pregnancy centers there is a similar emphasis on assertiveness. After volunteers have "earn[ed] the right to be heard" by demonstrating compassion and attentively listening to their clients' troubles, pregnancy center counselors are still required to "confront" their beliefs and behaviors. But leaders are also quick to remind volunteers, as those at Care Net do, that "the motive behind confrontation must be genuine love and concern. If there is any motivation such as anger, frustration, scorn, or the need to be assertive, the person will feel punished or rejected and the communication will not be effective. It will come across as condemnation." But even when motivated by love rather than other motives, Christian confrontation is not a simple matter. As Care Net leaders explain, confrontation "is not always easy. It requires balancing compassion with boldness." Yet volunteers are asked to maintain this love and acceptance even if their clients ultimately choose to have an abortion. And, here again, common assumptions about the relationship between Christianity and tolerance for the moral choices of other citizens is complicated by another fact. Care Net trainings ask volunteers to accept and love those women who choose abortion because "God's interest lies beyond outcomes." Instead, the Care Net training continues, "His interest is in our faithfulness and obedience. We cannot control what someone else will decide, but we can control how we educate, love, and accept someone."[56]

That many Christian leaders labor to build up the courage and confidence of at least some of their activists may strike readers as particularly surprising. After all, activists are often regarded as too belligerent rather than sheepish. It is less surprising, however, when we consider the nature of the activism just described, since it requires citizens to approach perfect strangers and confront them with arguments that commonly invite hostility or indifference. Such activism is quite different from the very familiar marches and demonstrations where citizens tend to be far less reticent. In these settings, activists draw on the support and camaraderie of other like-minded citizens rather than confront those who disagree with them. In fact, the morale-building that takes place in mass marches fuels the far more intimidating work of talking to other citizens.

Dialogue

Of course, civility is merely a necessary rather than sufficient condition for real deliberative discussion. As scholars such as Benjamin Barber and Adolf Gunderson have emphasized, citizens also need to listen carefully to one another and ask good questions.[57] Leaders in the Christian Right tend to agree. To cultivate and nurture conversations with other citizens, Christian leaders encourage activists to respect and understand the opinions of others by listening attentively and asking questions. While demonstrating respect for the views of other citizens builds rapport and credibility, actually understanding others allows Christian activists to develop persuasive responses.

To converse in a meaningful way with other citizens, activists must practice a careful attentiveness to what others are telling them. Accordingly, Christian Right organizations remind their activists to listen intently to those who disagree with them. The president of Concerned Women for America, for example, instructed her members to "[l]isten to the opposition. Know their arguments and reasons. You will be better at presenting your own point of view if you know what motivates their thinking. How can you expect them to listen to you if you don't listen to them?"[58] Providing similar advice, the Christian Coalition training seminars on citizen lobbying instructed activists as follows:

> Officials with an opposing view often can offer a perspective on an issue that you may have overlooked. Discuss the issue with the politician or activist on the other side. If you understand what your opponents are saying, you will be in a better position to counter their arguments. Do not discount your opponent's arguments as just being wrong. . . . While you personally may not agree with someone's views, your challenge is to gain insight into all aspects of the issue so you can build a winning coalition.[59]

Meanwhile, leaders at the Ohio Right to Life Society tell their extensive membership to "listen to your opponent respectfully and sincerely before telling your side. . . . In their view, if you're not really willing to listen to them, how smart or credible can you be."[60]

Listening to others is crucial precisely because activists—both on the Right and Left—often do not understand their opponents or ordinary Americans very well. Therefore, Christian leaders highlight the distance between devout believers and other Americans. As an official at the Leadership Institute informed me, the institute always emphasizes in its grassroots training school that conservative activists are strange characters and that political success requires "getting into the heads" of ordinary Americans.[61] Steve Wagner of Stand to Reason tells his students in training seminars that they need to become "normal," which involves building common ties to other citizens.[62] Far from a "moral majority," these training seminars remind Christian activists that they, no less than activists on the Left, are a radicalized minority.

Christian Right organizations that are devoted to moral suasion (as opposed to grassroots lobbying or electoral politics more broadly) are especially interested in building relationships with other citizens. Such organizations range from those that target university campuses, such as Justice for All, the Center for Bio-Ethical Reform, and Survivors, to sidewalk counseling groups and crisis pregnancy centers. In the case of the former, organization leaders train their volunteers to listen to students and ask probing questions rather than lecture or preach. As the director of the Center for Bio-Ethical Reform, Greg Cunningham, put it, "[W]e are very Socratic; we ask more questions than make declarative statements."[63] The appeal of the Socratic method for Christian leaders is that not only does it help build trust and credibility with other citizens, but it also helps Christian activists encourage their fellow citizens to think more thoughtfully and carefully about the morality of abortion. As Stand to Reason instructor Steve Wagner explained to a group of Justice for All volunteers, "[W]e need to create conversations by asking questions," which will help us "find common ground" with, as well as "clarify"and "challenge the views" of, pro-choice students. Wagner also warned volunteers not to assume knowledge of other students' beliefs or even the correct answer to all questions. As he put it to the assembled volunteers, "[P]lease don't assume that you know what the other person thinks. It is critical to listen to the other person's story." Finally, Wagner also encouraged the practice of humility since "we all have false beliefs."[64] Or as the training handout emphasized, "Remember that there are also problems with your thinking (if only you knew what they were, you could correct them!)."[65]

A similar perspective is common at evangelical colleges across the country, even small fundamentalist ones, such as Patrick Henry College. With a mission of training "Christian men and women who will lead our nation and shape our future,"[66] Patrick Henry College emphasizes to its students, a majority of whom were relatively isolated from secular influences in home school environments, that they need to listen to and understand the other side before they can engage the wider public. Michael Farris, the college's president and founder, recently argued that the "ability to argue both sides of a case is essential to winning a debate." Farris, like so many of his fellow evangelicals, further believes that Christ's command not to judge others involves "showing respect for their opinions, talking to them, [and] listening carefully."[67]

Among far less philosophically oriented sidewalk counselors, there is a similar dedication to building relationships with other citizens. For instance, in their zeal to prevent abortions, sidewalk counselors sometimes rush around patients as they approach the clinic and then talk all at once. But as leaders in the sidewalk counseling movement point out, such behavior often intimidates women and discourages them from talking to Christian activists. Accordingly, Operation Rescue West gives this advice to sidewalk counselors: "Only one at a time should speak. When too many try to talk, the woman cannot hear all that is being said. This often makes her feel frightened or harassed." And like organizations that target university students, Operation Rescue West also wants activists to ask questions that foster real understanding. In fact, the same training manual provides this instruction to promote dialogue: "Ask the woman questions that do not require 'yes' or 'no' responses. Try to ascertain her situation and find out what she needs to help her through this crisis in her life."[68] Similarly, Life and Liberty Ministries in Virginia tells its activists that they "must have a two-way conversation" and that "questions are ideal for getting conversations going and obtaining information."[69] Meanwhile, the leadership of Operation Rescue Boston instructs its sidewalk counselors to "talk to them on their terms. Find out where they are and lead them to the next step."[70]

When I spoke with Cheryl Sullenger, who trained hundreds of sidewalk counselors in San Diego County as the former director of the now-defunct California Life Coalition, she expressed a similar emphasis on building relationships with pregnant women. First and foremost, Sullenger tells activists that they should not "mob" women entering the clinic because it is intimidating. The second major point Sullenger highlights for sidewalk counselors is that they should "talk with them, not at them." As she described her approach, it is critical that activists "find out what [the patients'] problems are" so they can do their best to address them. Such information is very difficult if not impossible to acquire if the pro-life activist is doing most of the talking.[71]

Perhaps more than any other type of Christian leader, however, those who are devoted to training volunteers in crisis pregnancy centers are especially interested in equipping Christians to build relationships with other citizens. In fact, if the model for groups that lobby university students is Socrates, it is far closer to Oprah Winfrey for pregnancy center volunteers. This is because volunteers in such centers are something like a counselor—they want to help women sort through their feelings, build trust and rapport, and guide them toward pro-life options and faith. To build intimate relationships with pregnant women, pregnancy center volunteers are directed to listen carefully to their client. Care Net trainings, for example, provide this warning to volunteers: "Before the client can hear your solutions, she needs to know that you have heard and understood her problems." Proverbs 18:13 is invoked to reinforce this wisdom: "He who answers before listening—that is a folly and a shame." In addition to "active listening," as Care Net calls it, volunteers are also directed to ask for clarifications if they do not understand their client and to ask open-ended questions that deepen understanding.[72]

This new "woman-centered" approach, as pro-life activists often call it, did not come about over night, nor is it embraced in all centers. In fact, a significant minority of centers remain independent from an affiliate organization. The result of such independence, according to the director of Care Net, is that these centers tend to "have no professionally trained staff" and "mistakenly rely on a 'baby-focused' approach that emphasizes the need to use every means available to save the baby."[73] Such centers, however, have more in common with those of an earlier era than most contemporary pregnancy centers. As Julie Parton, who is responsible for providing resources to pregnancy centers at Focus on the Family, explains, "Initially there was too much emphasis on saving babies, which alienated the girls." Young women reasoned, Parton continued, "[W]hy should I listen to them if they don't listen to me?"[74]

This new woman-centered philosophy is laid out in great detail in Care Net trainings, which succinctly describe it this way: "A women-focused ministry is rooted in the understanding that our role is to minister to the client's needs, recognizing that it is she who must make the ultimate choices. When we instead try to focus our efforts on saving babies, we can easily lose sight of this role of ministry to the client." In fact, crisis pregnancy centers have been so devoted to this woman-centered approach that they have drawn criticism from other quarters of the pro-life movement for not investing in fetal life enough. One pro-life leader I spoke with even called crisis pregnancy centers "Planned Parenthood light." Parton acknowledged that perhaps there is some truth to this critique, but that the change from a baby- to a woman-centered approach was "vitally important" nonetheless.[75]

Theology

In academic circles, one of the most contentious issues has been the role of religious arguments in public forums. According to Amy Gutmann and Dennis Thompson, religious claims have no place in the public square since citizens must offer grounds for their views that are "mutually justifiable."[76] Christian Right elites, however, tend to agree with Gutmann and Thompson. Like other Christian movements in American history, the Christian Right has learned that religious arguments are unpersuasive to many of their fellow citizens.[77] Thus, Christian leaders tell their rank-and-file activists to carefully avoid religious arguments in public forums even as they look to scripture to justify deliberative norms.

It is often assumed that Christian activists reflexively resort to religious arguments in the public square. Yet one of the great ironies of the abortion debate is that it is actually the secular pro-choice movement that routinely frames abortion as a religious issue. It does so largely for strategic reasons. Advocates of abortion rights recognize that if the ontological status of the embryo is exclusively a theological question, then the state must treat abortion as a private, religious matter. After all, any effort to restrict abortion could only be an illegitimate assertion of sectarian metaphysics.

This was precisely John Kerry's position in the 2004 presidential campaign where he argued in stump speeches and in the debates that his personal pro-life view should have no influence on public policy because it was just an "article of faith."[78] Outside the Kerry campaign, NARAL Pro-Choice America, the National Organization for Women, and Planned Parenthood have argued for decades that abortion decisions are religious in nature since they should be left to a "woman, her doctor, and her God"—a mantra that is often repeated in the halls of Congress and editorial pages. Likewise, the Religious Coalition for Reproductive Choice concludes that abortion decisions are properly left to individuals because "of the wide range of religious beliefs on this sensitive issue." In fact, the coalition regards the unfettered freedom to make such choices as an "essential element of religious liberty."[79] Even *Roe v. Wade* itself grounded abortion rights partly on the sociological fact that various faith traditions disagree on the morality of abortion.

Partly in an effort to counter this strategy, nearly all pro-life organizations insist that their views cannot be dismissed as merely religious in nature. The leadership of Arizona Right to Life tells its membership that the pro-life cause cannot succeed "until we address the concerns of secular-minded citizens."[80] Dan Kennedy, the executive director of Human Life of Washington, offered similar advice to his rank-and-file activists: "To be heard, we must speak in a language that holds meaning for people . . . not simply in a style we think they should hear." Kennedy continued, "[W]e must reach out to all segments of society in a manner that is compelling and relevant to their lives."[81] Pat Chivers, the Director of Governmental Relations at Georgia Right to Life, is more blunt. According to Chivers, she simply tells her activists that they "can't preach!" when they contact public officials.[82]

At times pro-life leaders even become exasperated by the pro-choice movement's success as framing abortion as a religious issue. Such frustration was evident in the directives of Georgia Right to Life: "Do not be sidetracked by pro-abortion comments that typically come up. The most common is to dismiss the undeniable facts of prenatal life as merely a 'religious' issue. Do not allow your questioner to discount the scientific facts of life with misleading beside-the-point rhetoric. . . . While it may be tempting, and in some settings even appropriate, to engage in a discussion of the theological origins for a person's pro-life position, usually the religious arguments are just another attempt by pro-abortionists to evade the powerful truth you are presenting."[83] The media spokesperson for Maine Right to Life, Lisa Roche, was even more agitated. When I asked her about the pro-choice campaign in her state to frame a proposed ban on partial-birth abortion as a religious issue, she responded, "[I]t has nothing to do with religion!"[84] Meanwhile, Greg Koukl, the president of Stand to Reason, has been similarly irritated by the campaign on behalf of embryonic stem cell research. As Koukl explained to his supporters, "By labeling our view as 'theological belief' . . . [opponents have] tried to dismiss our ethical case, banning it to the wasteland of irrelevance."[85]

As this last example suggests, staffers at Stand to Reason aggressively discourage religious arguments in the public square. Paradoxically, Stand to Reason even describes a Christian ambassador as someone who does not talk like a Christian. Its "Ambassadors Creed" directs believers to be "careful with language, and not rely on Christian lingo." Instructors at Stand to Reason tend to defend their efforts to keep religious arguments out of the public square on pragmatic grounds. When I spoke to Scott Klusendorf, for example, he criticized Jerry Falwell for articulating scriptural arguments against homosexuality on the talk show *Donahue*. As Klusendorf explained, "[H]e should have made arguments based on the public good and not Deuteronomy" given the show's largely secular audience.[86] Making a similar case, I witnessed Stand to Reason instructor Steve Wagner encourage Justice for All volunteers at Arvada Covenant Church to eschew theological language when engaging college students. Wagner told his pupils that it was especially important not to refer to abortion as a "sin." Instead students should use the word "injustice" when discussing abortion. More generally, he instructed the volunteers never to mention scripture since it will have no effect on those who do not believe.[87]

It is not just the larger, more professionalized, pro-life organizations that emphasize secular discourse. At a recent meeting of First Right, a pro-life student organization at the University of Virginia, its leadership demonstrated the commitments of more-senior movement leaders. When the group's president described a presentation given the prior year on scriptural passages that students could use when arguing for a pro-life position, the former president called out from the audience, "*If* you're talking to a Christian!" The new president followed her lead and noted that since the University of Virginia is largely a secular campus, First Right members should deploy the good philosophical arguments that they had learned in other presentations.[88] In addition, pro-life student organizations at fourteen of America's most elite universities ran the same full-page ad in their respective student newspapers, which elaborated an extended philosophical apology for the pro-life position. The ad concluded with this defense: "Contrary to the claims of our opponents, none of our appeals have been personal, private, or religious. Our simple demand is for the equal protection of all human beings."[89]

Outside the pro-life movement, Christian Right elites articulate similar concerns. When its members contact public officials, Concerned Women for America routinely offers this strong directive: "Don't preach: remember, you want to influence your legislator's vote, not convert him to your religion."[90] Charles Colson was more colorful in the pages of *Citizen*, where he encouraged evangelicals to avoid speaking "Christianese." Colson continued, "Because Christian activists seek to change society, they must win the support of mainstream Americans, many of whom will be alienated by Christian imagery, theology and idiom."[91] In another issue of *Citizen*, evangelical readers were offered more concrete suggestions from Tom Minnery: "[W]hen Christian citizens make anti-pornography arguments, they shouldn't use Scripture. Instead, they should use moral arguments that make common sense to all. Pornography degrades women. Pornography desensitizes men to rape and other sexually violent behavior. Pornography shops attract prostitution and depress property values," and so on.[92] Kerby Anderson of Probe Ministries, a research-oriented organization that disseminates materials within the Christian Right, elaborated a similar point: "Christians should articulate the moral teachings of scripture in ways that are meaningful in a pluralistic society. . . . Scientific, social, legal, and ethical considerations can be useful in arguing for biblical principles in a secular culture."[93]

Reaching a larger evangelical audience, *Christianity Today* has echoed these appeals. Thomas Grey, the founder of the National Coalition Against Legalized Gambling, offered *Christianity Today* readers this advice in a recent issue: "In a pluralistic nation, the church is not in a position to dictate, 'Thou shall not gamble.' But we can ask the right questions: What is social morality? What is just economics? What is good uncorrupted government?"[94] Another article in *Christianity Today* even suggested that it is intrinsically wrong to deploy religious arguments in the public square: "When we speak in the public square . . . we can be faithful to Christ while using the language of the public square. . . . It would be insensitive as well as ineffective, for example, for Christians to exhort their Jewish, Muslim, or agnostic neighbors in terms of what Jesus would want us to do."[95]

Meanwhile, evangelical colleges across the country push their students to defend their biblical beliefs on secular grounds in a way that is consistent with a long Christian apologetic tradition. One of the principal goals of Patrick Henry College, for instance, is to "integrate the Christian worldview with the study of the liberal arts and sciences."[96] Or, as one professor put it more candidly, "'The Bible says so' is never the answer to [his] questions."[97]

Christian Right organizations, however, are not merely concerned with the introduction of theology into public forums; they even want to keep it out of internal organizational politics. Indeed, many leaders take precautions that help ensure that their political goals will not be compromised by internecine struggles over proper belief.

The National Right to Life Committee has always been nonsectarian because its founders did not want theological questions to divide the rank and file.[98] In general, NRLC's nonsectarian charter has served it well: few theological conflicts have arisen in an organization that aside from a handful of atheists and Jews in its ranks is roughly divided between evangelicals and Catholics. When occasional conflicts do occur, they often reinforce the nonsectarian commitments of organization leaders. For example, Barbara Listing, the director of Right to Life of Michigan (RLM), informed me that one local affiliate formally broke with the state organization because its members insisted that RLM's mission statement should restrict membership to Christians. Listing objected to such exclusivity partly because she got her start in Right to Life of Michigan under an atheist chapter leader. But Listing was also concerned that creating an explicitly Christian mission statement would introduce theological debate and schism into the state organization.[99] It is a concern, moreover, that is reflected in a handbook that is distributed to all presidents of local affiliates. It offers this admonition:

> It should be remembered that RLM as an organization was formed to promote the civil liberties of the unborn. Thus, within a RTL group there may be a wide spectrum of theological views and personal motivations for involvement. Leaders of affiliates should be sensitive to these differences and not allow them to undermine our ability to cooperate with others. The goal which unites us (the ultimate passage of a Human Life Amendment) should be the focus of our joint efforts.[100]

Suffering a similar fate, the executive director of the Pennsylvania Pro-Life Action League was dismayed by one local affiliate that broke from the parent organization because of its strong Catholic commitments. According to executive director Michael Ciccocioppo, the local affiliate objected to the mission of the state organization—which is exclusively focused on abortion, infanticide, and euthanasia—because it did not include a position on contraception. The Pennsylvania Pro-Life Action League, like all NRLC affiliates, does not include contraception among its core issues because many of its non-Catholic members have a different perspective on the issue.[101]

At Texas Right to Life (TRL), the commitment to keeping religious questions out of in-house debates is similarly strong. Unlike other state affiliates of National Right to Life, its concerns, however, spring from the experiences of another pro-life organization. As Joseph Graham, the TRL president, explained, Texans United for Life completely disintegrated after an explosion of activity because it was an extremely sectarian, evangelical organization. Its charismatic leader, Bill Price, simply could not sustain the religious zeal that birthed the organization and build a more ecumenical base of support.[102]

Efforts to minimize theological debate among rank-and-file activists were especially strenuous at the Christian Coalition. According to Mark Rozell, Christian Coalition leaders were mindful of the Moral Majority's failure to build a genuinely ecumenical political organization.[103] Their fear of theological infighting prompted Coalition leaders to be attentive to religious tensions and train rank-and-file members to keep theological questions out of chapter politics. One training seminar instructed activists to eschew theocratic impulses: "Avoid confrontations on theological issues. Our mission is to change the laws under which our nation is governed, not to establish religious doctrine." Chapter leaders were further told to "respect the differences between religious backgrounds and keep them in mind when asking volunteers to perform certain tasks." Christian Coalition training seminars also reminded members of the strategic utility of ecumenical cooperation: "In order to improve the social and political fabric of this nation, we must work side-by-side with other pro-family individuals. Allowing doctrinal issues to intrude into the local chapter will only strengthen those who oppose what we are trying to do."[104]

Although Christian organizations generally discourage their activists from making religious claims, it is certainly not true of all groups. Most crisis pregnancy centers, for example, explicitly have an evangelical mission. An important exception to this tendency is the affiliate Birthright, which is a mostly Catholic organization that oversees some 400 centers and explicitly forbids evangelism by charter. Most centers, however, regard Christ as the ultimate solution to their clients' troubles. As Care Net puts it, "The Gospel is the long-term solution to a client's problems in lifestyle, relationships, or pregnancy choices. The Gospel is what allows women who come to the center to make life-affirming decisions that have eternal consequences." Yet, consistent with these centers' woman-centered focus, there is nothing heavy-handed about their evangelism. Training seminars at Care Net, for example, instruct volunteers not to mention Christ until they have established a relationship with their client and demonstrated their love. Care Net's training manual reads, "Young people are not looking for a lecture about salvation; they are looking to see whether our lives, the way we speak, and the way we listen, reflect the compassion and love of Christ. . . . Once we have demonstrated the Gospel through our attitudes and actions, we are much more likely to be given the opportunity to share the salvation message." What is more, volunteers are also told not to push their faith on reluctant citizens. Instead, Care Net trainings provide this instruction: "If you begin to talk about Christ and you see that she is not interested, drop it and move on to the next part of your time together."[105]

Despite overwhelming evidence to the contrary, most critics continue to insist that Christian conservatives routinely articulate theological arguments in the public square. Most recently, editorials in the *Washington Post* and *New York Times* accused President George W. Bush and his allies of advocating "stem cell theology" in their case against embryonic stem cell research.[106] Yet, they offered almost no evidence for this assertion. The only exception was an editorial by Jerome Groopman, a professor at Harvard Medical School. Groopman highlighted the following remark by Tom DeLay as evidence for a stem cell theology: "An embryo is a person, a distinct, internally directed, self-integrating human organism. We were all at one time human embryos ourselves. So was Abraham. So was Muhammad. So was Jesus of Nazareth."[107] DeLay, however, was not elaborating a theological claim; he was doing precisely the opposite. In DeLay's view, theology has no relevance whatsoever to bioethics since, as he sees it, science shows that a human person exists at conception. Thus, regardless of whether one believes in Judaism, Christianity, or Islam, one should oppose embryonic stem cell research. The great search for a stem cell theology turned out to unearth a bit of counter-evidence.

As I have already emphasized, it is actually liberal advocates who often frame critical bioethical issues in religious terms. For example, when politicians insist that they cannot allow their private, religious convictions to influence bioethical policies, the clear implication is that science and philosophy can shed very little light on the moral status of the embryo. Such weighty questions are simply trapped in the darkness of religious metaphysics. Yet, those on the bioethical Left have provided no justification for taking such a dim view of human reason. Worse still, they have quietly undermined the entire enterprise of bioethics, which must begin with the assumption that human reason can shed light on such questions.

MORAL REASONING

Christian Right leaders recognize that it is not enough simply to avoid religious arguments to be persuasive—activists must also make well-reasoned and informed arguments. Such arguments help establish the credibility of activists and persuade other citizens. With this in mind, Christian elites tell their rank-and-file activists to avoid false or distorted claims as well as appeals to their personal feelings or emotions. Christian leaders, therefore, embrace the very heart of deliberation, which is traditionally defined as "reasoning on the merits of public policy."[108]

Christian leaders fear that over-zealous activists will compromise their organizations' credibility by spreading false or distorted information. In 1990 J. C. Willke, the former president of the National Right to Life Committee, pleaded with his membership in the organization's newspaper, saying, "Accuracy, please. Meticulous accuracy should be the order of the day in terms of factual happenings."[109] Willke's admonition is echoed in the NRLC's lobbying guidelines: "If the congressman or staff asks you a question that you don't know the answer to, don't guess. Tell him you'll provide that information later—and do so. If you give a congressman or his aid misinformation, it can erode your credibility and that of other pro-life lobbyists."[110] Focus on the Family is concerned about its credibility as well. An article in *Citizen* on the political consequences of spreading false information concluded, "Because errors are so common, it is hard to overemphasize the need for skepticism."[111] *Christianity Today* has gone further. One of its articles argued that dishonesty breaks God's commandments: "[T]he command to love has a particular obverse side: 'we may not bear false witness.' . . . After engaging in careful research, we may discover that we have misunderstood [our secular opponents], and if so, are duty bound to say so rather than continue misrepresenting them."[112] Finally, the Center for Reclaiming America cautioned Christian activists involved in school board politics to "[n]ever, never, never make an accusation or charge that you can't substantiate."[113]

Concerns over the accuracy of information have been especially prominent in organizations that have been sued by opponents on the Left. Leaders at the Christian Coalition, for example, have labored to protect the integrity of their voter guides, which have been the target of multiple lawsuits. The Coalition's director of voter education warned state leaders at a 1994 strategy briefing that "if you're not certain [as to a candidate's position] don't risk it. The credibility is on the line of your organization and of this tool [voter guides]."[114] Similarly, crisis pregnancy centers, which were once far less disciplined about providing undistorted information, have now changed their orientation after several lawsuits. Care Net trainings, for example, stress that volunteers "must avoid presenting information on abortion risks that contain inaccuracies, exaggerations, outdated statistics or any form of misleading information." The training even cautions against making statements that are vague and misleading but not false in any technical sense, such as "Many women die each year from abortion." Volunteers are also asked to admit that medical studies have not yet established a "definite linkage between abortion and breast cancer" and that whether or not a woman is likely to experience "post-abortion emotional difficulties" depends on many factors, including the "religious beliefs of the woman," the "circumstances surrounding the abortion," and the "stage of pregnancy when the abortion occurred."[115]

When I discussed all of these changes with the director of Pregnancy Resource Ministries at Focus on the Family, including the lawsuits from pro-choice advocates, she responded, "It's OK, it keeps us on our toes" and, in any case, "deception does not honor God."[116] That such heightened conflict has led, at least in the Christian Right, to greater devotion to making accurate statements should certainly cause us to question the claim that culture-war conflict invariably leads to greater distortion in public forums.

Christian leaders are just as worried their activists will build their case on personal emotional appeals without recourse to reasoned arguments. Sometimes they even become exasperated with activists who will not take the time to educate themselves. For example, Dauneen Dolce, director of the New Mexico Right to Life Committee, recently pleaded with her members to attend a state conference. "It is fine," she said, "to have a strong emotional feeling about being pro-life. However, you also need to have a strong knowledge base to accompany those feelings. Arguing on emotion usually doesn't affect the average person, but a good source of different facts that are able to 'push the right buttons' can convince others to the cause."[117] Likewise, the Ohio Right to Life Society gives this advice to activists before they contact public officials: "Resolve to take a *reasoned* (not emotional) approach to the matter."[118] Meanwhile, Texas Right to Life leaders encourage their rank-and-file activists to "provide legislators with objective evidence" since these lawmakers "want substantive reasons to defend their vote to themselves and others."[119]

Pat Chivers, the director of governmental relations at Georgia Right to Life, candidly recalled the excessive emotionalism of some Christian activists. In Chivers' account, activists sometimes become angry with their representatives and "just want to walk [into their offices] and tell them off." It is Chivers' job to prevent such outbursts by training her members. As she explained, "I help channel that energy" by providing talking points and reminding activists that they need to build a relationship.[120]

The emphasis has been similar at Concerned Women for America, the Center for Reclaiming America, and the Christian Coalition. CWA has even invoked the rationalism of Abraham Lincoln: "Reason, cold, calculating, unimpassioned reason, must furnish the materials of our future support and defense."[121] To facilitate such rationalism, CWA distributes pamphlets that explore the legal history of the church-state conflict, medical findings on RU-486, evidence for a potential link between breast cancer and abortion, and federal regulations on public schools.[122] The Center for Reclaiming America similarly instructs school board activists to "keep [their] emotions under a tight rein" and present "credible source materials" such as a "scientific journal."[123] Meanwhile, the Texas Christian Coalition encourages its activists to make requests that are "reasonable and possible to accomplish," devoid of "exaggeration," and not "argumentative or abrasive." Texas leaders believe that fidelity to these guidelines "will go a long way in opening up communication."[124] Staffers at South Carolina Christian Coalition also want to undermine moral zealotry. Its leadership tells local activists to be "constructive and suggest alternatives" and to "recognize that compromise is often an essential ingredient of the law-making process."[125] Likewise, the Christian Coalition of Oregon reminds its membership to "identify possible alternatives" and "accommodate other ideas."[126]

In some cases, evangelicals are prepared to engage in political and moral debates even before they enter political life. Patrick Henry College, which has the unique mission among evangelical colleges of training young people for public life, is especially interested in building Christian thinkers. Its students take a variety of courses that serve this end, including courses in logic, rhetoric, and philosophy. As Hanna Rosin, a reporter for the *New Yorker* put it, "[A]t Patrick Henry, debate plays roughly the same role that football is to Notre Dame."[127] The results of the college's mock debate competitions corroborate Rosin's account. In fact, as of 2005, Patrick Henry College was the national defending champions in moot court and even beat the Oxford law students on two occasions, once using British law and procedure. And most of its graduates do enter public life, often taking internships and jobs on Capitol Hill, the White House, and conservative think tanks. As the school's president, Michael Farris, has emphasized, Patrick Henry's internship program provides students with critical experience in the real, compromising world of politics.[128]

Perhaps more than any other Christian Right organization, staffers at Stand to Reason are most opposed to the emotionalism that sometimes dominates public life. Scott Klusendorf's criticisms of Christian Right politics even parallel Richard Hofstadter's view that American Christianity has an anti-intellectual tradition that values the spirit over intellectual rigor. When we met on the campus of Biola University, Klusendorf reported that Christian activists have been "good at shouting conclusions, not establishing facts."[129] He has made the same argument more gently to Christian activists: "[W]e have a pro-life movement that does pretty well at marches and rallies, but we're not doing so hot in terms of building Christian thinkers who can articulate a pro-life view."[130]

Klusendorf attempts to inspire greater intellectual engagement among his evangelical audiences, in keeping with 1 Peter 3:15–16, which requires Christians to "give reasons" for their beliefs. As he put it during one of James Dobson's radio broadcasts, "[S]cripture commands us to argue well."[131]

It should be emphasized, however, that many Christian leaders, even those at Stand to Reason, do not want to banish moral passions from public forums. Indeed, many groups, including Justice for All, the Center for Bio-Ethical Reform, and Survivors, are highly trained to make philosophical arguments in defense of fetal life *and* also bring provocative images of aborted fetuses to college campuses across the country. However, images that obviously stoke moral passions are not as at odds with rational moral discourse as some culture war critics contend.[132] In fact, proponents' defense of graphic images is essentially two-fold: they awaken moral intuitions and get people talking. Greg Cunningham, the director of the Center for Bio-Ethical Reform, has defended the images because they help to "stimulate a dialogue," adding, "but we want that dialogue to be well informed."[133] The leadership of Justice for All shares Cunningham's view. In fact, they are especially pleased when the images provoke pro-choice groups on campus to counter-demonstrate because it brings more of the student body to see the exhibit and talk to the pro-life activists.[134] On the first day of the Justice for All exhibit in Denver, for example, the group's director could hardly contain his glee when a prominent pro-choice display was erected in response.[135] In this way, the campus outreaches of the Center for Bio-Ethical Reform and Justice for All are really microcosms of this larger tension between a more participatory and deliberative democracy; moral passions must be provoked to excite political action, but deliberative norms shape it.

There is also an ongoing debate among pro-life leaders as to whether images of aborted fetuses are manipulative or informative. The former camp includes the leadership of Care Net and Birthright—two of the largest pregnancy center affiliates. According to the director of Care Net, such images possess an "inherent power . . . to distort rational thinking." Care Net further elaborates its ban on showing graphic images to clients in its Abortion Education Guidelines: "The primary impact of showing graphic images is to shock clients, not educate them. Such practices can be seen as a form of manipulation and coercion." On the other hand, Stand to Reason defends the use of graphic images in many settings, because they are thought to puncture the misconception that embryos and fetuses are merely clumps of undifferentiated tissue. As Scott Klusendorf put it, "The purpose of displaying these controversial images is not to manipulate people emotionally, but to convey truth better than words ever can."[136] Perhaps the foremost defender of graphic images, Gregg Cunningham of the

Center for Bio-Ethical Reform, similarly thinks of these images as revealing "facts" that would otherwise be ignored. According to Cunningham, "The culture is in massive denial about what abortion is and does. Social reformers have always had to force feed facts into the heads of people who resist evidence in their own complicity in injustice."[137]

However one views the pedagogical value of these images, nowhere in Christian politics have the efforts to inform the moral sentiments of activists been greater than in the pro-life movement. Whether it is Randy Alcorn's widely read *Pro-Life Answers to Pro-Choice Arguments*, education seminars within the state affiliates of the National Right to Life Committee, courses in bio-ethics at evangelical colleges, the campus outreaches of Justice for All and the Center for Bio-Ethical Reform, or Christian apologetics at Stand to Reason, the pro-life movement as a whole is diligently laboring to move the abortion debate beyond slogans and unreflective beliefs. What is more, pro-life leaders are gaining an intellectual confidence and sophistication that is especially surprising among evangelicals, who have been in a century-long intellectual retreat from the academy and its values.[138]

This newfound intellectual sophistication was in evidence at the training seminar I attended at Arvada Covenant Church. Steve Wagner of Stand to Reason emphasized to the assembled activists that they *should* accept permissive abortion laws *if* pro-choice students could demonstrate that the differences between fetuses and newborns were morally significant. Wagner continued that there were really just four differences between fetuses and newborns: size, level of development, environment, and dependency. None of these distinctions, in Wagner's view, was sufficient to change the ontological status of the embryo. The burden for pro-choice advocates, Wagner then explained, is to show that the value of a human being depends on the characteristics that he or she acquires rather than the kind of thing that it is. And contrary to the *Roe* decision, Wagner argued that we should err on the side of caution and protect the fetus if we are at all uncertain as to its ontological status. If it is possible that over forty million humans have perished since *Roe*, we should embrace philosophical caution.[139] Framed this way, Stand to Reason and other pro-life advocates want to place the philosophical burden of proof on the other side even as they offer their own evidence for the value of fetal life.

• • •

This survey of elite messages found that Christian Right leaders in the pro-life movement overwhelmingly emphasize four important deliberative norms: promoting public civility, practicing careful listening and dialogue, avoiding theological arguments, and embracing moral reasoning.

The teaching of these norms has been a massive though relatively unnoticed undertaking. In fact, the evidence in this chapter scratches only the surface of such efforts. Yet, despite the prevalence of democratic education in the Christian Right, there are important sources of Christian radicalism. For this reason, the next chapter examines the enduring influence and importance of such radicalism and explores its causes.

CHAPTER TWO

Christian Radicalism

As PREVALENT AS DEMOCRATIC EDUCATION has become in the Christian Right, there are important and enduring sources of radicalism. Indeed, strident radicalism can be found within the relatively moderate organizations discussed at length in the previous chapter. To survive, these groups need to mobilize the passions of uninvolved citizens and maintain the moral conviction of their rank-and-file activists. This reality exposes a clear dilemma for many Christian leaders: they must excite and sustain the moral convictions of citizens to build an activist base on the one hand; but, on the other, they must also discipline and educate the passions of mobilized activists before they practice public advocacy. As will be discussed at greater length in chapter 6, these countervailing pressures highlight an even greater tension between the ideal of a participatory and a deliberative democracy.

Outside of mainstream organizations, militant fundamentalists have been an important and volatile source of Christian radicalism. The Moral Majority under the leadership of Jerry Falwell and Operation Rescue under Randall Terry exemplified such militancy. But not only did such radical organizations come relatively late to the culture wars, they also are now on the decline and can currently claim very few Christian activists. This is partly because their militancy alienates conservative Christians and because fundamentalist leaders have been very ambivalent about politics.

These lingering sources of radicalism have been magnified by a hostile media that tends to characterize the Right in a negative way and focus on its most militant activists. Yet despite all of the legitimate complaints of a liberal media bias in conservative circles, it is also true that Christian media often projects a strident image of the Christian Right to the larger public. This is because Christian media personalities are primarily interested in exhorting their base. But unlike political mobilization in mainstream organizations, the moral exhortations of media personalities are far more visible. Therefore, they must embrace a public radicalism in a way that leaders of interest groups do not.

MOBILIZING THE FAITHFUL

Although Christian elites generally do not explicitly tell their rank-and-file activists to behave contrary to deliberative norms, they nonetheless exhort them in ways that excite their passions and prejudices. For citizens to give their time, energy, and dollars to a cause that brings them no material reward, their moral passions need to be excited and sustained. The most important mobilization tool in the pro-life movement has been images of aborted fetuses, while direct mail has been critical to the survival of Christian Right organizations more broadly. In fact, direct mail has become a staple of nearly all public interest groups. Paul Johnson's study of public interest groups found that direct mail was "the single most important method" of contacting and recruiting new members.[1]

This is not to suggest that strident or militant language is neatly confined to appeals directed to uninvolved citizens. The moral passions of leaders and activists alike need to be continually stoked. Annual marches, for all their excesses, serve this function well by drawing battle-weary activists together. Likewise, "everyday talk" (to borrow Jane Mansbridge's term) in the circles of Christian Right activists is full of strident language and harsh characterizations of opponents in particular.[2] Liberal activists are routinely called by such epithets as "baby-killers" and "pro-aborts." It is likely that these almost-reflexive tendencies compromise the ability of Christian leaders and activists to embrace deliberative norms in the public square. But they also no doubt sustain the moral passions that compel Christian citizens to participate.

Observers of the culture wars have tended to single out direct mail for promoting radicalism and coarsening public life. They do so for good reason, since direct mail is unusually vitriolic and hysterical. Mailings in Christian Right organizations are certainly no exception.[3] In stark contrast to the communications reviewed in the previous chapter, direct mail routinely describes liberal opponents with terms that tend to emphasize their extremism, such as "abortionists," "radical special interests," "militant homosexuals," and "ultra-feminists."[4]

The Right's political opponents are not simply characterized as extreme. They also are reputed to seek patently depraved ends and do so through immoral means. Among other evils, the Left is charged with attempting to "destroy marriage," promoting "baby harvesting," corrupting the "innocence of children," and laboring toward "the wholesale destruction of parental authority."[5] These objectives, in turn, are pursued through deceit and dishonesty. According to the Christian Coalition, liberals use "oppressive and unconscionable tactics," do "everything possible to misrepresent our concerns and positions," and are "masters of misinformation and confusion."[6] CWA likewise informs citizens that liberal activists "grotesquely distort the truth," perpetrate "horrible deceptions," and are "masters of dishonest rhetoric."[7] Liberals further are said to resort to "vicious political ploys" and happily "use any political tactic conceivable."[8] Christian Right organizations also return liberal charges of intolerance and bigotry. Christian Coalition and CWA mailings routinely accuse liberal groups of religious "bigotry" and attempting to "silence" or marginalize Christian voices.[9]

Just as the critics of the culture wars rightly insist, approximately half of Christian Coalition and CWA mailings (taken from the sample that dates between 1993 and 2001) compared our moral conflicts to a war. These rightist groups often insist that if religious conservatives are to "win the war" against "liberal forces," they must continue "fighting battles," launching "powerful counter-strikes," and training its "army of neighborhood captains."[10] In a handful of these mailings, the Christian Coalition and especially CWA even suggest that compromise is not an option. In the 1990s, CWA's president described moderation in the Republican Party this way: "I am angry, appalled, and disgusted by this weak and compromising 'leadership.'" Reaching for even stronger language in another mailing, CWA vowed that it "will never compromise Christian values."[11] Meanwhile, the Christian Coalition told its current and prospective members to "get involved and prove that a growing 'outrage' still exists among the electorate."[12]

Despite the insistence that Christian citizens should not use religious arguments in the public square, the Christian Coalition and CWA did not shrink from theocratic language in their direct mailings. In its campaign against the Freedom of Choice Act, for example, one CWA letter warned: "We cannot allow such ungodly laws to rule our society."[13] CWA further exhorted evangelicals to resist "those who oppose God's laws and commandments" since they want to "destroy His purpose."[14] The Christian Coalition even invoked revolutionary language in at least one of its mailings: "*Never again* will we be subject to a government that dishonors our Lord."[15] After the election of Bill Clinton in 1992, the Christian Coalition offered this prophetic message as consolation: "Remember, God sent Moses and his people into the wilderness for a time before delivering them to the Promised Land."[16] More commonly, these groups cite scripture to support political arguments and appeal in a general way to a "Judeo-Christian heritage," "godly standards," and "biblical values."[17]

But even direct mail is constrained by the imperatives of successful public activism. Although the authors of direct mail often exaggerate the potential consequences of a given piece of legislation and characterize their opponents in harsh terms, they are much more cautious when reporting the details of pending legislation or current policies. The Christian Coalition and CWA provide these facts precisely because they do not want their members to be ill informed if they decide to contact their representative. In fact, when such details are provided, it is generally part of a larger effort to mobilize grassroots lobbying. Typically, these letters discuss the details of pending legislation, such as the bill number and sponsor, key provisions, and legislative history. Some even attach the language of the bill itself to the letter or detailed voting records of members of Congress.[18] This juxtaposition of hyperbolic claims about the effects of pending legislation and scrupulously accurate details of the same legislation highlights the tension between the twin goals of mobilization and thoughtful activism. On the one hand, appeals often exaggerate because this is vital to mobilizing otherwise passive citizens. On the other hand, mobilized activists need to be well informed and avoid distortion if they are to be successful lobbyists.

Critics of the moral conflict often point to direct mail as emblematic of everything that is wrong with today's culture wars. Yet they overestimate both the significance and function of direct mail. Amitai Etzioni, for example, suggests that direct mail represents all "in-house communications" at the Christian Coalition.[19] James Hunter further argues that direct mail is a good reflection of public discourse. In *Culture Wars*, Hunter concludes,

> Direct mail copy can be viewed quite literally as a form of public discourse; the letters themselves a mechanism for communicating publicly about issues of social and political consequence. In this capacity, direct solicitations also are instruments of civic education; a device for the prejudicial instruction of large segments of the population in the dynamics of contemporary social and political life.[20]

To be sure, direct mail is "*a form* of public discourse." But it does not represent the kind of discourses that take place between citizens in a wide variety of public settings, including state houses, city council meetings, colleges, and abortion clinics. Rather, direct mailings are carefully targeted solicitations to individuals who sympathize with particular causes. Direct mail is so strident, therefore, because it is preaching to the choir. Above all, these mailings do not model the way Christian Right organizations want their rank-and-file activists to behave in the public square.

Nonetheless polemical exhortations certainly inspire political radicalism. Even so, they cannot be abandoned. Movement leaders are correct to conclude that impassioned calls to action are critically necessary to the survival of their organizations. In James Hunter's critical account of the cultural wars, he interviewed activists on both sides who repeatedly defended their polemics on participatory grounds. A pro-choice activist claimed Planned Parenthood used "colorful" rhetoric to "get the attention of the American public who don't focus on this issue." Likewise, a pro-life activist defended the use of images of aborted fetuses by arguing that they "are very, very powerful tools for motivating people who may be pro-life, but are ambivalent or not activated."[21] If activists on both sides of the culture war agree on nothing else, it is the necessity of dramatic appeals.

The Rise and Fall of Organized Fundamentalism

When the modern culture wars first erupted over abortion, many conservative evangelicals remained isolated and estranged from politics, while Catholics took the lead by advancing philosophical and scientific claims rather than theological or strident ones. As Keith Cassidy has demonstrated, the National Right to Life Committee (NRLC), which was first formed in 1967 as an arm of the U.S. Conference of Bishops, has consistently made secular, scientific, and philosophical appeals since its founding. Meanwhile, other early works, such as Charles Rice's *The Vanishing Right to Life* and Germain Grisez's *Abortion: The Myths, Realities, and Arguments*, rejected theological claims in favor of natural law, a tradition that has been continued by Catholic intellectuals such as Robert George and Patrick Lee.[22]

Meanwhile, even the rescue movement, which would become famous for its belligerence and violence by the 1980s, was a peaceful campaign in the 1970s. Faced with the futility of electoral politics in a post-*Roe* America, the rescue movement was pioneered by leftist Catholics. Veterans of the 1960s antiwar movement, they were inspired by the examples of David Thoreau, Mahatma Gandhi, Martin Luther King, and Thomas Merton, and by Catholic teachings on the sanctity of human life. Beginning in the mid-1970s, these young radicals orchestrated nonviolent "sit-ins" in front of abortion clinics in the Washington, D.C., and St. Louis areas. However, the rescue movement (as it came to be called by its evangelical heirs) never made deep inroads into the American Left despite the best efforts of its founders.

By the 1980s, fundamentalists such as Jerry Falwell and Randall Terry radically changed Christian politics and its public image. A true fundamentalist, Falwell tended toward political militancy even as the incentives of interest-group politics steered him in a more moderate direction. Political inexperience and distrust of those outside the Baptist Bible Fellowship further undermined the public image and success of the Moral Majority. According to Mark Rozell, the Moral Majority never managed to build a grassroots organization because it failed to defuse religious factionalism within the Religious Right and forge friendly ties within the Republican Party.[23] In addition, the lobbying efforts of the Moral Majority often failed because the organization's goals were unrealistic and its tactics unsophisticated. As Matthew Moen explains in his study, the movement "ran simplistic pressure campaigns, bullied friends and allies, failed to unite behind legislative proposals, [and] squandered valuable time and resources on quixotic tasks" among other shortcomings.[24] In 1989 the Moral Majority collapsed, prompting some observers to write the movement's obituary.[25]

Although *New York Times* articles and other liberal exposés of the New Right chronicled Jerry Falwell and the Moral Majority with hyperbolic alarm, evangelicals themselves hardly noticed them. In addition, most evangelicals who were aware of Falwell and the Moral Majority were not impressed. Stuart Rothenberg and Frank Newport's 1983 survey of evangelicals demonstrates that slightly more than half of evangelicals did not even have an opinion of Jerry Falwell. Meanwhile, those evangelicals who did volunteer an opinion reported an unfavorable one.[26] James Hunter's interviews with evangelical college and seminary students led him to conclude that the Moral Majority faired no better in the eyes of evangelical citizens. Hunter found that in spite of natural political affinities between the new Christian Right organizations and evangelicals, most of the young students he interviewed reported that these groups "exceed[ed] the limits of political decorum by attempting to impose their will on an unwilling majority." In fact, even though Hunter identified significant diversity among evangelicals in other respects, he concluded that their low opinion of the Moral Majority and its new allies was "ubiquitous."[27]

Another study, by James Guth, found that a plurality of Southern Baptist ministers described themselves as opponents of the Moral Majority. Meanwhile, many sympathetic ministers nonetheless reported serious reservations about the group's tactics and goals.[28] More recently, Christian Smith's qualitative fieldwork unearthed similar disaffection among evangelicals.[29]

Opposition to Christian militancy was not confined to ordinary, nominally political evangelicals. The militant radicals who found their way into the Christian Coalition also alienated more mainstream evangelical activists. A case study of twenty-six Ohio chapters of the Christian Coalition found that the chapters that were really thriving embraced the Coalition's pragmatic approach to politics. Meanwhile, chapters with limited operations were much more radical and purist in their orientation.[30]

Partly because the Moral Majority could not even command the respect of a majority of evangelicals, it never managed to build a truly grassroots organization. Like other public interest groups, most of its support came from a diffuse group of members whose donations were solicited through direct mail. As Jeffrey Hadden and his colleagues concluded in their 1987 study, "[T]he Moral Majority was primarily an organization for grabbing media attention, built and supported by direct-mail technology."[31]

To the extent that there were local chapters in the Moral Majority, they were led by fiercely independent Bible Fellowship ministers. These ministers were far more invested in building and maintaining their churches than in organizing political movements. According to Clyde Wilcox and others, they were also particularly averse to ecumenical cooperation and even intolerant of fellow evangelicals.[32] James Ault's remarkable ethnographic study of one such pastor's church in Massachusetts corroborates these findings. Despite the fact that this particular pastor served as vice president of the state chapter of the Moral Majority, Ault found that even many "core members" were simply unfamiliar with the organization. Ault concluded that "the Moral Majority itself, rather than being a powerful machine . . . represented little more than a loose network of like-minded pastors who kept one another abreast of relevant issues."[33]

The Christian radicalism that was so characteristics of the 1980s has led some scholars' to make a sharp contrast between a first generation of Christian activists, represented by sensationalistic figures such as Falwell and Pat Robertson, and a second generation, epitomized by the pragmatic Ralph Reed of the Christian Coalition. This account accords with the standard sociological view that social movements become more pragmatic and organized as they mature. As Clyde Wilcox and Mark Rozell explain, the "Christian Right of the late 1970s and 80s was a social movement characterized by disorganization, decentralization, and a lack of fully developed institutional structures." Yet by the 1990s, Wilcox and Rozell conclude, "the Christian Right built far more effective organizational structures, far larger and more inclusive coalitions, and began to adapt more pragmatic strategies."[34] This thesis is also consistent with survey data that suggests that Christian Right activists become more compromising and tolerant through political participation. For instance, one survey of Virginia GOP delegates found that senior Christian Right activists were much more likely to disagree with the statement "compromise is not necessary" than new activists. They were also more likely to disagree with the view that there is "only one correct Christian position."[35]

To be sure, organizations such as the Christian Coalition were *far* better at mobilizing Christians than any prior group had been and certainly more compromising and pragmatic than the Moral Majority. This emphasis on a radical break, however, does not account for a number of other important developments.

First, it obscures the relative moderation and conservatism of Christian Right politics in the 1960s and '70s. Opposition to liberalized abortion laws, for instance, began in and through established institutions, especially Catholic parishes and the National Conference of Catholic Bishops (NCCB). The NCCB founded the National Right to Life Committee, which became an umbrella organization for the various pro-life state organizations that grew out of Catholic parishes.[36] As the historian John McGreevy explains, "With an instant network of parishes, parish bulletins, newspapers, copy machines, staplers, and, most important, volunteers, Catholic institutions became the grid upon which the anti-abortion movement sprung to life."[37] The Catholic Church was hardly an institution that lent itself to militant or disorganized radicalism. Rather it fostered a moderate, organized, and incremental interest-group politics—a fact that inspired militancy in the rescue movement. Would-be militants simply grew impatient with the slow progress accepted by the Catholic Church and the NRLC.

Second, despite the considerable failings of Christian Right organizations in the 1980s, many moderate voices were articulating an alternative vision of Christian politics. In fact, pleas for civil discourse and moderation were coming from within the Moral Majority itself in the early 1980s precisely because the organization was attempting to influence lawmakers and improve its public image. Cal Thomas, the vice president of the Moral Majority, reported in 1983 that Christian activists "need to stay away from inflammatory rhetoric, like calling people who support legalized abortion 'murderers and baby killers.' . . . Negative campaigns contribute to a lack of discourse on the issues. That's hurt us in the past."[38] A year earlier, the Moral Majority and Free Congress Foundation held Family Forum II, which was a conference that attempted to educate some five hundred activists on how to influence politics. At the Forum, activists were encouraged to be sensitive about how they raise family policies with feminists. And, in an effort to reach out to African Americans, they also emphasized that blacks should be regarded as victims of American welfare policy rather than undeserving beneficiaries. Michael Lerner, a liberal activist and leader of Friends of Families, was also invited to the Family Forum to debate the merits of liberal and conservative approaches to family policy—a move that even brought some tepid praise from at least one *Washington Post* editorial.[39]

Outside the Moral Majority, democratic education efforts had already gained a far greater foothold by the 1980s. Beverly LaHaye of Concerned Women for America, for example, reported that her organization trained thousands of activists throughout the decade to "share their convictions with graciousness."[40] Phyllis Schlafly also held annual conferences as the president of Eagle Forum, which included mock debates for participating activists and careful instructions on how to behave in public forums.[41] Of perhaps greater significance, the Leadership Institute, which conducts seminars for conservatives on grassroots organizing, public speaking, and campaigns, among other topics, actually opened its doors in 1979.[42] Meanwhile, the National Right to Life Committee continued to embrace philosophical and scientific objections to abortion, as it had always done since its founding.

And while Francis Schaffer's *A Christian Manifesto* was inspiring evangelical fundamentalists to lay their bodies down in front of abortion clinics, a more conciliatory group of evangelicals authored books that encouraged activists to be civil, compromising, and to frame issues in terms of the larger public good rather than biblical mandates.[43] To highlight just a couple of examples, legal scholar John Eidsmore instructed Christian activists in *God and Caesar* to "[t]ry to remember, though, that a politician must deal with political realities. Politics is the art of the possible, it is said, and sometimes this requires compromise. It is much easier to be dogmatic in a pulpit, in a classroom, or in an armchair at home than in a position of public trust where you are responsible for the lives and interests of many people."[44] In a similar vein, James Robison, an otherwise dogmatic fundamentalist from Texas, directed Christian activists to avoid grounding their policy positions on religious doctrine and language when communicating with public officials and other nonbelievers. Instead, Christians should "think through the issues and understand how they relate to the good of the individual and the good of the community. . . . Then we can communicate with the public official or media person in a language he understands." Robison also attempted to persuade activists to compromise: "Getting things done within a political party requires compromise of a sort, but giving in on an objectionable issue need not be condoned. It can be fought and defeated later. As the old saying goes, half a loaf is better than none—particularly when you may get the other half, too, if you try long enough."[45]

Given this interest in educating rank-and-file activists throughout the 1980s, it is not clear that the Christian Coalition's dedication to civility and moderation in the 1990s represented a radical transformation in Christian Right politics.[46] To be sure, the efforts of Ralph Reed at the Christian Coalition did constitute progress if the leadership of Jerry Falwell is used as the point of comparison. But the reality is that efforts to educate and inform the passions of Christian activists were well under way in the 1980s, and the failures of the Moral Majority only confirmed the wisdom of more conciliatory voices.

Meanwhile, even as the Christian Coalition was emerging in the wake of the Moral Majority's collapse, other fundamentalists were transforming the rescue movement into something large and militant. The largest rescues were orchestrated in the late 1980s and early 1990s. In addition, clinic physicians were not targeted for execution until the 1990s, precisely when the Christian Coalition was training thousands of evangelical activists to embrace deliberative norms.

Although the rescue movement began as peaceful civil disobedience modeled on the example of the civil rights movement, it was dramatically transformed in the 1980s by conservative Catholics, such as Joseph Scheidler of the Pro-Life Action League, and especially by charismatic evangelical fundamentalists, such as Randall Terry of Operation Rescue.[47] All told, the National Abortion Federation reports that there were over 600 blockades and 33,000 arrests between 1977 and 1993.[48]

The nonviolent arm of the rescue movement was largely ended in 1994 by the Federal Freedom of Clinics Entrance Act (FACE), which levied massive fines for blockading clinics. Even before the passage of FACE, there is evidence that the rescue movement was losing steam. The leadership of Operation Rescue faced large court-imposed fines by 1989, while its activists suffered from more frequent use of "pain compliance" techniques to clear abortion clinic entrances and from longer prison sentences.[49] According to William Cotter, who is the current director of Operation Rescue Boston and was deeply involved in the early activities of Operation Rescue, activists could not keep staging rescues because the prison sentences demanded too much time away from their jobs and everyday lives. Activists simply exhausted their vacation time and financial resources.[50] Operation Rescue further suffered from internecine fights between organization leaders and the autocratic mismanagement of Randall Terry.[51]

Thus, direct action efforts were declining even before the passage of FACE. Between 1989 and 1990, for example, the number of clinic blockades plummeted from 201 to 34. After a modest rebound in subsequent years, there were only five blockades the year after FACE became the law of the land.[52]

The result was that Operation Rescue collapsed altogether in 1994, which spawned many local groups that embraced its name, such as Operation Rescue Dallas, San Diego, Los Angeles, and many others. But few activists remained in these scattered organizations. A 1997 survey of Christian Right activists reveals that only 4 percent were members of Operation Rescue compared to 40 percent in the Christian Coalition, 33 percent in Focus on the Family, 18 percent in CWA, and 16 percent in the National Right to Life Committee. And although two-thirds to nearly 90 percent of activists reported a "very favorable" opinion of these larger organizations, only 31 percent reported the same opinion of Operation Rescue.[53] Today most of the local groups have collapsed as well, leaving only three organizations that embrace its name if not its tactics. They include Operation Rescue West, Operation Save America, and Operation Rescue Boston.

Likewise, the violent faction of the rescue movement is now on the decline after a long history that began with property destruction. Between 1977 and 1993 the National Abortion Federation reported 39 bombings, 99 acid attacks, and 154 arson cases. It was not until the murder of Dr. David Gunn in March of 1993, however, that abortion providers were actually targeted for execution. Since Gunn's death, six other clinic employees have been murdered—four in 1994 and two in 1998. But in spite of this disturbing escalation of violence in the 1990s, violent radicals

TABLE 2.1
Property Violence at Abortion Clinics in the United States and Canada, 1977–2004

	1977–1990	1991–1992	1993–1994	1995–1996	1997–1998	1999–2000	2001–2002	2003–2004	Change from 1991–1992
Bombing	26	1	2	3	7	1	1	0	–100%
Arson	74	27	23	17	12	10	· 3	5	–81%
Invasion	266	55	26	4	12	7	3	0	–100%
Vandalism	270	160	155	60	151	119	118	97	–39%
Acid attacks	57	23	1	19	0	0	0	0	–100%
Burglary	22	6	6	9	12	9	7	14	+133%

Source: National Abortion Federation, "NAF Violence and Disruption Statistics," accessed on the website of the National Abortion Federation at http://www.prochoice.org/pubs_research/publications/downloads/about_abortion/violence_statistics.pdf, 13 December 2006.

seem to be disappearing. Property violence declined precipitously throughout the 1990s (see table 2.1) and there have been no murders for nearly a decade.[54]

Exactly why these radicals are vanishing is not clear. But despite the participation of some violent militants in Operation Rescue, it would be a mistake to see the organization itself as a catalyst for violence. In fact, the success of its civil disobedience and influence of peaceful activists actually helped control violence-prone activists. As Christopher Keleher has observed, throughout the 1980s "the drop in the number of violent incidents correlated with the increase in the number of nonviolent protests." Moreover, the collapse of Operation Rescue disbanded and isolated violent factions, leaving them to embrace their own worst impulses.[55] Making a similar claim, the editors of the Harvard Law Review have argued that the federal crackdown on peaceful clinic blockades closed one of the few remaining "safety valve[s]" for democratic dissent. According to its editors, "By foreclosing all democratic outlets for the deep passions this issue arouses, by banishing the issue from the political forum that gives all participants, even the losers, the satisfaction of a fair hearing and an honest fight . . . the Court merely prolongs and intensifies the anguish."[56]

Although the rescue movement is largely history, the most vital remnant of the movement can be found in Wichita, Kansas, where Troy Newman and his staff at Operation Rescue West have learned to adapt to the new federal restrictions. Taking their inspiration from Joseph Scheidler's Closed: 99 Ways to Close Abortion Clinics, Operation Rescue West is devoted to shutting down abortion clinics largely by harassing abortion providers. After moving operations from San Diego, where Operation Rescue West closed eighteen abortion clinics in collaboration with the now-defunct California Life Coalition, Newman and his staff have set their sights on what is easily regarded as the most infamous abortion clinic in pro-life circles.

The clinic is Dr. George Tiller's Women's Health Care Services, which specializes in late-term abortions and attracts patients from around the country and even abroad. Many aspects of the clinic particularly invite the outrage of activists. For example, Tiller apparently reported at a National Abortion Federation meeting that only 800 of the 10,000 abortions on fetuses at twenty-four to thirty-six weeks' gestation that his clinic oversaw during a five-year period were done because of a genetic anomaly.[57] Adding further fuel to pro-life opposition, Tiller disposes of the fetuses in a crematorium. He also retains a Christian chaplain on staff to perform "spiritual sacraments such as baptism . . . and blessings for the aborted fetus." "Remembrances" are offered as well, such as footprints and handprints, an urn for ashes, and a certificate of premature miscarriage.[58] This attempt to consecrate abortion deeply distresses the devout Christians who make up the bulk of the pro-life movement.

I witnessed the methods of Operation Rescue West first hand during a series of trainings that the organization held in St. Louis. Troy Newman explained to a group of activists gathered in a downtown Holiday Inn that a basic method of shutting down clinics is to "collect dirt" on them and then disseminate the information. The first step involves significant research, including the acquisition of knowledge about zoning laws and codes on medical waste as well as any lawsuits or health department violations that have been filed against the abortion provider. Then, he said, this information should be brought to the attention of public officials, local media, and women entering the clinic.[59]

But perhaps the most important method that Operation Rescue West advocates is harassing the abortion providers in their neighborhoods and places of business. The staffers believe that this method works because often abortion providers do not want their neighbors to know what they do for a living.[60] For example, the field director of Operation Rescue West, who gave a similar presentation at the Church of St. Louis, reported that one abortion provider in San Diego had informed his neighbors that he was a weight loss specialist.[61] Or as Newman put it, "Abortion providers must be pursued in their neighborhoods and private life. We must constantly hold the evil of abortion up in their face. To make them crack and give up, evil must be uprooted from its rat hole and exposed."[62]

Although Operation Rescue staffers have enjoyed some success closing clinics, the organization has no real grassroots presence. As Troy Newman explained rather candidly, "We have no base." This reality can partly

Table 2.2
Disruption and Harassment at Abortion Clinics in the United States and Canada, 1977–2004

	1977–1990	1991–1992	1993–1994	1995–1996	1997–1998	1999–2000	2001–2002	2003–2004	Change from 1991–1992
Stalking	N/A	N/A	210	113	80	30	22	18	–91%
Harassing calls/mail	213	611	1009	860	3744	2657	634	855	+40%
Picketing	892	3190	3686	5294	15920	17205	21589	22988	+621%

Source: National Abortion Federation, "NAF Violence and Disruption Statistics," accessed on the website of the National Abortion Federation at http://www.prochoice.org/pubs_research/publications/downloads/about_abortion/violence_statistics.pdf, 13 December 2006.

be explained by the unpopularity of direct action within the pro-life movement itself. Operation Rescue West is also weak organizationally because its leadership's very radicalism undermines interest in organization-building and maintenance. As Newman pointed out, most pro-life leaders spend a great deal of time and energy maintaining their organizations at the expense of actually fighting abortion.[63] Such antagonism to organization-building, moreover, was evident from the very beginnings of Operation Rescue, which was always more of a movement than an organization and largely sustained by its charismatic founder, Randall Terry.

There is some evidence that harassment has become more popular in what remains of the rescue movement as clinic blockades and property violence have declined. The National Abortion Federation reports that some forms of harassment of abortion providers have increased in recent years. While abortion clinics reported 213 incidents of harassing phone calls and mail between 1977 and 1990, they complained of 10,370 such actions between 1991 and 2004. On the other hand, one of Operation Rescue West's favorite tactics—stalking abortion providers in their private lives—has actually declined significantly since the collapse of the rescue movement. There were some 201 reports of such incidents in 1993–1994, but only 18 in 2003–2004. To be sure, picketing has increased substantially as clinic blockades declined. It is currently the most popular form of clinic activism by far. But such picketing is generally relatively moderate and includes peaceful sidewalk counseling.

The radicalism of those in the rescue movement is partly grounded in a profoundly different understanding of Christianity from that of more moderate activists. Parting ways both with notions of Christian ambassadorship that currently pervade Christian politics as well as with the early pioneers of the rescue movement who emphasized a "peaceful presence," the evangelical fundamentalists who came to dominate the leadership of Operation Rescue imagined a vengeful Christ. As James Risen and Judy Thomas explained in their excellent and unusually balanced study of the rescue movement, fundamentalist activists believed that obeying God's law required a militant disregard for civil authorities. Violent extremists imagined a "wrathful Son of God who could overturn the money changing tables" rather than a "merciful, suffering Christ." Many were also inspired by a hard version of Calvinism, which encouraged activists to see themselves as the rightful instruments of God's justice.[64]

Unlike advocates of deliberative modes of politics, radicals in the rescue movement tended to find their greatest inspiration from a handful of passages in the Old Testament rather than the New, which tended to stand in the way of political militancy. The single most important biblical passage in the rescue movement is Proverbs 24:11: "Rescue those being led away to death; hold back those staggering toward slaughter." This passage did much to undermine the respect for governmental authority that is evident throughout the New Testament, such as Paul's instruction to "be subordinate to the higher authorities" and Christ's saying, "Render unto Caesar what is Caesar's."[65] The handful of activists who supported the murder of abortion clinic staff found justification in Genesis 9:6: "If anyone sheds the blood of man, by man shall his blood be shed." This bellicose reading of the Old Testament is at odds with the emphasis on Christian love that has heavily influenced moderate Christian leaders.

It is this biblically based militancy and defiance of governmental authority that makes radicals allergic to the deliberative norms that are embraced by most Christian Right groups—a fact that further alienates them from mainstream leaders. Randall Terry, for example, often antagonized Christian leaders and activists because he would regularly accuse them of selling out the cause. When moderate organizations in the Christian Right were on the ascent, Terry blasted them in a *Washington Post* editorial: "[N]ow certain 'Christian leaders' are 'inspiring' droves of Christians to move into the 'big tent' of the Republican Party—a happy tent housing child-killers and sodomites." Repudiating compromise as sinful, Terry continued, "The Ten Commandments are not on the auction block. We will not auction away the eternal, flawless law of heaven for temporary, flawed political gains."[66] Operation Save America, which sees itself as a kind of prophetic witness against abortion, echoes Terry's criticism. Recently, its leaders argued that pragmatism "is the primary reason that we still have abortion in our land today. It has caused us to believe that we can legislate this evil out of our culture slowly but surely by education, sound reasoning, and political maneuvering. . . . The battle for the lives of children will never be won by educating and seeking common ground with those who refuse to see the truth."[67]

Elites within the mainstream Christian Right have reciprocated such criticisms by expressing their own unfavorable views of these radicals. As the president of Americans United for Life argued in *Christianity Today,* "Some of the more strident activists of the pro-life movement have yet to understand that they discourage rather than encourage a pro-life consensus in the public mind. . . . Operation Rescue leader Randall Terry helps the pro-abortion cause when he advocates what sounds like a lot of theocracy to humanistic and otherwise pluralistic ears."[68] Making a similar point, a New York pastor protested Operation Rescue's local campaign in *Christianity Today:* "The intensity of the rhetoric, the disruptions of order in the community, and the skewing of truth only seemed to polarize people further on the issue. One hopes that the consciousness-raising work they accomplished . . . will find productive redirection."[69]

The division between radical and mainstream organizations, however, is not always as sharp as these barbs suggest. The reason is that some groups embrace strategies that draw from both camps. Survivors, for example, is a pro-life organization based in Southern California that embraces deliberative norms when its activists visit college campuses, but can also become confrontational when it decides to picket the neighborhood of an abortion provider or protest the Democratic National Convention. For this reason, one pro-life leader called them "somewhat of a renegade bunch." Similarly, the Center for Bio-Ethical Reform has drawn much criticism from pro-life leaders—especially from within the National Right to Life Committee—for driving a fleet of trucks paneled with images of aborted fetuses, but much praise for its use of Socratic methods in its college outreaches. Finally, even leaders at Operation Rescue West advocate many deliberative norms to sidewalk counselors, but not to those determined to close abortion clinics. These somewhat unusual cases should highlight a deeper regularity, which is the close relationship between different political strategies and the educative interests of group leaders.

THE MEDIA AND THE RIGHT

Popular and academic conceptions of the Right are overwhelmingly negative not just because of militant fundamentalism. They are also shaped by the media, which tends to characterize Christian activists as extreme and intolerant. For all the unfounded paranoia over a liberal media bias, coverage of social issues and abortion in particular, has been biased. This bias was first revealed over a decade ago when the *Los Angeles Times* conducted a comprehensive study that drew upon over one hundred interviews with journalists and abortion activists as well as content analysis of abortion coverage. According to a summary of this research by *Los Angeles Times* journalist David Shaw, pro-choice advocates are "quoted more frequently and characterized more favorably" than pro-life activists. For example, pro-life advocates are often described as "strident" or "militant"—terms that are rarely used to describe pro-choice advocates. Other examples of systematic bias include the printing of editorials in favor of abortion rights by a margin of two-to-one in America's major daily newspapers and selectively ignoring issues and events favorable to the pro-life movement.[70]

Perhaps the greatest measure of the press's support for abortion rights, however, is found in its lack of interest in otherwise newsworthy, even sensationalistic events that happen to be favorable to the pro-life cause. During the height of the rescue movement, for example, pro-life advocates regularly reported excessive force by the police, which was corroborated both by other witnesses and videotape. In one such case, an elderly bishop's shoulders were dislocated and some seventeen female college students were forced to strip, walk around, and even crawl naked while in prison. Yet, with only a handful of exceptions, the media simply failed to investigate or even report such charges. As James Hunter noted with deliberate understatement, "[O]ne might think that these facts would be of passing interest to journalists."[71]

Such bias has not been confined to the abortion issue. Louis Bolce and Gerald De Maio's content analysis of *New York Times* and *Washington Post* articles and editorials between 1987 and 2004 reveals that evangelicals are nearly always described as politically extreme. On over 400 occasions these papers characterized evangelicals as "hard right," "extreme right," "Religious Right," or "Christian Right." Meanwhile, an ideological label was attributed to secularists much less often. On only three occasions were secularists described as "left." In addition, while evangelicals were described as "intolerant" in over 420 articles, secularists were never characterized as intolerant.[72]

What is more, Bolce and De Maio found substantial evidence that the media has influenced the opinions of the mass electorate. Drawing upon the standard feeling thermometer scale (that runs from 0 to 100) in National Election Studies surveys, Bolce and De Maio reveal that those citizens who are more politically attentive are about twice as likely to harbor strongly negative sentiments toward "fundamentalists." Approximately one-third of politically attentive nonfundamentalists reported intensely negative feelings toward "fundamentalists," and fully 11 percent gave the lowest score permissible—a zero. By way of contrast, not a single politically attentive non-Catholic or non-Jew gave Catholics or Jews a score of zero, and only a very small fraction of them might be classified as anti-Catholic or anti-Semitic.[73]

Bolce and De Maio further found that 44 percent of those who are most attentive to political media reported that if their party nominated an otherwise qualified Christian fundamentalist for president, they would oppose him or her. Only 16 percent of all other respondents held the same opinion. Likewise, politically aware citizens were far more likely to regard Christian fundamentalists as "extremely" conservative and "intolerant." This media effect held independent of other potentially influential variables, such as cultural orientation, ideology, and partisanship. Bolce and De Maio conclude, "[A]nti-Christian fundamentalism has become a very fashionable prejudice of the sophisticated classes."[74]

But if the "thinking classes" find the Right to be extreme and intolerant, it is partly because radical Christian Right groups enjoy far more coverage than the more moderate and substantial mainstream organizations. I conducted a content analysis of coverage of pro-life organizations in major elite newspapers (*New York Times, Washington Post,* and *Los Angeles Times*) and magazines (*Time, Newsweek,* and *U.S. News and World Report*). Between 1989 (the year Operation Rescue was founded) and June 2006, this survey records every article in which a major pro-life organization is mentioned, including the National Right to Life Committee, Operation Rescue, crisis pregnancy centers, and campus groups such as the Center for Bio-Ethical Reform and Justice for All.

What I found was a predominance of coverage of Operation Rescue despite the fact that the organization collapsed in 1994 and that the other groups represent the most important players in the pro-life movement. For that matter, since 1989 Operation Rescue has accounted for two-thirds of all coverage of pro-life organizations in elite newspapers and more than twice the coverage of the National Right to Life Committee, the largest pro-life organization in the country (see table 2.3). Crisis pregnancy centers have hardly enjoyed any coverage—a mere eight stories in seventeen years—even though there are some 2,300 such centers in existence, a figure that outstrips the number of abortion clinics. And despite their wide reach, campus groups such as the Center for Bio-Ethical Reform and Justice for All, enjoyed a single story in elite newspapers.

Reporting in major magazines has been somewhat more balanced (see table 2.4). In fact, Operation Rescue accounted for slightly less than half of all coverage of pro-life organizations. The National Right to Life Committee even enjoyed marginally more coverage. Crisis pregnancy centers and campus outreaches, however, were equally ignored in these magazines.

On the other hand, it is also true that coverage of Operation Rescue has diminished since its collapse in 1994 (see table 2.5). Between 1989 and 1994, Operation Rescue's sensational and dramatic tactics excited

TABLE 2.3
Coverage of Pro-Life Organizations in Elite Newspapers, 1989–2006

	Operation Rescue	NRLC	Crisis pregnancy center	Campus group
New York Times	155	103	6	1
Washington Post	60	28	2	0
Los Angeles Times	95	15	0	0
Total	310	146	8	1
Percent	67	31	2	0

Source: InfoTrac database.

TABLE 2.4
Coverage of Pro-Life Organizations in Elite Magazines, 1989–2006

	Operation Rescue	NRLC	Crisis pregnancy center	Campus group
Time	37	32	3	0
Newsweek	10	16	3	0
U.S. News & World Report	21	26	1	0
Total	68	74	7	0
Percent	46	50	4	0

Source: InfoTrac database.

an explosion of coverage. In fact, in the elite newspapers and magazines surveyed here, some 282 articles were written on Operation Rescue in this period, accounting for nearly 80 percent of all coverage of pro-life organizations. Notably, media interest declined significantly after Operation Rescue's collapse. Yet it still remained remarkably high compared to extant organizations. Between 1995–2000 and 2001–2006, for instance, Operation Rescue accounted for 46 percent and 30 percent of all coverage of pro-life organizations, respectively.

It is even possible that the media inadvertently contributed to the radicalization of the pro-life movement in the 1980s. While the peaceful and largely Catholic sit-ins routinely failed to inspire much press attention,

TABLE 2.5
Trends in Coverage of Pro-Life Organizations in Elite Newspapers
and Magazines, 1989–2006 (percents are in parentheses)

	1989–1994	1995–2000	2001–2006
Operation Rescue	282 (79)	57 (46)	39 (30)
NRLC	74 (21)	66 (53)	79 (61)
Crisis preg. center	3 (1)	2 (2)	10 (8)
Campus groups	0 (0)	0 (0)	1 (1)
Total	359	125	129

Source: InfoTrac database.

others soon discovered that a more combative politics would. James Risen and Judy Thomas emphasize that the Chicago militant Joseph Scheidler quickly ascended as the rescue movement's "national spokesman" because he served the press "outrageous and combative sound bites." As Risen and Thomas explain, "[T]o the chagrin of mainstream leaders, Scheidler used his notoriety and celebrity to cajole and prod the movement toward militancy and away from political compromise, accommodation, and marginal victories that the National Right to Life Committee and Catholic Church had come to expect by the late 1970s."[75]

Meanwhile, those who advocated a "peaceful preference" in an effort to share the "vulnerability of the unborn" were simply ignored. In one dramatic case, John O'Keefe, the founder of rescue, taught a workshop on civil disobedience at the annual meeting of the National Right to Life Committee in 1978 and "watched as, one by one, the local television news crews, turned off their lights and packed up their gear." As Risen and Thomas explain, "Reporters had come hoping for fiery sound bites of fiery rhetoric endorsing violence, not O'Keefe's intellectual meanderings about a 'peaceful presence.' "[76]

Whether the media actually contributed to the radicalization of the Christian Right or not, it has certainly focused on its most radical leaders and activists partly because they make for entertaining news. Michael Gerson, a policy advisor to President George W. Bush and contributor to *Newsweek*, emphasized a similar point, "There is a tendency to elevate the most irresponsible and strident religious figures, mostly because it makes for better cable TV."[77] In this respect, the media has not indulged a liberal bias. New Left activist Todd Gitlin complained of the same perverse dynamic in the antiwar movement. As E. J. Dionne observed, "Gitlin contends that the mass media were so fascinated with the violent minority of the New Left they played up extremist views within the movement to the exclusion of virtually all others."[78]

While a liberal media bias has also clearly contributed to the negative public image of Christian activists, it is also true that Christian media itself often complements the caricatures of the *New York Times* and *Washington Post*. For all the justified complaints of a liberal media bias in the Christian Right, its own media has not always projected a moderate and compassionate image.

As fundamentalists such as Falwell and Terry have faded from the limelight, media personalities, such as Pat Robertson and James Dobson, have emerged as the most newsworthy representatives of the Christian Right and are famous for their polemical claims. Christian media personalities are primarily interested in exhorting their listeners. Unlike mobilization in political organizations, however, the moral exhortations of media personalities are, of course, far more visible. Thus, they must accept and even embrace a public radicalism in a way that leaders of interest groups do not.

Both Robertson and Dobson are some of the most well-known personalities in the Christian Right and therefore deserve some sustained attention. Yet precisely because they have enjoyed such a disproportionate share of media attention, their significance has been greatly exaggerated. Although they both have been influential in their capacities as Christian media personalities, their direct influence over Christian Right political organizations has been rather attenuated.

Pat Robertson's life is something of a paradox. He has long been infamous for his incredible and offensive statements, but nonetheless he was president for many years of the Christian Coalition, which was famous for its pragmatism and sophistication. This puzzle is explained by the fact that Robertson had little to no control over the day-to-day operations of the Christian Coalition. Instead, Ralph Reed adroitly managed the organization and institutionalized a thoroughgoing democratic education for rank-and-file activists before a clash with Robertson caused him to resign.

While Reed oversaw the operations of the Christian Coalition at its height, Robertson's comments on his television program marred its image and that of the Christian Right in general. A comprehensive list of every strident and offensive comment Robertson ever uttered would fill many volumes, so a few must suffice. In one of his stranger remarks, Robertson once equated Satanism and Nazism with homosexuality: "Many of those people involved [with] Adolf Hitler were Satanists, many of them were homosexuals—the two things seem to go together." And on the *700 Club* he has been anything but ecumenical to other Protestants: "You say you're supposed to be nice to the Episcopalians and the Presbyterians and the Methodists and this, that, and the other thing. Nonsense. I don't have to be nice to the spirit of the Antichrist." He has also called secularists "termites" and has embraced conspiracy theories that rival those on the far Left. For instance, he claimed that European bankers were behind the assassination of Abraham Lincoln since they wanted to "nip the American populist experiment [interest-free currency] in the bud." This particular belief is part of a much larger conspiracy theory described in *The New World Order*, in which many interests are conspiring to form "a godless and collectivist dictatorship."[79]

Robertson's militant and idiosyncratic politics has certainly not gone unnoticed by Christian leaders. In fact, state leaders in the Christian Coalition itself have expressed their irritation with Robertson to me. These reports have been corroborated by Michael Cromartie, director of an evangelical studies project at the Ethics and Public Policy Center, who recently reflected, "I don't know a religious conservative leader— Protestant, Catholic or Jewish—who has not run out of patience with Mr. Robertson's comments." Even National Public Radio has conceded that Robertson is now "swimming outside the evangelical mainstream" and primarily uses his television program *The 700 Club* primarily as "a showcase for his particular take on Pentecostalism."[80]

James Dobson's case is equally complicated. Currently Dobson enjoys much more influence than Robertson. He also is much more politic and attentive to how his message will be received by secular listeners. In fact, he routinely consults Robert George, a professor at Princeton University, for advice on articulating his position on such issues as stem cell research, abortion, and gay marriage. As the previous chapter demonstrated, he also encourages his listeners to be civil and reasonable in the public square.[81] Focus on the Family also supports debates and programs, such as Christian worldview training for college students, which promote the values of public reason.

Although Dobson is more combative than Ralph Reed was at the Christian Coalition, he has shown a strong willingness to compromise. His outspoken support for President Bush's nomination of Harriet Miers for the Supreme Court despite an avalanche of criticism from other parts of the Republican coalition is a good example. Such behavior is consistent with Clyde Wilcox's proposition that evangelicals have actually been the most compromising faction of the GOP. In his account, the Christian Right might be the "ultimate cheap date" of the business community. As Wilcox explains, GOP elites "did not anticipate how easily evangelicals could be convinced that any Republican candidate was better than a Democrat. . . . They did not expect that movement to settle so quickly for symbolic assurances, rather than concrete victories."[82] This view has even found some support on the hard Left. One of the unnoticed ironies of

Thomas Frank's polemic against Christian conservatives is the charge that they have been *too willing to compromise* their social agenda.[83]

Despite all the attention showered on Dobson's behavior, however, it should not be forgotten that politics is a relatively minor concern of Focus on the Family. It is true that Dobson will occasionally devote a radio broadcast to political questions and that the mainstream news media often seek out his views on matters of politics. But the vast majority of his programs are devoted to Christian family life and Christian parenting in particular. A psychologist by training, Dobson's real claim to fame in the evangelical world is the therapeutic advice he passes on to stay-at-home moms.

For all their differences, Robertson and Dobson do have something important in common—they both sit on top of media empires and make a living selling their own distinct charismatic personalities. And because of their visibility and polemics, they also routinely find themselves in the press. It is striking to note, for example, that there are no visible spokespersons in the National Right to Life Committee, even though it is currently the largest grassroots Christian Right organization in America. Meanwhile, Robertson and Dobson do capture the media's attention, even though they are principally Christian media personalities and do not have any direct control over a grassroots political organization.

• • •

However one weighs the radicalism discussed in this chapter against the moderation presented in chapter 1, both chapters say very little about how rank-and-file activists respond to Christian elites. Yet, of critical importance is the actual behavior of rank-and-file activists. After all, the demands of moderate leaders could be ignored altogether or perhaps mobilization efforts render the task of disciplining activists too difficult. More broadly, before we can critically assess this tension thoroughly between participatory and deliberative ideals, it would certainly help to know how successful the Christian Right has been at mobilizing Christian citizens and getting them to practice deliberative norms. For this reason, the following chapters turn our attention to rank-and-file activists. Chapter 5 principally uses survey data to assess the Right's success at mobilizing citizens, while the next chapter examines the actual behavior of Christian activists in a wide variety of public forums through participant observation.

CHAPTER THREE

The Varieties of Pro-Life Activism

FOR ALL THE OPPROBRIUM CAST on activists of all ideological stripes, remarkably little is known about how they behave in public forums. Certainly, Christian conservatives have never been systematically observed as they practice public activism. Even some of the most well-received works on contemporary moral conflict, such as James Hunter's *Culture Wars* and Kristen Luker's *Abortion and the Politics of Motherhood*, do not draw on participant observation or what Richard Fenno once called "soaking and poking."[1]

This chapter sheds empirical light on how Christian activists conduct themselves in public forums largely by observing them in their own element—on city streets, in front of abortion clinics, at college campuses, and in other public places. In so doing, I hope to determine whether or not the democratic education discussed in chapter 1 really has political consequences. For example, how faithfully do activists embrace deliberative norms? How do activists understand these norms in terms of their faith? And how much influence do leaders actually possess?

I focus exclusively on pro-life activism for a number of reasons. As a practical matter, pro-life activism is far easier to observe than other varieties of Christian activism for two reasons. First, the pro-life movement has remained vital and strong while the major multipurpose Christian Right organizations, such as the Christian Coalition and Concerned Women of America, are in sharp decline. In most states these once-large grassroots organizations do not have an organization at all, and the Christian Coalition does not even have an organization in Pat Robertson's home state of Virginia. By way of contrast, the National Right to Life Committee has organizations in every state, many of which are thriving. Second, pro-life activists are also more visible to social scientists as well as ordinary citizens, because *Roe v. Wade* has effectively pushed abortion politics from state houses out into the streets.

This fact is underscored by the finding that some 45 percent of respondents in the Citizens Participation Survey who reported participating in a national protest did so because of abortion. What is more, nearly three-quarters of all abortion-issue protesters are pro-life, an unsurprising fact given that the pro-life movement is challenging rather than defending the current policy regime. Meanwhile, all other social issues, including pornography, gay rights, school prayer, and sex education, account for only 3 percent of all national protest activity.[2]

Some might reasonably argue that Christian Right activism is less abortion-oriented than it was at the time of the last Citizens Participation Survey and that it now places more emphasis on other issues like gay marriage. Yet even in 2006, at the height of the movement for gay marriage, political scientists Dana Patton and Sara Zeigler found that abortion politics dominated the agendas of state legislatures compared to gay rights. According to their study, some 295 abortion bills were introduced in 2006 compared to 83 gay-related bills.[3] Abortion politics is clearly the most visible and dominant type of Christian Right activism.

As this data suggest, pro-life activism is also an ideal case because abortion remains the single most contentious moral issue in American politics. As James Hunter argues, abortion "remains the knottiest moral and political dilemma of the larger culture war, contested now for more than two decades with little hope of a satisfying resolution."[4] Likewise, Amy Gutmann and Dennis Thompson write that the abortion debate has created disagreement that appears "fundamental and irresolvable."[5]

Of course, the problems of selection bias do not end here since there is simply no way to assure that the pro-life activism I observe is representative of all such activism. I have tried to mitigate this problem by examining a broad cross-section of pro-life activism, including campus outreaches, sidewalk counseling at abortion clinics, marches, counter-demonstrations, and direct action. These cases oversample the radicals. Missing from this study are the far less visible grassroots lobbying efforts of the rather moderate National Right to Life Committee and moral suasion inside crisis pregnancy centers. Therefore, even if many Christian activists actually do embrace deliberative norms and regard public belligerency as contrary to their faith, we still might expect them to be particularly scarce in many of the groups that I examine.

In addition, rather than examining pro-life activism in a particular city or state as is often done, this study looks at activism in a wide variety of social settings. Some of the cases I examine are set in very liberal locations, such as San Francisco, Boston, and Washington, D.C., while others are found in conservative cities, including St. Louis and Denver. In addition to these urban settings, I also observe one case in the relatively small and working-class town of Granite City, Illinois. But like all qualitative research, breadth is invariably sacrificed for depth.

There are equally difficult sampling problems out in the field. At a large march or abortion clinic protest, for example, there is no scientific way to sample exchanges between pro-life advocates and other citizens. But

I have tried especially hard to record carefully any behavior that is contrary to deliberative norms, such as religious appeals or public belligerency. In any case, strident activists are hard to ignore because they tend to be more visible and demonstrative than those who practice deliberative norms. Therefore, here, too, incidents of Christian radicalism are oversampled.

In addition to close participant observation, I also draw upon sixty personal interviews with pro-life leaders and rank-and-file activists. In most cases, I approached activists after observing them for some time and was then able to acquire a better sense of how they understand their public behavior. Interviews ranged from ten minutes to many hours in length, depending partly on the willingness of these Christians to share their lives with an inquiring academic. In some cases, I benefited greatly from other accounts, such as media sources and well over one hundred written reflections by activists themselves.

This chapter organizes pro-life politics into three basic categories—deliberative, disjointed, and radical. Deliberative politics is found within campus outreaches where activists are careful to practice civility, avoid theological appeals, and ground their claims in philosophy and science. They are also Socratic in method in the sense that volunteers ask more questions than make philosophical declarations. Such activism is also highly coordinated, professionally organized, and tightly regulated by pro-life leaders. Disjointed politics, on the other hand, mixes a wide variety of civic appeals, including the secular and religious, civil and belligerent. It includes sidewalk counseling, marches, counter-demonstrations and tends to be only very loosely organized at best. In such cases, moreover, the behavior of aggressive activists is very difficult to control and regulate. Finally, radical politics can be found in the broken remnants of the rescue movement. Activists in the rescue movement systematically harass abortion providers in an effort to close abortion clinics. In many respects it is the exact opposite of deliberative politics, except for the fact that it too is highly coordinated and organized.

In all these cases, however, Christianity plays a central role in how activists understand what they are doing. In practicing civility, deliberative activists believe that they are sharing the love of Christ. And, in reflecting God's love, they regard their behavior as a soft form of evangelism in addition to an efficacious means of changing minds on the morality of abortion. At the other end of spectrum, radicals understand their belligerency through a Christian framework as well. For the handful of pro-life activists who practice direct action, true Christian love demands unflinching public condemnation so that the souls of abortion providers might be saved and America might be spared the wrathful hand of God.

DELIBERATIVE POLITICS

Pro-life groups, including Justice for All (JFA) and the Center for Bio-Ethical Reform (CBR), have initiated what is easily the most ambitious effort to engage ordinary citizens in deliberative discussions. Combined JFA and CBR have reached well over one million students at more than one hundred different college campuses. In fact, this is a rather conservative estimate since both groups have visited many of these campuses more than once. As discussed in chapter 1, these organizations set up large displays that feature images of embryos and aborted fetuses on college campuses in an effort to provoke discussion and moral sentiments. Activists then initiate deliberative discussions. In doing so, they avoid grounding claims in scripture, ask many more questions than express opinions, appeal to public reason, and are remarkably civil even in the face of hostility.

Yet, even for these deliberative democrats, pro-life activism is understood through a Christian worldview. Civil behavior, for example, is not merely strategic; it is also a means of expressing the love of Christ. In fact, such civility is embraced with so much devotion partly because these Christian activists cannot evangelize in a traditional sense. That is, precisely because they cannot speak directly about Christ, they are so committed to revealing him indirectly through their patience and compassion.

The following case study examines a Justice for All outreach at the Auraria campus in downtown Denver, which is home to the University of Colorado at Denver, the Metropolitan State College of Denver, and the Community College of Denver. During my time there, I sat in on an activist training session, observed conversations, conducted interviews, attended a Justice for All staff meeting, and shared meals with activists and staffers. I also benefited from the acquisition of eighty-eight "volunteer reflections," which JFA routinely administers to all of its volunteers.[6] In the reflections, volunteers described their experiences as a JFA activist. What follows, then, is principally a layering of these sources.

Justice for All

Although there is no vast right-wing conspiracy, conservative institutions do show unusual coordination every year at Colorado-area campuses. Once a semester, the Focus on the Family Institute (FFI) in Colorado Springs, where evangelical college students learn how to defend a Christian worldview, provides upward of one hundred volunteers for a Justice for All outreach. Local area Christian high schools further supplement FFI's contribution with some of their own student volunteers. Stand to Reason, the Christian apologetic organization discussed at length in chapter 1, is then contracted to train these volunteers on how to defend a pro-life view philosophically and scientifically. Housing for these students is even provided by university-area families, and local businesses cater lunches free of charge.

I helped Justice for All staffers set up their large, triangular display in the quad of the Auraria campus one icy Denver morning in April. As staffers quietly went about this work, a pro-choice student busily chalked up the surrounding sidewalk with such epithets as "Nazi Scum," "Hatred of Women 50 Feet Ahead," and "Taliban." To my surprise, the JFA activists were remarkably unaffected by this demonstration.[7] In fact, when I asked one African American activist what he thought about this kind of hostility, he said, "I just pray that God will soften their hearts."[8] And once the display had been erected, the staffers formed a circle and collectively offered the same prayer.

This civility was also evident in the actions of more than two hundred student volunteers. Rarely did volunteers raise their voices or interrupt others. After the first day some students were laughing with one another even as they disagreed, and their conversations wandered well beyond the topic of abortion. The most dramatic gesture of civility came on the second day of the exhibit, however, when several of the JFA volunteers helped pro-choice counter-demonstrators as they struggled to erect their large, cumbersome display. It featured silhouettes of shapely women and read "Keep Your Laws off Our Bodies" and "We Won't Go Back." JFA volunteers also warmly greeted the pro-choice demonstrators as they set up their display each morning.[9]

Reflecting back on the outreach, some student volunteers emphasized the strategic utility of approaching pro-choice students with such civility and compassion. As David explained, "It was very helpful to learn the arguments but more helpful to hear the reiteration to be compassionate. Lives are not saved just because I could out-debate anyone." Rachel, a less intellectually confident volunteer, found that compassion helped to compensate for her philosophical shortcomings. She reflected, "I was a bit fearful, despite our training, that extremely intellectual people would just rip me apart. I discovered that if you approach people with a kind, caring, non-argumentative demeanor, you are far more likely to make progress with that person." Likewise, Lillian observed, "I think that what made the outreach so effective was the willingness of volunteers to talk with students—and the loving way that they did so. It made a world of difference for the students to feel as though they were not being condemned but were being loved and listened to."[10]

Other volunteers believed that JFA's embrace of civility challenged popular stereotypes of evangelicals, if not abortion opinion. For instance, Mark explained that students expected "to hear from a militant, extremist group." But quickly "they realize that they are speaking to someone [who] is loving, has a compassionate heart, and speaks convincingly without shouting. They have come with every defense and wall in place, and often leave with their walls broken down." Kimberley likewise noted that because the JFA volunteers really listened and were respectful to pro-choice students, "perhaps their views of pro-lifers, and even Christians [were] changed for the better." Making a cognate point, Amanda reported more succinctly, "Arguing and changing minds without anger or excessive emotion I think made JFA look good." Meanwhile, Stephanie thought that perhaps the volunteers' minds had changed as well. As she put it, "[A] lot of stereotypes are broken on both sides when there is dialogue."[11]

Most JFA volunteers, however, did not view public civility through a purely strategic lens. In fact, most emphasized that it served as a soft form of evangelism, which allowed them to be authentically Christian in a secular arena in which they could not readily appeal to their faith. One of the volunteers who helped the pro-choice counterdemonstrators set their display up believed that the gesture provided him with an opportunity to "show Christ's love." Likewise April found that "the most important aspect of JFA for me was the availability and willingness of the staff and volunteers to listen and invest and love people by those conversations, an active way to exemplify Christ to a lost world." Echoing April's sentiments, Patricia reported, "For me the outreach effectively emphasized the underlying purpose and reason we are on this earth: to bring God's glory by engaging our culture in a way that Christ himself modeled for us." Meanwhile, Elaine contrasted the soft evangelism at the JFA exhibit from more direct and traditional varieties: "Whether or not I spoke the name of Jesus did not matter. My entire countenance should have spoken louder than anything else." Crystal similarly reported that the love and compassion of JFA volunteers were the qualities that distinguished them from secular activists. As she put it, the ultimate end of the outreach was "expressing God's love. . . . Without that we would be no different than other pro-choice or even some pro-life arguers." Making an identical point, Audrey observed that "personal attacks are never effective and they simply lower us to using the same tools that the world uses even though God has offered us so much more."[12]

Although the students who approached the exhibit often reciprocated the kindness of pro-life activists, such behavior was less common among the counterdemonstrators themselves. In fact, when the JFA display was disassembled on the final day of the exhibit, some activists cheered and then chanted "pro-life fascists, get your asses off campus!" Another student activist with the anarchist group Creative Resistance mocked JFA volunteers by yelling, "Cult members are welcome at my parties once the deprogramming is over." JFA signs that had been posted some distance from the exhibit in an effort to warn students about the graphic nature of the images were also ripped and destroyed—a repeat of vandalism that had occurred at Baylor and UCLA. Yet another student wrote on JFA's "free speech board" each morning "Get the fuck of our campus." But the worst offender was probably Channey, who screamed at a few female volunteers and then walked away without giving them an opportunity to respond. At a press conference held by the Feminist Alliance, she then accused JFA volunteers of "shouting" at other students and of even trying to "provoke a violent incident." Then Channey added, "Fortunately we've all kept our cool."[13]

JFA staff members took this treatment in stride and were accustomed to this kind of response from counter-demonstrators. One staff member informed me that a pro-choice group at the University of Missouri worked hard to maintain the prevailing cultural image of pro-life activists by reporting to the student newspaper that JFA staff and volunteers had hurled aborted fetuses at students and yelled "You're going to hell." Staffers in general, however, reported that pro-choice professors were often the worst offenders. At the University of Colorado at Boulder, for example, a literature professor took his entire class out to see the JFA exhibit and then proceeded to shout invective at staffers while his students snickered in the background.[14] Likewise, an instructor at the University of New Mexico yelled at JFA volunteers, "You are the American Taliban."[15] Professors at the University of Texas at Austin also routinely screamed obscenities at JFA staff as well. As one of the offending professors at Austin confessed, "I am incandescent with rage."[16] Most professors, however, keep a low profile when JFA visits and those who are vocal tend to come from the most politicized quarters of the academy, such as English and Women's Studies departments.

Other pro-choice activists at the Auraria campus, however, were clearly disarmed by the civility of JFA volunteers. Stephanie, a Mennonite from Los Angeles, reported that a lesbian student responded with disbelief at the discovery that she was a Christian conservative. According to Stephanie, she said, "I don't understand—you're so nice."[17] Another activist with the student group Feminist Alliance realized that pro-life activists were "regular kids" rather than "monsters with horns."[18] Meanwhile, Michael, a heavily tattooed anarchist and active member of Creative Resistance, claimed he even came to respect some of them, especially those who participated in humanitarian work abroad.[19] And Mishka, a lesbian pro-choice activist, found the JFA activists friendly and could muster no enmity toward them.[20]

When I asked JFA volunteers how they remained civil and gracious even in the face of hostility, they invariably attributed it to God's grace rather than their own efforts. One dramatic example was a young student named Mary, whose hands were deformed due to a genetic disorder. Mary kept her deformity concealed throughout the exhibit with the long sleeves of her shirt. When a student told her that embryos and fetuses with deformities should be aborted, Mary remained calm. In fact, when Mary provided a full account of the exchange she said that a week ago such a claim would have made her "really angry." But because she "found grace," Mary reported that instead she quietly revealed the deformity to the offending student and "changed her heart."[21] Likewise, Lisa ventured over to the pro-choice camp of counter-demonstrators "where a man was yelling and proclaiming that the pictures were forced upon him" and using "foul language." Lisa reported that she listened to him and remained calm because she wanted to share "Christ's love" and because she saw someone who was "hurting, who needed the Lord."[22]

It is easy to see, moreover, why such volunteers would readily accept Stand to Reason's instruction to be "ambassadors for Christ, as though God were entering through us," since it fits so easily with their own sense of God in their lives. Throughout the volunteer testimonies, students described themselves as "vessels" for God's love, grace, and wisdom—a belief that subdued public fears and frustrations. Elaine reported, "In many ways it is a relief because we do not really have to do anything but be willing, and the Lord is faithful to do the rest. When I opened myself up to be a vessel, the Lord gave me words, direction, and wisdom." Crystal also believed that she was emboldened by God's presence despite doubts about her ability to engage others. As she put it, "I trusted that if I opened my mouth, God would fill it just with what was needed. He is faithful and can glorify Himself, even through the weakest vessels." Similarly, Katherine confessed that she "experienced a weakness that caused me to humbly depend on the power of the Spirit of God."[23]

So strong was this supernatural orientation, that many JFA volunteers did not believe that they were even responsible for their own deliberative behavior. As Joy explained: "My only part was in being there, and willing to say what God put in my heart. He took care of the rest, giving me the wisdom to counter lies, the words to say, and the grace to debate with love." Elaine also attributed her compassion to God's grace. As she put it, the "Lord was faithful to help control my tongue, frustration, facial expressions, and body language that the person talking to me would feel safe to share their heart on the subject of abortion." Indeed, JFA volunteers further believed that, as vessels for God's love, it was the Holy Spirit rather than their own efforts that would ultimately change the hearts and minds of pro-choice students. Patricia made the following observation: "The staff taught us and showed us that . . . we were people talking to people and we needed to remember that God's love and grace could and would penetrate the hearts and lives we were speaking truth to."[24]

On the final day of the JFA exhibit, however, the tolerance (or grace) of at least one staff member, Corrine Cords, was waning. Moments earlier she had been identified as a JFA staff member by a student bustling past who reported into her cell phone, "Oh, no wonder she's pro-life, she's a blonde." Cords then asked Tammy Cook, the director of field operations, if she could cheer when the counter-demonstrators marched past with their pro-choice display in tow. Cook responded, "Absolutely not!" and Cords obeyed.[25]

What was most striking about the JFA exhibit, however, was how much dialogue it generated. Over the course of three days, thousands of students lingered around the exhibit. Although some simply gazed silently at the images while others passed unaffected, the majority of students stopped and talked to a JFA volunteer or staff member. Some conversations lasted for hours and ultimately spilled into classrooms, university cafés, and the student newspaper. That so many students were drawn into discussions about abortion is partly due to the creativity of JFA's tactics. For example, a "free speech board" was placed near the exhibit, where students were encouraged to express their views. When pro-choice students wrote their opinion on this board, JFA volunteers approached them and asked them to explain their views more fully. Therefore, the free speech board is set up as a catalyst for moral dialogue rather than an outlet for student opinion. Similarly, a polling station was set up where students could vote on whether or not abortion should remain legal. Here, too, the point of the poll is to create conversations since volunteers were trained to engage those students who voted on behalf of abortion rights.

On the opening day of the exhibit, JFA volunteers were forbidden from talking to other students for the first hour. Instead, they were instructed to observe the more expert JFA staff and their conversations with students. In this way, the training discussed in chapter 1 was actually extended into the first hours of the JFA exhibit. Only when students felt comfortable were they encouraged to approach others. Some students immediately began talking to other students once the ban was lifted, while others spent as much as half the day watching and learning from JFA staff members.[26]

The staff members proved to be great examples to the many volunteers huddled around them and clearly outmatched and impressed the undergraduates they talked to. JFA staff member Jeremy Alder engaged one young student as she busily scribbled something on the free speech board. She responded, "[T]here is no point in talking because we cannot change each other's minds." Alder replied, "I think you could change my mind if you can demonstrate that the fetus is not a human being." They then talked for approximately forty-five minutes. Another Auraria student approached Alder and asked "OK, but what about a child that's going to be born into a family where he'll be terribly abused?" Alder responded, "I agree that's a terrible, terrible situation." And then he pointed to an image of the remains of a first-trimester abortion and asked, "But is that the most humane solution to that problem? Is that the best we can do as a society?" Meanwhile, fellow staff member David France, an African American evangelical from Minneapolis, challenged two students' contention that the fetus must not be valuable because we do not grieve miscarriages in the sense that we mourn the loss of born children. France, like many black pro-life activists, was quick to draw parallels to racial injustice and asked whether a society's feelings about a class of people should determine their value. Later, France engaged two young women who quickly reported that they were pro-choice because "women have a right to control their own bodies." France then pointed to an image of an aborted fetus and asked, "But what about her body?" Clearly disarmed by this query, one of the women responded, "Oh, I see your point."[27]

As the volunteers begin engaging students on their own, it became clear that they were not nearly as expert as JFA staff despite their training. Consistent with their training, however, volunteers were generally good at asking questions rather than stating their own opinions. They also labored to focus their conversations on ontological questions. One common tactic volunteers used, for example, was to refer pro-choice students to a panel of the JFA exhibit that showed the development of human organisms at different levels of gestation (e.g., fertilization, implantation, four-week embryo, and so on). Volunteers would then ask students at what point human life should be protected and to justify their position. When students offered such answers as when a fetus begins to have a heartbeat, brain activity, or feel pain, volunteers would then ask why these various developmental markers were morally relevant criteria for separating valuable from disposable human life. For most Auraria students, it appeared that this intellectual exercise was altogether new and that most had never thought about the ontology of the fetus before.[28]

JFA volunteers were especially careful to avoid defending their views with Christianity. As one bewildered anarchist and counter-demonstrator put it to me, "They seem loath to talk about Jesus." He further explained that he had tried to raise religion with the JFA volunteers, but they avoided the subject. Mystified, he then asked, "Have they been trained?"[29] Making the same observation, a JFA volunteer reported that the handful of untrained pro-life students who spontaneously decided to participate in the campus outreach tended to play "the religious card."[30] According to Audrey, one such outside activist who spoke to a student kept "[focusing] on God's wrath and judgment." Audrey further reported, "He had no evidence to back up his claims, but the Gospel." However, she was able to steer the student to a quiet bench where she "had a chance to do some damage control." Reflecting back on the episode, Audrey found that it "permanently reinforced in my mind the need to present the scientific, philosophical arguments for the pro-life cause and to do that completely in love."[31]

Throughout the JFA reflections, volunteers consistently expressed enthusiasm for secular arguments. Ashley, for example, reported that "it was great to be equipped with sound and logical explanations and refutations for why abortion is wrong rather than Biblical or emotional reasoning." Matthew shared Ashley's enthusiasm: "I love[d] using reason and logic to prove right and wrong instead of forc[ing] faith and scripture down people's throats. . . . Many people thanked me, whether they agreed with me or not, for not pushing religion on them." Another volunteer named Sarah spoke with a girl who had an abortion but became pro-life after seeing the exhibit. Sarah described the efficacy of JFA's embrace of public reason this way: "She told us that she supports Justice for All because [it does] not [have a] 'religious' approach. She didn't seem to know that we were Christians. Five of us were talking to her but not one of us said anything about our faith in Christ." Yet another volunteer named Valerie shared her support for secular arguments more succinctly: "I really appreciated how we did not use Bible verses to argue, but philosophy."

This did not mean that volunteers viewed their embrace of secular philosophy as contrary to Biblical mandates. In fact, some students argued that their avoidance of scripture is in fact grounded in the Bible. Sandy found that the most effective part of the JFA outreach was "sharing and asking questions in love, not arguing but reasoning with them like Paul did for Christ's sake." Michelle even rooted the Socratic method in Christ's example. As she explained, "I love to present people with questions. Jesus rarely lectured at them."[32]

Other volunteers shared cognate opinions when they emphasized the virtues of philosophy over sentiment. Michelle, for instance, thought the JFA exhibit was effective because "an atmosphere was created where it was easy to bring up a controversial topic to engage people's thinking, not just their emotions." A fellow volunteer named Cynthia similarly observed, "The most effective aspect of the outreach is its appeal to the intellect and logical side of the abortion debate." Meanwhile, Eve elaborated the same point in her JFA reflection: "Many times I was told that the exhibit was factual, logical, and scientifically sound. I feel that was beneficial to the outreach because an appeal [was] not made to emotions or feelings, but to scientific and philosophical principles."[33]

JFA volunteers were not excited by their newfound philosophical sophistication simply because they could be more persuasive in the public square. Their training also gave them the public confidence and courage to approach secular students. Therefore, although a deliberative education does temper the passions of some pro-life activists, for many others it emboldens. One such volunteer was Evelyn, who reported, "I think the reason I felt the desire [to engage people] was not only God prompting me, but I felt well prepared to speak to the people. I believed that my argument had validity and a scientific basis. I had a *reason* for the people to believe what I was saying." Likewise, Barbara noted in her reflection that "I know now how to answer people and give reasons, proof, and concrete answers [for] why abortion is wrong. I can feel confident that I am equipped enough to speak up and not get shot down immediately. I have something to say besides quoting a Bible verse or simply saying that God values life." Echoing the same point, Leah reported, "I really loved just talking to people, knowing my arguments had grounding and could stand criticism. It also helped me to be able to engage, because I wasn't worried about having my argument fail." For others, the training helped to direct and temper their moral passions. Joanna, for instance, explained, "I never knew how to effectively argue my position until the training took place. Since I am a very emotional person, knowing the scientific data helped me to be more concrete in my arguments."[34]

JFA volunteers did sometimes raise their faith when conversations moved beyond a philosophical debate about abortion into friendly personal exchanges about life more generally. These conversations tended to last many hours and were sometimes extended into the following day. A couple of JFA volunteers gifted their new friends with C. S. Lewis's *Mere Christianity*, which they purchased from the student bookstore. In other cases, conversations about abortion quickly slid into larger metaphysical debates about natural law and postmodernism. Ashley found, for example, that conversations moved quickly from abortion to larger discussions about "relativism, worldviews, and morality." Ruth similarly reported that her conversations often drifted from abortion into "a debate over moral relativism and postmodernism." And Loren had an extended conversation that pivoted around whether or not anything exists external to human beings that confers worth on them.[35]

Not all students, however, were willing to talk to the JFA volunteers. In fact, many Auraria students eschewed conversation, especially the counter-demonstrators. Two pro-choice students, for example, walked away from three volunteers in disgust. At that point, one of the JFA volunteers pleaded, "Please don't walk away."[36] I spoke with two pro-choice activists with the Feminist Alliance who refused to talk to any of the JFA volunteers. They set up a booth near the pro-choice display and circulated a petition to have the exhibit removed from campus because it was "obscene" and created "a hostile environment." Because they grounded abortion opinion in "personal experience," these feminists also regarded conversation with JFA volunteers as "a waste of time." Unlike many of the counter-demonstrators who did engage the JFA volunteers, these women retained their negative stereotypes of Christian activists. According to one, the pro-lifers were "preachy" and just "trying to push religion on us."[37]

Another counter-demonstrating feminist who was approached by a JFA staff member said that it was a waste of their time to talk since neither would be able to persuade the other. When the staff member responded, "I think you can convince me," the counter-demonstrator called him "brainwashed" and walked away.[38]

The reluctance of the pro-choice activists to discuss abortion was further highlighted at a news conference held by the Feminist Alliance. At the press conference, members of the Feminist Alliance called on university officials to remove the JFA exhibit from campus because it was "obscene" and "disruptive to the learning environment." After a local press member questioned this reasoning, an agitated professor responded, "We are not here to debate."[39]

When I asked JFA staff members about pro-choice activists' reluctance to engage in dialogue, they said that it was common but that there have been important exceptions. For instance, David France reported that when JFA visited the University of Minnesota, volunteers and staff members managed to immerse themselves in a large crowd of pro-choice activists. After a short period, this organized counter-demonstration disintegrated into small circles of students peacefully sitting together and talking about abortion.[40]

Pro-Choice Resistance

Such dialogue between activists is rare, however, and the reluctance of the Auraria pro-choice activists to debate their pro-life opponents is actually part of a much broader phenomenon. Pro-life student groups at the University of Texas, University of North Carolina, University of Virginia, and the University of Albany, to name a few examples, complain that pro-choice campus groups will not debate them. As one student from the University of Albany put it when I asked him about the reluctance of pro-choice students to discuss abortion, "we have to beg them."[41] Such frustration is fueled by NARAL Pro-Choice America and Planned Parenthood, whose elites discourage their campus affiliates from debating or even talking to pro-life students. NARAL's "Campus Kit for Pro-Choice Organizers," for example, gives this categorical instruction: "Don't waste time talking to anti-choice people."[42] Meanwhile, Jamia Wilson, the campus organizer at Planned Parenthood, recently informed me that she "discourages direct debate."[43] And Scott Klusendorf, the former director of bioethics at Stand to Reason, reports that he rarely succeeds in getting pro-choice advocates to debate him on college campuses. The leadership of the Canadian based Pro-Choice Action Network recently corroborated Klusendorf's account with the following admission: "Along with most other pro-choice groups, we do not engage in debates with the anti-choice."[44] It is surprising that such a strong aversion to dialogue has not been unearthed by other scholars, especially since pro-choice leaders are often aggressive about asserting their opposition to public debates.

One organization that has managed to soften opposition to public discussions in the pro-choice movement has been Feminists for Life, a group that has had far-reaching effects on pro-life campus groups. Its president, Serrin Foster, emphasizes in her stump speech prepared for college audiences that "no women should have to choose between sacrificing her education and career plans and sacrificing her child." Instead, colleges should see to it that women have the requisite childcare and health coverage so that they can really exercise meaningful choices. As she sees it, mainstream feminists have not pushed for these kinds of services because they have accepted the proposition that women could only be successful if they "fit into a man's world on men's terms," which above all means not "troubling employers with their fertility problems." "Women," as Foster and her staff at Feminists for Life are fond of saying, "deserve better than abortion."[45]

Foster's message has been warmly embraced by pro-life campus groups and has paved the way for dialogue with pro-choice student organizations. Georgetown University Right to Life organized a Pregnancy Resource Forum that brought together pro-choice students and campus administrators. As a result of the forum, Georgetown hired a full-time employee who coordinates pregnancy services, expanded its Health Education Services department, and created a childcare center. The forum has also become an annual event and a model for other campuses, such as University of California Berkeley, University of Chicago, Oberlin College, Old Dominion University, and the University of Virginia. Yet, even at these campuses, pro-choice advocates have remained steadfast in their opposition to debating bioethics. Despite multiple visits by Serrin Foster to the University of Virginia, for instance, the campus Planned Parenthood group has categorically objected to debate.

DISJOINTED POLITICS

To be sure, not all pro-life activism is as deliberative or as well organized as campus outreaches. Much pro-life activism, especially sidewalk counseling, marches, and counter-demonstrations, are rather disjointed and loosely organized at best. Partly because of this lack of coordination, the kind of secular messages found in the campus outreaches mix with overtly religious appeals, and belligerent activists on the fringes are often hard to control. What is more, the citizens who participate in this kind of activism, especially sidewalk counseling and counter-demonstrations, are drawn from the most committed and zealous wing of the pro-life movement. They are also self-mobilized and participate for different reasons— some want to evangelize and be a Christian witness, while others carefully avoid religious appeals in an effort to reach secular citizens. Yet, for all these difficulties, pro-life activists do try and reform belligerent activists with varying degrees of success. And like the volunteers who participate in campus outreaches, many activists attribute their civility to their Christian faith and strategic motives.

Sidewalk Counseling

Whereas the campus outreaches grew out of a commitment to public reason, sidewalk counseling emerged from the ashes of the most radical wing of the pro-life movement—the rescue movement. Once activists in the rescue movement could no longer physically prevent citizens from seeking abortions without incurring huge fines, they found that they had to persuade them instead. As a result, activists had to appeal to the concerns of the men and women who sought abortions and to do so in a gentle way. The change from coercive obstruction to soft persuasion is even evident in the term "counseling" itself. Unlike rescuing, which underscores the physical boldness and bravery that clinic obstruction demands, one who counsels must establish a relationship with others and offer compassion.

Sidewalk counselors, however, remain among the most committed and radical activists in the pro-life movement. They are, after all, on the "front lines," and they sometimes regard the patient lobbying efforts of the National Right to Life Committee and its annual conferences in luxury hotels as wasted time at best. As some sidewalk counselors see it, they are "saving babies" today rather than laboring for the quixotic dream of a Human Life Amendment to the Constitution. It is a fact that is often unappreciated among the media elite and academics that those who are truly invested in overturning *Roe v. Wade* are the moderates, not the radicals. If many radicals had their way, lobbying efforts and litigation would be abandoned altogether, and their fellow pro-lifers would join them in the trenches.

Like the rescuers before them, sidewalk counselors are also often uninterested in careful organizing. This does not mean that sidewalk counseling organizations do not exist or that activists are never formally trained. In most cities, however, sidewalk counseling is only very loosely organized as new activists learn the ropes from more senior counselors. And because no real chain of command exists, those activists who are committed to public civility are often left to control wayward and belligerent activists themselves, but with little authority to do so.

This collective weakness was evident at the Hope Clinic for Women in Granite City, Illinois—an economically depressed and drug-infested town just across the Mississippi River from St. Louis. I spoke to Nolen, a retired, working-class evangelical, who shared some of his concerns and frustrations. Although Nolen tries to approach clients with a "Christian spirit," not all activists follow his example. Nolen singled out John in particular as an aggressive and confrontational activist.[46] Many of Nolen's fellow activists have tried to encourage John to be more compassionate with the men and women who seek abortions, but they have now given up. This collective resignation is encouraged by the conclusion that John is mentally ill. As one activist put it, "He's crazy!"[47] And, indeed, John did not seem well. Glued to the front of his yellow hardhat is a plastic baby that is spotted with red paint. "The sky is falling" is printed along the side of John's hat, and nearly every inch of his pickup truck is covered with pro-life bumper stickers.[48]

Other Christian activists at the Hope Clinic, however, share Nolen's tactics and concerns. Jessica, who is a soft-spoken working class evangelical, reported that she attempts to be "compassionate" and "kindhearted." She also believes that aggressive behavior does not dissuade clients from entering abortion clinics. In fact, Jessica further speculated that if she sought an abortion and an activist approached her in an aggressive manner, then she would be even more likely to follow through with the procedure because of her "stubbornness."[49] Likewise, Heather, an evangelical college student, emphasized the importance of Christian love toward women seeking abortions. When I asked her if she thought some activists behave in unchristian ways, she responded emphatically "yes!" Heather especially dislikes it when Christians call other citizens "baby killers" or attempt to frighten them by talking about the "judgment" of God. She was also one of many activists who had labored to control John and longed for more coordination with her fellow activists.[50] Michaela, a pregnant Charismatic Catholic who has spent much of her adult life in front of abortion clinics, approached clients as they exited their cars and is so soft-spoken that I have trouble hearing her some ten feet away. She, too, hates it when Christians accuse women of "baby-killing." According to Michaela, women who seek abortions are "very fragile" and therefore need to be reached out to rather than condemned.[51]

Unlike hopeless cases such as John's, other activists seem capable of personal reform. When I spoke with Chuck, a thirty-something Catholic, he confessed that he became "more merciful" after a year of pro-life activism. Chuck explained that activists should be more "loving" and "tone down their rhetoric." He also noted that Christians should care far more for the "broken souls" of those who exit abortion clinics rather than only for the unborn life that enters them.[52] On the other hand, even the most veteran activists can lose their temper. Nolen, for instance, reported that he sometimes lost his temper with unusually confrontational clients, such as one who ripped his Bible from his hands and threw it to the ground.[53]

Activists use different methods to get the attention of the young men and women entering Hope Clinic. Many, for example, simply asked, "Is it okay if we talk to you for a few minutes?" Other activists shouted, "Please do not go in there, we can help you." Most clients walked past without paying any attention to the sidewalk counselors, while a few were hostile and told the activists to "fuck off!"[54] Yet there have been success stories, which are recorded by local activists. Angela Michaels, who heads a local sidewalk counseling organization called Small Victories, estimates that there has been over one thousand "saves" since 2000.[55] It is, to be sure, a small fraction of those who enter Hope Clinic, but enough to sustain the energies of local activists.

When sidewalk counselor actually talked to the clients, they emphasized that medical services were available and that clients should explore all their options before agreeing to an abortion. Angela Michaels, for example, placed her arms around one young woman who was having second thoughts and invited her to participate in an ultrasound. Michaels then directed the ambivalent woman to her beat-up van, which was equipped with an ultrasound machine. After viewing the ultrasound, the woman changed her mind (at least temporarily), and Michaels then directed her to Christian doctors just across the street from Hope Clinic, who treat without charge any of the women the sidewalk counselors can divert into their offices.[56] The process for Michaels appeared routine.

As clients neared the clinic entrance, several activists became more shrill and desperate. Some activists yelled, "Do you know that your baby can feel pain?" Others made appeals that were explicitly directed toward men, such as "Be a man, care for your woman and her child" and "If he really loved you, he wouldn't be bringing you to this place." And, in stark contrast to the campus outreaches, Christian imagery and messages were everywhere. Nolen handed out copies of the New Testament to anyone who would take them, while some Catholics quietly prayed the rosary. Meanwhile, one evangelical activist held a large flag with a cross on it, and yet another sported a hat that simply read "Jesus." Other activists shouted "Jesus saves," "God will forgive you," and "God hates the shedding of innocent blood."[57] Meanwhile, John is very subdued and the local activists attribute this fact to medication. As one put it, "He must have taken his meds today."[58]

Across the Mississippi River in St. Louis, sidewalk counseling is shaped by the concerns of African American activists. In a blighted, heavily black neighborhood, I observed some forty activists gather at a downtown Planned Parenthood. Many of the African American activists accused clinic staff of "black genocide." Like many black pro-life activists, they are angered by the fact that abortion clinics are often placed in minority neighborhoods and that African Americans account for some 36 percent of all abortions but represent only 12 percent of the population. Zena—who showed up with all twelve of her children, eight of whom are adopted—recited these figures to women entering the clinic. She also repeatedly emphasized that Planned Parenthood was founded by Margaret Sanger, a "white supremacist" who wanted to "eliminate blacks" through abortion.[59] Connie, a working-class African American and Salvation Army member, agreed. She explained to me that the practice of abortion in America was both "classist" and "racist."[60] Meanwhile, another African American man named Leonard shouted to black citizens who walked passed the clinic, "Do you know that they are killing black babies in there? Black genocide is taking place!"[61] These arguments, it should be noted, are circulated widely within the pro-life movement and are especially well known to black activists.

Activists were much louder at the St. Louis Planned Parenthood, partly because they are fenced out of the parking lot used by clinic clients. In Granite City, sidewalk counselors could quietly approach clients as they exited their cars in an adjacent, public parking lot. But here in St. Louis activists had to shout to be heard above the iron fence that separates them from Planned Parenthood's enclosed parking lot. The result is that soft-spoken activists cannot be heard at all. Here and elsewhere the very layout of abortion clinics significantly shapes pro-life activism. In fact, one of the great ironies of abortion politics is that the more difficult abortion providers make it for pro-life activists to speak to their clients, the louder and more confrontational sidewalk counselors become.

Although no dialogue took place between Christian activists and Planned Parenthood's clients, African American activists enjoyed some success in talking to pedestrians, all of whom were black. The neighborhood residents and local police officers seemed respectful and listened as sidewalk counselors stressed the racist dimensions of the abortion industry. White activists, meanwhile, expressed their gratitude since they could not have come into an African American neighborhood and commanded the same attention and trust.[62]

These important departures aside, though, the Christian activism at Hope Clinic and Planned Parenthood was equally disjointed and unorganized. While African American activists, for example, expressed rather secular claims of "black genocide," a small group of Catholics quietly prayed the rosary and a group of evangelicals sang with the aid of an acoustic guitar. Meanwhile, an especially passionate black evangelical named David preached to the Planned Parenthood escorts from the Book of Revelation. The white college students who volunteered as Planned Parenthood escorts were clearly amused and laughed at this exercise. Below the din of this motley group were activists who gently labored to reach out to the young women seeking abortions.[63]

From abortion clinics in the blighted neighborhoods of Granite City and St. Louis to a Planned Parenthood in the affluent city of Boston, abortion clinic activism appears much the same. Early one July morning, a torrential rain pounded the solemn gathering of some sixty activists outside of a Planned Parenthood on Commonwealth Avenue in Boston. The gathering was unusually large because pro-life activists were in the city to protest the Democratic National Convention. An elderly activist named Ruth departed from the low-key tactics of other activists by yelling at young women as they entered the clinic, much as John did in Granite City.[64] When I asked Tony, a Catholic retiree, about Ruth's methods, he responded that there was simply little that others could do to control her.[65] Danny, who is the president of Boston Rock for Life, was much less critical. He shrugged his shoulders and said "different strokes, for different folks." But Danny also said that sidewalk counselors are only successful when they approach others with "compassion" and an "open heart."[66] Amid the downpour I spoke to Phil, who is a member of Albany Rock for Life. Ruth reminded Phil of a sidewalk counselor from Albany who is similarly belligerent. Phil reported that he and his fellow activists do their best to marginalize this radical by not inviting him to their activities.[67]

I also caught up with the director of Operation Rescue Boston, Bill Cotter. With the demise of the rescue movement, Cotter's organization principally organizes what remains of the sidewalk counseling activity in the Boston area. According to Cotter, Operation Rescue Boston periodically conducts training seminars for local activists. Although seminars emphasize that activists should be "representatives of Christ," Cotter reported that some Christians still misbehave. In these cases, he has found that one's ability to control activists ultimately depends on one's "personal credibility."[68]

Before the activists disbanded for the day, they gathered together and offered a prayer, which was both conciliatory and judgmental, for the clinic escorts who were within earshot: "We know that these escorts believe that they are doing the right thing and are good people. But please Lord soften their hearts so that they will turn away from baby-killing." It was prayer that clearly distinguished between the sin ("baby-killing") and the sinner ("good people").[69]

As in Granite City and St. Louis, sidewalk counseling in Boston is greatly affected by the layout of area abortion clinics. This particular Planned Parenthood abuts a busy city street, and it is often very difficult for local activists to determine which approaching pedestrians are headed inside. In fact, activists such as Lorraine, a middle-age Catholic, believes that some patients further attempt to evade sidewalk counselors by pretending that they are not Planned Parenthood–bound until they dart inside at the last moment.[70] And, of course, many of those headed inside are not seeking abortions. Unlike the Granite City clinic, which only performs abortions, Planned Parenthood clinics provide a wide variety of other services. Many Boston activists, therefore, are pleased if they can simply get citizens to take some of their literature, and actual conversations are rare. Making matters perhaps more difficult for local activists is the fact that this is Boston and residents are not, in general, very sympathetic to pro-life activists. Unlike the working-class, Bible-belt town of Granite City, where activists often enjoyed the vocal support of the surrounding community, here on Commonwealth Avenue I noticed many angry looks from the Bostonians who strolled by.[71]

Many local sidewalk counselors do their best to pitch their message to Boston citizens. Bill, a Catholic retiree, asked women as they approached Planned Parenthood, "Did you know that abortion can cause breast cancer?"[72] Meanwhile, sidewalk counselors attempted to give Planned Parenthood's clients a pamphlet that reads, "Women at Risk . . . Abortion increases the risk of breast cancer by fifty percent." This is not to suggest that these pro-lifers are embracing a woman-centered approach only for strategic reasons. As Theresa, another Catholic retiree, informed me with much sincerity, "The greatest lie is that abortion helps women."[73] But in general these pleas fell on deaf ears. After three mornings in front of Planned Parenthood I noticed only one actual conversation with a sympathetic African American who thanked activists for being there.

From the cold rain showers of Boston to the icy January snow of Washington, D.C., I later witnessed hundreds of activists gathered in front of a downtown Planned Parenthood to sidewalk counsel days before the annual pro-life march. The activists were primarily from Rock for Life and Saving Arrows, which are youth organizations with members who are far hipper than the Catholic retirees who frequent Boston-area abortion clinics. Many are clad in black, grungy, heavily pierced, and look much like the leftist youth found on Berkeley's Telegraph Avenue asking for spare change. Their political opinions are also more varied. Some are vegans, opposed to the Iraq War, and against the death penalty. But all are deeply committed to ending abortion and are devout Christians.

I talked at length with Courtney and Laura, both of whom are members of Rock for Life and are very active sidewalk counselors in Ashland,

North Carolina. They emphasized that they always try to be "loving" and "not condemn" any of the women entering abortion clinics. When I asked them if activists are ever too aggressive or judgmental, Courtney informed me that such activists are "regulated" by the leaders of Life Advocate, the local sidewalk counseling group in Ashland. By "regulated" she meant that all new activists are instructed in sidewalk counseling protocols and tactics. But she also conceded that such organization is unusual. In Charlotte, N.C., she was aware of "one or two" belligerent activists who compromise the pro-life mission and image.[74] It is a dynamic that appears very commonplace.

The pro-choice escorts showed up in force. Some thirty escorts lined the clinic, and as many as five or six surrounded patients who approached the clinic's doors. In addition, chain link barricades were erected the night before, which pushed the pro-life activists even further onto the street. The result was that the entire outreach became less of a sidewalk counseling outreach and more of a prayer vigil. It also took on a decidedly Catholic character as mostly female college students prayed the rosary. Many kneeled down on the icy sidewalk to pray as the escorts shuttled Planned Parenthood's clients indoors. They also softly sung hymns such as "Amazing Grace" and "This Little Light of Mine." Such displays invited wry smiles from the escorts, but no words except for an occasional "keep the street clear!" As with all escorts at Planned Parenthood, they have been instructed not to speak to the pro-lifers.

Across the street, pro-life activists gathered in prayer before they departed on a vigil to the Supreme Court. One activist prayed that the womb would become "a sanctuary again" and another asked the Holy Spirit to bring "a revival" in the hearts and minds of Americans so that they might see the injustice of abortion.[75]

Marches

Unlike other varieties of pro-life activism, the annual March for Life in Washington, D.C., is not principally intended to change the hearts and minds of the American public. Instead, the march helps to sustain the difficult and sometimes dispiriting work of activism at colleges, crisis pregnancy centers, and abortion clinics by lifting the morale of pro-life activists. It is a chance for activists to network, feel their own strength, and be reminded that they are part of a national movement.

The thirty-second annual March for Life began as it always does at the Ellipse with a host of speakers. Since Ronald Reagan was elected in 1980, every Republican president has addressed the annual march from a safe distance, and this year was no exception. From Camp David, George W. Bush addressed some one hundred thousand activists with a speech that was largely secular in message and even hit some liberal notes. The president advocated a "culture that will protect the most innocent among us and the voiceless" and one in which there is "compassion for women and their unborn babies." Although Bush did highlight some of his administration's legislative successes, such as a partial-birth abortion ban, he also stressed that abortion will not end through legislative means. Instead, Bush declared, "We need most of all to change hearts."[76]

The march down Constitution Avenue itself was relatively calm and quiet. When chants did occasionally break out among a small number of marches, they would die just as quickly. One such chant went: "What do we want? Babies! How do we want them? Alive!" There is, after all, very little to celebrate for these activists. The temperature was well below freezing, *Roe v. Wade* has survived another year, and as they see it well over a million human beings are now dead as a result.[77] The march had almost nothing in common with the celebratory, almost carnival-like atmosphere of the March for Women's Lives the previous spring.[78]

Nor was there any organized counter-protest to raise the collective energy of the marchers, although there were one or two lone pro-choice activists along Constitution Avenue. What did excite pro-life activists more was one woman seated at a bench who held a sign that read "35 percent of abortionists are Jews." Activists continually broke from the march to speak to her, some calmly, others with more heated words. The episode was a reminder of how difficult it is to control the worst and most extreme elements of the pro-life movement. Further down Constitution Avenue another radical antagonized the marchers who paraded by with a violent appeal. He held a large sign that highlighted the single most important scriptural passage to the violent fringe: "Whoever sheds the blood of man by man shall his blood be shed."[79] Yet, the fact that these activists were outside the march itself is symbolic of their marginalization from the pro-life movement.

Christian messages were everywhere, particularly Catholic and Orthodox ones. Groups of students, for example, held banners that displayed the name of their Catholic high school or local parish. A large papier-mâché of the Virgin Mary was hoisted above the shoulders of several men and many other Catholics prayed to Mary: "Hail Mary, full of grace, pray for us sinners now and at the hour of our death." Another group of activists carried three giant wooden crosses, representing Christ's crucifixion on Calvary. Eastern Orthodox Christians meanwhile carried icons of Mary, Christ, and various saints. And two teenagers just behind me were talking about Augustine's theology.[80]

Mixed with these religious appeals are more secular, even woman-centered messages. For example, many marchers carried Feminists for Life signs that read "Women Deserve Better than Abortion" and "No More

Children Die, No More Women Cry," while other women held signs that read "I Regret My Abortion." Other secular appeals included the ubiquitous Rock for Life and Knights of Columbus signs that simply read "Face It, Abortion Kills!" and "Defend Life," respectively.[81]

Bubba Garret, an activist with the Center for Bio-Ethical Reform, expressed his disappointment with how fractured the annual pro-life marches are. Before his first march Garret imagined that everyone would embrace the same chants and songs, not unlike the civil rights marches. What he found instead was small pockets of groups marching to their own beat—a fact that he regarded as symbolic of the larger disunity of the pro-life movement as a whole.[82] Or as Scott Klusendorf once responded more generally to the charge of a vast right-wing conspiracy: "I only wish it were true."[83]

However, not all pro-life marches are as disjointed or emphasize religious appeals and themes to the extent that the Washington march does. In San Francisco that same weekend a smaller pro-life march of some 6,000 activists was decidedly more woman centered. The main speaker at the Walk for Life West Coast was Sally Winn, the vice-president of Feminists for Life. In her speech, Winn expressed the core conviction of Feminists for Life: "Pro-life feminists demand that society support the unique life-giving capacity of women so that no woman feels that she has no choice other than abortion." Winn added, "Abortion is not the emancipation of women. Abortion is the ultimate degradation of women." Complimenting Winn's message, Georgette Forney, the president of Silent No More, claimed that her organization "want[s] women and men to know help is available if you are hurting from your abortion." As Forney delivered her speech, moreover, women surrounded her with signs that read "I Regret My Abortion."

Other speakers, meanwhile, struck equally liberal notes, albeit not necessarily feminist ones. Clenard Childress, the director of a black pro-life organization called Life Educational and Resource Network (LEARN), declared: "We are standing for those who are denied the dream of life, liberty, and the pursuit of happiness." Likewise, Carol Crossed, the president of Democrats of Life, propounded: "We Democrats need to return to our roots and protect the vulnerable—and that includes the most vulnerable, pregnant women and their children."[84] Video footage revealed a march that was unusually coordinated and on message. Although evidence of the activists' faith could certainly be found, the vast majority of marchers held Feminists for Life signs that read "Women Deserve Better than Abortion."[85]

The pro-choice citizens of San Francisco, however, were not softened by these liberal appeals. In fact, in response to the march, the City and County Board of Supervisors unanimously declared January 22 "Stand Up for

Choice Day" and officially declared San Francisco a pro-choice city. They also played an active role in planning a counter-demonstration in consultation with pro-choice organizations. Supervisor Bevan Duffy even insisted that pro-life activists were "not welcome in San Francisco."[86] Likewise, Supervisor Tom Ammiano bemoaned the boldness of pro-life activists. He complained that pro-life activists "think they can come to our fair city and demonstrate." Dian Harrison, president of Golden Gate chapter of Planned Parenthood, fretted that Christian activists have "been so emboldened that they believe that their message will be tolerated here."[87]

These declarations set the tone for one of the largest, but hardly noted, confrontations between Christian conservatives and secular liberals in the larger culture wars. Some three thousand counter-demonstrators greeted the pro-life activists by hurling condoms, shouting obscenities, spitting, extending their middle fingers, and chanting, "Pro-life, your name's a lie! You don't care if women die!" Meanwhile, the pro-life activists, who were reminded beforehand by an organizer to "return any sort of agitation with a smile," did not retaliate.[88] Afterwards, a surprised *San Francisco Chronicle* reported that "the pro-choice contingent . . . berated the larger [pro-life] group with insults," while "antiabortion ignored taunts from pro-choice marchers, smiling politely in response to jeers, flashing peace signs, and singing 'God Bless America.' "[89]

The entire affair was repeated the following year at what was again an unusually large confrontation between pro-life and pro-choice activists. Journalists at the *San Francisco Chronicle* once again described the pro-life march as "subdued," while pro-choice counter protestors were "loud and confrontational" and "jeered and taunted the marchers."[90] The counter-demonstrators yelled such slurs as "bigots go home" and held signs that read "Fight the Fascist Right," "Fuck Your Agenda," "No to Women Hating Christian Fascist Theocracy," "Religious Terrorists," "Abort More Christians," "Kill Your Kids Motherfucker," and "Catholic Taliban."[91]

Partly the discrepancies between pro-life and pro-choice activists in San Francisco can be attributed to the nature of counter-demonstrations, which tend to be more confrontational than marches. And, in fact, some of the pro-life demonstrators at the March for Women's Lives the year before were belligerent. The *Washington Post* reported that some pro-life activists yelled "you're murdering innocent babies," "choice kills," and "you're killing babies."[92] Likewise, *USA Today* reported that one counter-demonstrator blared "It's a good thing you didn't kill her" to a pro-choice marcher carrying her small child."[93]

However, those who counter protested at the March for Women's Lives described a reception by pro-choice marchers that was strikingly similar to the one in San Francisco. And like those who participated in the Walk for Life West Coast, many pro-life activists were simply shocked by the behavior of pro-choice marchers in Washington, D.C. When the president of Boston Rock for Life arrived at Union Station wearing a pro-life t-shirt, one pro-choice activist yelled, "I hope you die!"[94] Meanwhile, Sarah, who ventured to Washington from Hanover, PA reported: "Pro-choice marchers old and young shouted phrases such as 'I hope you get raped' as middle fingers popped up right in front of our faces. Others criticized belief in God and the bible, calling for the abortion of Christ." Fred of Centerville, Ohio, likewise reflected on the anger and hostility of the marchers as follows: "Priests were mocked and asked 'how many little boys did you f—k today?' Mothers with infants were ridiculed and insulted. We were continually given 'the finger' or told 'f—k you!' " Fred was apparently so uncomfortable with this language that he couldn't even write the word "fuck" in a written reflection, much less utter it in public. John and Sandy of Manassas Park, Va., echoed Fred's account: "We watched in astonishment as we were angrily spit on, yelled at, cursed, cussed and accused of a wide range of ridiculous things. We did not respond in kind."[95] Pro-choice activists similarly dismayed Michael Ciccocioppo, the executive director of the Pennsylvania Pro-Life Action League. Ciccocioppo explained that although he was upset to hear reports of belligerent pro-lifers, in general he was saddened and struck by the "total lack of charity" from pro-choice activists.[96] Finally, Reverend Childress, the director of LEARN, made the trip as well with some one hundred members of his African American church in New Jersey. According to Childress, he has never heard as many "expletives" directed his way in his life.[97]

Counter-Demonstrations

However the average pro-life demonstrator compares to her pro-choice counterpart, it is certainly true that pro-life counter-protests can be very confrontational. Partly for this reason, they attract a far smaller number of activists than marches tend to. And because counter-demonstrations provoke contentious encounters, they represent some of the best evidence for the culture-war thesis.

Counter-demonstrations are also relatively disorganized, mixing appeals that are secular and religious, civil and strident. The disjointed nature of counter-demonstrations was on display in Boston where pro-life activists protested the National Democratic Convention in the summer of 2004. As activists marched down the city sidewalks with signs and graphic images of aborted fetuses, Pat Mahoney of the Christian Defense Coalition yelled into a megaphone, "What is going on in Iraq is terrible and tragic, but we are killing children within our own borders. Please look at these images. This is what choice looks like. Just look at the terrible mangled bodies, this is what Kerry supports." Other activists embraced a more woman-centered approach. Some activists held signs that read "Abortion Hurts Women" and "Women Deserve Better than Abortion." Others made religious appeals. Many Catholic demonstrators sported shirts and held signs that read "You can't be Catholic and Pro-Choice" and another woman had a sign that said "Abortion. God Calls It Murder."[98]

This motley variety of messages reflects deeper tactical divisions within the pro-life movement itself and, in general, the younger activists I spoke with were opposed to religious messages in the public square. One such activist was Paul, who served as president of a pro-life group at the University of Albany. As we walked the streets of downtown Boston, he explained, "The perception that abortion is just a religious issue has been a disaster for the pro-life movement" and has "alienated" liberal Americans who otherwise respect life in other contexts. Paul then concluded, "We have to find a way to work with these people, or else abortion will continue for another thirty, even sixty years."[99]

Phil of Albany Rock for Life shares this general view. Like a growing number of young pro-life activists, he does not look even remotely like a stereotypical Christian conservative. Phil's finger nails are painted black and he is sporting torn camouflage pants. Like Paul, he is also a vegan who is opposed to the Iraq War. In fact, he has even participated in antiwar demonstrations. When I asked him about the utility of religious appeals in the public square, Phil made an astute observation: "Christians often get involved to oppose abortion and evangelize, but doing so may imperil both goals." Yet many Christians, Phil continued, simply do not see it this way. From the perspective of many believers, "Conversion opens the door to respect for life and becoming pro-life opens one's heart to Christ."[100]

Likewise, Melissa and Joy, two activists with Saving Arrows, firmly share Phil's orientation. In addition to being devout evangelicals, they are tattooed, heavily pierced, and Melissa has dreadlocks. As we sat together in the Boston Commons, these activists shared their frustration with some pro-life activists, especially their facile acceptance of the war.[101]

As the activists rolled through the streets of Boston, it was evident that such demonstrations simply do not provoke conversations the way that campus outreaches or even sidewalk counseling does. But occasional exchanges did occur. For instance, Danny, the president of Boston Rock for Life, was approached by a young woman who asked him, "How can you take that position if you are not a woman?" When Danny responded, "Because I believe that life begins at conception," she turned and walked away. Other interactions, however, were more encouraging. Brandi Swindell, the director of Generation Life Boise, encountered a pro-choice woman who insisted that pro-life activists did not really care for women or their children. When Swindell protested that her claim wasn't true, she yelled, "I doubt it!" and proceeded to walk away. Moments later, the woman stopped, turned, and challenged, "How many children have you adopted?" Swindell informed her that she had not adopted any children, but that she had started an adoption referral program in her church. The tenor of the conversation then changed instantly and the two women had what appeared to be a long, respectful discussion and even embraced as they parted ways.[102]

At times there were more serious efforts to cultivate actual dialogue, but they were halfhearted and poorly organized. Pat Mahoney stood in front of some assembled pro-life activists at Quincy Market, where he used his bullhorn to inform pedestrians, "This is what democracy is all about, coming together and having a serious, civil discussion about great moral questions. We just want to dialogue. We are nice, friendly people." Mahoney continued, "Please explain to us why you think abortion should remain legal." Unlike the campus outreaches, however, these pro-life activists had no way of drawing a crowd and no clever devices for creating conversations. The Bostonians simply ignored them.[103]

The lack of commitment to dialogue was underscored by what was easily the most confrontational incident of the weekend. Pro-life activists decided to counter-demonstrate in front of the very posh Harvard Club, where the Feminist Majority was honoring a prominent feminist. Outside the club about a dozen members of the Feminist Majority greeted guests as they arrived. The pro-lifers showed up in waves, including a large contingent of Catholics and many young and confrontational activists from Survivors—a California based, student pro-life organization. One such activist was Johanna, an eighteen-year-old evangelical from Sacramento, California. As the feminists entered the Harvard Club, Johanna extended her hand and offered this greeting: "Thank you for killing a third of my generation." Meanwhile, Jeff White, who played an important role in organizing clinic blockades for Operation Rescue, scolded arriving guests with "Shame on you!" Some of the feminists lost their composure. One man shoved Brandi Swindell's bullhorn into her face and another woman recited a favorite chant of pro-choice activists: "Pro-life, that's a lie! You don't care if women live or die!" The pedestrians were similarly belligerent as one yelled "Get the fuck out of our town!" and another very well-dressed Bostonian screamed "Rednecks!"[104]

During all of this commotion, Pat Mahoney grabbed the bullhorn, but then quickly decided that a woman should be the face of the pro-life demonstration. Mahoney passed the bullhorn to Sauna, a seventeen-year old evangelical from Southern California, who proceeded to deliver a critique of pro-choice feminism. Sauna belted into the bullhorn, "Do you know why men love abortion? Because they don't have to take responsibility for getting women pregnant, because they can have free access to women's bodies." After catching her breath, Sauna continued, "Why doesn't the Feminist Majority, NOW, and NARAL give a single penny to poor women. . . . Is that all you can offer women? An abortion! I'm a feminist and pro-life! Please tell me that you can offer me more than an abortion!"[105]

Like much of the counter-demonstrations, Sauna's very secular pleas sat somewhat uncomfortably with the religious messages that swirled around her. A group of Catholics, who are far less vocal and confrontational than the evangelicals with Survivors, quietly prayed to Mary and said the Lord's Prayer. Another man held up large tablets of the Ten Commandments and staffers from Operation Rescue West instructed the feminists to "repent" as they circled Commonwealth Avenue in their "truth trucks," which are paneled with images of aborted fetuses.[106]

Estranged from the main pro-life demonstrations was Randall Terry of Operation Rescue fame. According to those who coordinated the major pro-life protests, Terry was simply not welcome to participate because he divorced his wife to remarry a younger woman. The several dozen activists who made the trek with him to Boston further highlighted his fall from the center of movement politics. These devoted activists were members of Terry's newly launched Society for Truth and Justice. As Terry exited the metro with his activists and headed toward the Democratic National Convention, he looked rather glum and certainly not like a man eager or ready to confront the liberal establishment. Terry's group arrived at the "free speech zone," which was a steel pen set aside by the City of Boston for political demonstrations. The steel walls of the enclosure were lined with razor wire and armed guards are perched above on metal beams.[107] It was the closest activists could get to the Fleet Center, where the convention was getting underway.

Once Terry arrived at the "free speech zone," his spirits rose under the glare of the media attention. A remarkably charismatic personality, Terry quickly incited laughter with lines such as "The Democratic Party likes pluralism, until someone disagrees with [it]. Then [it] puts them in a cage with razor wire." With the cadence of an evangelical preacher, Terry continued, "I'm not sure how much more freedom I can take! . . . I'd feel better if that sniper got a little closer." Terry's antics were so disarming that even one journalist who had mumbled "fucking idiots" under her breath when she caught sight of the pro-lifers was now enjoying his humor.[108] As Terry's right-hand man, Gary McCullough, rightly commented, "Terry's gift is words."[109] Terry's gift was also a reminder that in the recent past he was at the very center of the largest campaign of civil disobedience since the 1960s.

The small demonstration also highlighted just how far Terry had drifted from the radicalism of Operation Rescue. Like most of the pro-life movement, he encouraged his activists to be civil and to love their neighbors. As chapter 1 noted, the Society for Truth and Justice activists must promise to be "gracious" and "peaceful in word and deed" before they are allowed to participate in group activities. Terry's activists, moreover, seemed to follow these instructions. Jeff, a pro-life evangelical from Cincinnati, Ohio, approached a gay activist who was sporting a button that read "I'm Part of the Oral Majority." Although the activist accused evangelicals of bigotry, Jeff expressed his concern over the effects of AIDS on the gay community and reported that he harbored no ill will toward homosexuals. The two men parted with a handshake and pat on one another's backs.[110]

RADICAL POLITICS

Although Randall Terry has long since abandoned direct action and with it political radicalism, others have not. But what remains of the rescue movement can be found only in very small outposts, the most significant of which is Operation Rescue West (ORW)—an organization devoted to harassing abortion providers in an attempt to close clinics. Unlike the varieties of disjointed activism just described, radicals are not nuisances to be regulated and controlled. Nor is Christian faith considered contrary to public belligerency.

Direct Action

Operation Rescue West is located in Wichita, Kansas, where its primary mission is to close Dr. George Tiller's late-term abortion clinic. However, ORW's presence is felt beyond Tiller's clinic. In fact, I met ORW staff and activists in St. Louis, where they were organizing "rescue outreaches" at area abortion clinics. The term "outreaches," however, does not really capture ORW's brand of direct action. Outside the Hope Clinic for Women, Troy Newman, the director of ORW, showed the ropes to local activists interested in ORW's methods. Newman yelled at the clinic director, Sally Burgess, "Sally, we're going to expose you in your neighborhood if you don't stop taking blood money!" He then added, "You're a profiteer on the blood of babies, Sally" and "You're going to go down in history with the slave owners and Nazis." Cheryl Sullenger, the field director for ORW, then entered the mix and struck a less judgmental note when asking, "How is this helping women?"[111]

Yelling in front of abortion clinics, however, is not really ORW's bread and butter. Instead, staffers at ORW like to target abortion providers in their private lives, away from their clinics. As ORW sees it, such exposure will bring public shame on abortion providers, and they will be compelled to quit. It also has the virtue of making abortion providers feel like they can't leave their clinic and escape the harassment of activists. As Troy Newman informed me at a Steak and Shake in downtown St. Louis, "Evil must be uprooted from its rat hole and exposed."[112] In support of this view, Newman especially likes to cite Ephesians 5:11–12: "Take no part in the fruitless works of darkness; rather expose them, for it is a shameful even to mention the things done by them in secret."

I followed ORW staffers and activists to Dr. Shah's private office some miles away from the Hope Clinic. In an adjacent public parking lot, ORW parked its "truth truck," which is paneled with images of aborted fetuses. Meanwhile, pro-life activists lined the street in front of Shah's office holding the same images. Newman, never one to mince words, picked up a bullhorn and yelled, "Dr. Shah is an abortionist and child murderer, he has killed 100,000 babies!" Newman then turned his attention to the wider community and asked, "When will the community stand up and refuse to tolerate child murder?" Obviously agitated, Shah's office quickly called the police, and one nurse came out to investigate. The response from locals in Granite City was more mixed as some honked their horns in support while one woman rolled down her window and screamed "Fuck you!"[113]

Yet, for all the strident and judgmental rhetoric, ORW is actually rather calculating and systematic in its methods. For this reason, its staffers should not be confused with the occasional, self-mobilized radicals who scream at women entering abortion clinics. Instead, ORW applies very systematic methods to a concrete end, which is shutting down abortion clinics. For instance, one favorite method of ORW is sending postcards to abortion providers' neighbors. In one recent case, ORW sent postcards that contained an image of an aborted fetus and a note that read, "Your neighbor Sara Phares participates in killing babies like these." The postcard also asked Sara's neighbors to call her and suggest that she get out of the abortion business. Another postcard soon followed and made this request: "Beg her to quit, pretty please." Some time latter, ORW staff and activists showed up with the "truth trucks" in Sara's neighborhood.[114]

Newman especially likes to catch abortion providers precisely when they feel most protected from public scrutiny. Newman reported that he shows up at Dr. Tiller's home on major holidays, such as Christmas and Easter. Similarly, Newman attended a conference for abortion providers in Washington, D.C. Just as Dr. Tiller helped himself to a drink at the bar, Newman approached him, shook his hand, and said, "Why don't you get out of the baby-killing business?"[115] It is this kind of relentless and systematic harassment that is at the center of ORW's strategy.

In addition to clinic staff, ORW also targets employers who do business with Tiller's clinic. In fact, Newman and his staff just recently compiled a list of 200 "abortion collaborators." The goal is to pressure these businesses into severing ties with Tiller's clinic so that it can no longer function. Some of these "collaborators" include large corporations, such as Wesley Medical Center, where clinic patients are taken when an abortion procedure results in complications. The list also includes small businesses where even more personal and community pressure can be exerted, such as cab companies and cleaners.

Such harassment, moreover, requires more than just the relentless stalking of citizens in their private lives. It also demands considerable research and intelligence gathering. After all, ORW must somehow discover the names and addresses of clinic staff and their ties to local businesses. And some of this research is not especially enticing, such as combing through the garbage of clinic staff for information.

To be sure, Newman and his staff are well aware that most pro-life activists do not regard their methods as Christian. Newman reported that Christians often give him this response: "I'm Christian and pro-life but what you people are doing is not loving." Staffers at ORW, however, argue that their public condemnations are "really an open act of love" and point to Proverbs 27:5, which reads, "Open rebuke is better than hidden love." Such rebukes, according to Newman, give sinners an opportunity to turn away from evil. ORW staffers further argued that too many pro-life citizens emphasize the importance of mercy and grace at the expense of justice. As Newman put it, "Christians are often quick to appeal to grace but slow to seek justice." Those who embrace direct action are not simply trying to save the souls of abortion providers and their patients; they are also seeking their own salvation and the nation's. As they see it, all citizens have blood on their hands because they are complicit in the crime of abortion. This bloodguilt, moreover, can be absolved only through public condemnation and rebuke. Only direct action can stay God's wrathful hand.[116]

• • •

Despite renegades like Troy Newman, this chapter suggests that much of the received wisdom about the Christian Right is untrue. What is most striking about the varied world of pro-life activism is not the belligerency of Christian activists, but the degree to which they embrace the deliberative norm of civility. This follows from activists' own strategic incentives and a Christian commitment to demonstrate love and compassion for others. Indeed, as we have seen, even direct-action radicals try to square this value with their public belligerency. Their insistence that aggressive harassment is "really an open act of love" is a measure of the centrality and limitations of this Christian ideal.

Not all deliberative norms, however, are respected equally. Although Christian activists find that promoting civil dialogue is easy to reconcile with their faith, avoiding religious appeals is more difficult to square with the Gospels. For this reason many activists, especially sidewalk counselors and those who participate in marches and demonstrations, often make public professions of faith. And however much activists embrace philosophical reasoning, they do not become the kind of moral skeptics championed by deliberative democrats. Indeed, even in the most deliberative organizations, such as Justice for All, activists' confrontation with secular knowledge may leave them even more confident in their views. Whether these departures from deliberative ideals represent the Christian Right's democratic failings or are the inevitable cost of a more participatory democracy is a question this book will return to in chapter 6.

The next chapter, however, will turn to a more pressing question: Why are pro-life activists more committed to creating spaces for civil dialogue than their pro-choice opponents?

CHAPTER FOUR

Deliberation and Abortion Politics

THE SINGLE MOST SURPRISING FINDING of the last chapter was the pro-choice movement's opposition to carving out public spaces for civil and deliberative discussions. Yet if pro-life activists tend to be more civil and open to dialogue than their pro-choice opponents in many settings, they have also been far more belligerent in some quarters of the rescue movement. Pro-choice activists, therefore, are neither as deliberative as pro-life activists in Justice for All nor as militant as the stalkers in Operation Rescue West.

These discrepancies can be partially explained by the fact that both movements confront a different set of political incentives. Paradoxically, most pro-life leaders are deeply invested in encouraging deliberative norms precisely because outsiders' view their movement as reactionary and intolerant. And, of course, this poor image is partly due to violent radicals. Because the right-to-life movement seeks revolutionary change in American abortion policy, it is also committed to changing public opinion and policy to a far greater extent than the pro-choice movement. This has led both to violent, direct action tactics *and* a variety of relatively deliberative modes of moral suasion. Meanwhile, the pro-choice movement is a conservative movement that defends the status quo. Pro-choicers have little to gain from engaging its opponents and from the deliberative norms that facilitate persuasion. And, of course, they are not interested in what so many rescuers used to describe as "breaking the system."

In addition to these strategic incentives, the cultures of both movements matter as well. Although the women's movement is not trying to change radically public opinion and policy, it is (like many of the movements that came out of the New Left) seeking the personal empowerment of its members. Directing and controlling the behavior of their rank and file flies in the face of this fundamental value. There is nothing comparable to this commitment to participatory egalitarianism on the Right. While the pro-choice movement's commitment to participatory freedom undermines the authority necessary to discipline radical activists, Christianity provides conservative leaders with a powerful resource to shore up deliberative norms and excite militancy.

CIVILITY AND STRATEGIC INCENTIVES

To the extent that pro-life activists are more civil in public forums than their pro-choice opponents, this discrepancy may be explained by different incentives that are created by the larger political system.

Unlike pro-choice activists, pro-lifers are always fighting a very negative public image that has been shaped by militant radicalism and a hostile media.[1] As chapter 1 revealed, pro-life leaders often encourage their activists to be civil and gracious in public forums precisely because of the movement's negative public image. They are also well aware that the media is partly to blame.[2] Lori Kehoe, the president of New York State Right to Life, explained that a major part of her work is simply trying to convince journalists that pro-life activists are "normal."[3] It is hard to imagine a pro-choice leader describing her work this way. To the contrary, pro-choice advocates seem well aware that they have allies in the media. In the *Los Angeles Times* study on abortion bias, one pro-choice advocate confessed, "We've loved having the media's support, but we're wondering when someone would finally blow the whistle."[4] And because the worst a pro-choice advocate might be called in the media is an "activist," movement leaders simply have far less incentive to encourage deliberative norms.

The conservatism of the pro-choice movement also undermines its interest in deliberative norms. Its central concern is protecting the status quo as enshrined by *Roe v. Wade* and removing regulations on abortion, such as parental consent laws and bans on the partial-birth abortion procedure. Most of these fights take place among a fairly elite group of advocates within legislatures and courtrooms. Rank-and-file activists, meanwhile, participate in very occasional marches and counter-demonstrations, where the rewards are largely symbolic and the stakes are extremely low. Such activism fuels the passions of pro-choice activists and thereby helps to keep the more elite campaigns of national organizations well funded.

The conservatism of the pro-choice movement has not gone unnoticed by other scholars. Abortion rights advocate Eileen McDonagh argues that even the pro-choice movements greatest organizational successes, such as the March for Women's Lives, are essentially "defensive," since they seek to "preserve *Roe* and to overturn, or ban, the policies pro-life organizations have already enacted."[5] Thus, the pro-choice movement in McDonagh's view is a reactionary one.

Empirical studies have corroborated McDonagh's account. Political scientists Dana Patton and Sara Zeigler found a "relative dearth of pro-choice bills" compared to pro-life legislation. After examining abortion bills in the state legislatures in 2006, Patton and Zeigler conclude that some 215 pro-life bills were introduced compared to only eighty pro-choice bills. On gay rights, however, where the Left is challenging the status quo, it is conservatives who are less active. Patton and Zeigler found that there were forty-six "pro-gay" bills compared to only thirty-seven "anti-gay" ones.[6]

The pro-life movement, on the other hand, is committed to effecting radical change in public opinion and policy. As such, it is far more invested in moral suasion. Moreover, a lot is at stake in every act of moral suasion for pro-life activists. It is not uncommon to find sidewalk counselors or participants in college outreaches reflecting back on failed exchanges with other citizens with deep regret. If only they would have approached others a little differently, these pro-life activists reason, a life might have been spared. There is nothing analogous to this kind of moral suasion in the pro-choice movement. Pro-choice advocates do not really care, at least not very deeply, whether the abortion rate rises or falls from year to year or whether those who disagree with them change their minds. Their central concern is protecting *Roe* and its companion decisions.

But if challenging the status quo has encouraged deliberative modes of moral suasion, it has also excited violence and aggressive forms of direct action. Like the Christian elites who promote public reason at Justice for All, pro-life radicals have concluded that something must be done to reduce abortion rates in a country in which abortion laws are firmly entrenched and unlikely to change. *Roe*, therefore, has inspired both a deliberative politics as well as political violence.

CIVILITY AND THE POLITICS OF MOTHERHOOD

It is often assumed that culture shapes moral conflict. The importance of culture, however, has been overemphasized. As I argued in the introduction, the thesis that American moral conflict is driven by an inherently irrational, even pathological defense of symbols, status, cultures, and worldviews has clouded our understanding of social movements.

The scholarship on abortion politics is no exception. Kristen Luker's canonical *Abortion and the Politics of Motherhood* is the most important work to treat abortion politics as a symbolic conflict over worldviews. According to Luker, neither side fundamentally views abortion as a civil rights issue. Instead, pro-life and pro-choice activists alike are fighting over the value and definition of motherhood. As she puts it, "While on the surface it is the embryo's fate that seems to be at stake, the abortion debate is actually about the meaning of *women's* lives." To paraphrase Luker only slightly, abortion is merely the tip of a much larger cultural iceberg.[7] It is a view, moreover, that is reinforced by the almost universal description of the abortion conflict as a *culture* war.

Luker's argument is troubled both theoretically and methodologically. At a theoretical level, it simply does not follow, as she asserts, that a symbolic explanation must be sought in order to understand why the abortion debate is so "passionate and hard-fought." A more plausible and straightforward explanation is simply that pro-life activists are so passionate because they really believe over 40 million human beings have been exterminated since *Roe v. Wade*. It is difficult to place this view at the tip of any cultural iceberg even if it is often bound together with other beliefs that collectively make for a distinctive worldview. Instead, as pro-life advocates see it, the loss of this much human life rivals the greatest state-sanctioned crimes of the past century. And precisely because so much is at stake, most pro-life activists are committed to the deliberative ideals that further persuasion, while others are driven to violence.

Methodologically, Luker's work is equally troubled. Although Luker does a good job of describing the beliefs of devout Catholic housewives in the 1970s and early 1980s on a wide range of related issues (including sex, birth control, abortion, and motherhood), she cannot explain why the women in her sample decided to become active in pro-life politics while millions of other citizens who share this Catholic "worldview" did not.

When activists are asked why they became involved in the pro-life movement, they most commonly report that they viewed a graphic depiction of aborted human life. Cynthia Gorney, a professor of journalism at Berkeley and an unusually even-handed observer of abortion politics, has found that graphic images in Barbara Willke's *Abortion Handbook* inspired the first generation of pro-life movement activists. As Gorney explained in the pages of *Harper's Magazine*, "To this day, when asked whether there was an epiphany that brought them into the movement, many right-to-life veterans will recall their first look at Willke's pictures."[8]

The current generation of activists is far more likely to point to videos such as the *Silent Scream* and *Hard Truth*. Scott Klusendorf, the former director of bioethics at Stand to Reason and current director of the newly launched Life Training Institute, was formerly a Baptist pastor in Southern California. Klusendorf dropped everything to do pro-life work after watching *Hard Truth*. As he put it, the images "just broke me."[9] Likewise, Cheryl Sullenger began sidewalk counseling only after she watched the *Silent Scream*. Sullenger went on to found the California Life Coalition and currently works for Operation Rescue West.[10]

Because many movement leaders became committed to the pro-life cause only after they viewed the remains of aborted fetuses, such images continue to be embraced as the principal means of mobilizing pro-life

Christians. Stand to Reason, for example, routinely shows a brief portion of the *Hard Truth* to its Christian audiences in churches and religious schools. I witnessed one such presentation at a Christian school in Fredericksburg, Virginia, where hundreds of students were moved to tears.[11] Such images, moreover, continue to haunt the consciences of pro-life activists. One vivid example was a young activist and member of Rock for Life Boston who reported to me that when she first visited a Planned Parenthood to sidewalk counsel, she imagined blood flooding out the clinic's doors.[12] It is difficult to explain such reports if the "embryo's fate" was not at stake.

To appreciate fully the utility and power of these graphic images as a mobilization tool, it is important to highlight their effects on "converts"—a term that is frequently used to describe those who embraced pro-life activism after being philosophically, even actively, pro-choice. The pro-life movement is full of such activists, some of whom became very prominent movement leaders. Joan Appleton became a pro-life activist after spending much of her life as a NOW activist and head nurse at a large abortion facility in Falls Church, Virginia. According to Appleton, she became a "convert" after watching a first trimester ultrasound abortion. As she puts it, "I saw the baby pull away. I saw the baby open its mouth. . . . After the procedure I was shaking literally."[13] Dr. Joseph Randall, who participated in some 32,000 abortions, began to abandon his pro-choice commitments as ultrasound technology improved. Like Appleton, he reported that "the greatest thing that got to us was the ultrasound. . . . The picture of the baby on the ultrasound bothered me more than anything."[14] Feminist and Planned Parenthood clinic worker Judith Fetrow's pro-choice position also softened when she began performing the Jewish mourning ritual of "sitting shiva" over aborted remains. Fetrow, who was responsible for disposing of fetal bodies, described naming each fetus and saying "prayers for the dead."[15] Finally, Kathy Sparks, an OB nurse at an abortion clinic, reports that after seeing the remains of a fetus at twenty-three weeks' gestation she "began weeping, uncontrollably." Rebuked by the recovery nurse for not being "professional," Sparks left and embraced pro-life activism.[16]

Of course, not all "converts" changed their minds because of their confrontation with fetal remains. Some experienced a conversion of the more traditional variety, while others still became pro-life for philosophical reasons. While the former camp is not inconsistent with the symbolic-politics thesis, the latter converts are. Easily the most famous such case is that of Bernard Nathanson, the cofounder of NARAL Pro-Choice America and director of what was then the largest abortion facility in the Western world. Nathanson, a nonpracticing Jew and atheist, did eventually embrace Catholicism, but only decades after he began to rethink the morality of abortion. In fact, Nathanson's journey to faith parallels that of many "converts" in that his pro-life conversion led him to Christianity rather than vice versa. As he would later explain, "I was looking for a way to wash away my sins."[17] And then there are cases in which pro-choice Christians simply changed their minds about abortion, which equally complicates the politics of motherhood. Robin Hoffman, now president of Florida Right to Life, informed me that she was a Baptist who had a pro-life "conversion" after talking to sidewalk counselors.[18] Meanwhile, Phil, an evangelical and president of Albany Rock for Life, became pro-life after he was persuaded by an abortion debate in high school.[19]

The current demographic makeup of the pro-life movement also confounds the politics of motherhood. To a great extent, Luker's thesis rested on the fact that many of the pro-life activists in her sample were Catholic housewives. But as the previous chapter demonstrated, contemporary activists are drawn from a wide variety of demographic backgrounds and some, especially at elite universities, regard themselves as feminists and are very career oriented. Others gave up professional careers to do pro-life work full-time. The movement's general sympathy to feminist concerns is corroborated by survey data, which find that pro-life citizens are only moderately less likely to be "very concerned" about women's rights than pro-choice respondents.[20] In addition, Luker is one of the very few academics to overestimate the role of women in pro-life politics. It is certainly true that there are more women than men in the pro-life movement, but by no means is it a women's movement. The pro-life movement is actually quite diverse, and abortion politics more generally does not pit working-class Catholic housewives against professional, career-oriented women.

The rescue movement is especially difficult to understand as a cultural cause for at least two reasons. First, if the pro-life movement is best understood as a defense of traditional gender roles, then why was the movement's most radical wing pioneered by anti-war liberals? It is true that these liberals eventually allied with Christians who were quite socially conservative. But those who pioneered the rescue movement can hardly be described as conservative on gender issues. In fact, John O'Keefe, the founder of rescue, even took his wife's name, changing it to Cavanaugh-O'Keefe in 1976.[21] Second, it is hard to square the passion and sacrifice of the rescue movement with the politics of motherhood. Recall from chapter 2 that the rescue movement led to some 33,000 arrests between 1977 and 1993.[22] Are we to believe, then, that these citizens really spent time in jail, suffered "pain compliance" at the hands of local police, and used all of their vacation time for such activism for the politics of motherhood? Did they vandalize abortion equipment and lay their bodies in front of moving vehicles for the politics of motherhood? Did the violent fringe of the rescue movement bomb abortion clinics and even shoot abortion providers because motherhood had become undervalued culturally? And do the current rescuers at Operation Rescue West stalk and harass abortion providers because of the same cultural anxieties? It is simply implausible that the politics of motherhood can account for this degree of devotion and sacrifice to the pro-life cause.

Christian leaders sometimes even explicitly contrast abortion from the host of cultural issues that are arguably more symbolic. On a recent Focus on the Family radio broadcast, James Dobson discussed his organization's effort to equip crisis pregnancy centers with ultrasound machines. Dobson further expressed how easy it has been to raise money for this project because the abortion issue does not involve "some abstraction, it's a human being."[23]

Arguably, Luker's thesis might make more sense when applied to the pro-choice movement. But here again there is cause for skepticism. After all, a common symbol used in pro-choice demonstrations is the coat hanger and activists often chant "Pro-life, that's a lie! You don't care if women live or die!" Pro-choice activists seem to believe that human life is at stake no less than their opponents.

The great moral conflicts in American history, especially slavery, civil rights, and abortion, have been unusually hard fought and passionate because they cannot be understood as symbolic fights over different worldviews or cultures. Instead, they are better understood as clashes over how common liberal values should be extended to different categories of humans. These conflicts have been disagreements over who counts as a human person.

Whether or not the pro-life movement is on firm moral ground, it understands itself as today's civil rights movement. A failure to grasp this truth renders the movement almost incomprehensible to outside observers. Once scholars appreciate the pro-life movement's own self-conception, then its commitment to deliberative dialogue, its militant fringe, and its passion make sense. It also helps us understand why the issue of abortion has dominated the "culture wars."

Given the implausibility of Luker's account, why has it been so appealing to academics? As I have already emphasized, part of the explanation is the general tendency to see moral campaigns as symbolic defenses of cultural worldviews. The sociology of the academy, however, may matter as well. Perhaps Luker's book has been so appealing to academics because they do not want to entertain the possibility that these conservative reactionaries *might* be agents in progressive history. Central to the self-understanding of liberalism is the belief that the Left cares about justice and human rights, while the Right is obsessed with crabbed cultural preoccupations such as gay lifestyles, pornography, and traditional gender roles.

Conservatives, in this view, must be seen as reactionaries to the civil rights movements rather than its heirs. If this is right, Luker's book may say more about contemporary American liberalism than it does about abortion politics.

CIVILITY, CHRISTIANITY, AND AUTHENTICITY

If the abortion conflict cannot be understood as a symbolic fight over worldviews, culture might still shape abortion politics. As this book has shown, Christian Right leaders routinely anchor secular, deliberative norms in their faith. However cynically one is inclined to regard this elite behavior, it is likely that Christian faith does help shore up deliberative norms among rank-and-file activists just as it has inspired militancy in the rescue movement.

To the degree that Christianity can shore up deliberative ideals, it is consistent with one of Charles Taylor's central arguments in his classic work on modern identity. According to Taylor, the Western world is saddled with the very high moral standards of universal benevolence and justice, but with little to sustain the quest to make those same standards real. This dilemma creates the temptation to blame the failure to realize such standards on "some other people, or group." Taylor explains it this way: "My conscience is clear because I oppose them, but what can I do? They stand in the way of universal benevolence; they must be liquidated." The Christian notion of *agape*, on the other hand, lessens this temptation because it provides citizens with a belief in the intrinsic goodness and worth of all humans independent of their perceived unworthiness.[24]

In the end, of course, it is difficult to assess the influence of Christianity. On the one hand, some evidence suggests that strategic incentives are more important. For instance, most Christian leaders happily depart from deliberative norms in the context of mobilization or in the privacy of their own social circles. On the other hand, it is also true that Christian fundamentalists are drawn to a much more militant style of politics that has alienated most conservative evangelicals and Catholics. Therefore, the kind of Christianity that citizens practice influences the style of politics they are drawn to.

A larger and more important issue is how the answer to this question might matter. Some may assume that we should be troubled if Christians are being inauthentic. After all, if they do not sincerely believe in these norms, then they are simply manipulating other citizens to achieve their own ends. Perhaps this is right. But before accepting this argument, we should reconsider Richard Sennett's thesis in *The Fall of Public Man*.

According to Sennett, public life is only possible when there is a separation between the authentic, intimate self and the public, inauthentic one. In fact, Sennett argued that civility is inauthentic by definition. As he explains, "Wearing a mask is the essence of civility. Masks permit pure sociability detached from the . . . private feelings of those who wear them." Moreover, Sennett concluded that our public life has declined because we have insisted that even our politics should be marked by intimate, authentic relationships. Civility, according to Sennett, is destroyed as a result: "[C]ivilized relations between selves can only proceed insofar as the nasty little secrets of desire, greed, and envy are kept locked up."[25]

It is precisely this emphasis on authentic public expression that characterizes New Left–inspired movements, and it has had real implications for how they are organized. The women's movement, for instance, has sought more than simply policy objectives. Like other movements that came out of the New Left, it has also pursued more personal rewards, such as empowerment, authenticity, and liberation. As a result, feminist leaders have been very reluctant to control belligerent activists on the ground. Such heavy-handedness would compromise their commitment to participatory freedom in the public square. Thus, even if pro-choice leaders did have stronger strategic incentives to control their rank and file, they would still be reluctant to do so given their deep commitment to participatory freedom.

This conclusion finds support in Jane Mansbridge's study of the politics surrounding the Equal Rights Amendment (ERA). According to Mansbridge, "Among ERA forces, the decision not to organize hierarchically was explicit, conscious, and almost unanimous." After all, Mansbridge continues, " 'Empowering women' was a goal as important as the ERA." But in the words of one pro-ERA supporter in the Illinois House, the result was an " 'uncontrollable mess.' " Pro-ERA groups, for example, did not have any power over spontaneous acts of civil disobedience.[26]

Maryann Barakso's research corroborates Mansbridge's findings. According to Barakso, elites at NOW encouraged rank-and-file activists to do "whatever you feel will pass the ERA. . . . The choice will be yours. You are wise." Moreover, NOW continues to be guided by this radically democratic ethos. As Barakso explains, "Now chapters are highly autonomous, working for only those goals relevant to . . . their activists' interests." Or, as Kim Gandy, the president of NOW lamented, "NOW is excruciatingly democratic."[27]

The larger feminist movement shares the democratic commitments of the National Organization of Women. Anne Slater, an organizer for Seattle Radical Women, reported that grassroots democracy is compromised when there are "dictates from the top." And when political organizations improperly issue such dictates, Slater continued, "someone has a fear that things might get out of control."[28] More recently, the movement's commitment to unencumbered self-expression and participatory freedom was evident at the March for Women's Lives, which attracted hundreds of thousands of pro-choice demonstrators. In fact, its carnivalesque quality landed it in the Style pages of the *Washington Post*.[29]

To be sure, such participatory egalitarianism is not just found in the women's movement. After talking to many community organizers, David Broder reported that they had a "genuine discomfort with the idea of exercising real power." Broder even found that such organizers "go to extraordinary lengths to deny the obvious fact that they are the leaders of the organizations they have brought into being."[30] Today the global justice movement has been especially hostile to authority in its own political organizations and even considers itself a leaderless movement.[31]

The historical roots of this kind of leaderless politics originated in Students for a Democratic Society (SDS) in the early 1960s. Activists at SDS believed that only a truly democratic society could cultivate citizens' authenticity. As the historian Doug Rossinow argued, "The search for authenticity lay at the heart of the new left."[32] Former New Left activist Paul Berman later described the movement's "deepest promise" as the empowerment of "people who felt empty of identity."[33] Moreover, E. J. Dionne claimed that such "spiritual concerns" were "central to how the movement saw itself, to what made it new." At times, according to Dionne, the *Port Huron Statement* even sounded more like a papal encyclical than a political manifesto or treatise.[34]

Because SDS's mission was fundamentally one of personal liberation and authenticity, its very organization (or lack of it) was not designed with political efficacy in mind. Thus, SDS enjoyed no chain of command or procedural means of coming to group decisions. It was instead the kind of radically democratic organization that promised personal authenticity. From the inside, Paul Berman reported that "a Quaker-like cult of consensus stole across the world of student radicalism, as if to hold votes or to build an organization with rules and regulations and leaders and followers was to impose some kind of horrible dictatorship over the rank and file." Furthermore, "Suspicion of leaders became so intense that after a while [Tom] Hayden and other people who were, in fact, leaders began to pretend that they weren't." The result of such participatory egalitarianism, according to Berman, was "sheer madness." For frustrated student activists, however, there was no way to reform the organization without compromising their spiritual mission. As Berman put it, "[A]narchy in SDS was precisely how the movement delivered on its deepest promise."[35]

Although many scholars of the New Left have emphasized its participatory egalitarianism, they have not appreciated how it compromised a long tradition of democratic education in American social movements. Elites and activists alike in the abolitionist, temperance, civil rights, labor, and Christian Right movements have all accepted the need for organizational authority. This authority, in turn, has made the kind of democratic education discussed in chapter 1 possible.

The example of the New Left further suggests that Richard Sennett was right to argue that authenticity in public life paves the way for incivility. What all citizens need, in Sennett's view, are "masks" so that they do not continue "burdening others" with themselves.[36]

DIALOGUE AND ABORTION

The reluctance of pro-choice activists to debate is more difficult to explain. Pro-choice advocates themselves offer a wide variety of explanations. On college campuses, pro-choice groups sometimes claim that they will not debate their pro-life counterparts because an abortion exhibit offended them. However, many campus pro-life groups agree to participate in such exhibits after—and partly because—pro-choice groups refuse to debate them. Other pro-choice advocates argue that it is pointless to engage pro-life activists since neither camp will change its mind. NARAL Pro-Choice America, for example, encourages its student activists not to talk to pro-life students because "neither of you will change the other's mind."[37] Of course, public discussion is not really for the benefit of the activists—it is for the larger, more ambivalent public. The Pro-Choice Action Network, on the other hand, claimed that pro-choice groups avoid debate because "abortion is not debatable" since the "provision of basic human rights is not open to debate." [38] Yet pro-choice groups exist only because the right to an abortion is such a politically contested issue.

Such reluctance to engage the other side must be understood in light of the pro-choice movement's conservatism. As a movement that wants to preserve the status quo, it simply has nothing to gain from engaging its opponents, especially on college campuses where the pro-choice view is a default, progressive position for many students. But the pro-choice movement does have something to lose if bested in public debates. Moreover, pro-choice advocates know very well that even the minds of activists in their ranks can be changed. Prominent examples include abortion providers and the cofounder of NARAL Pro-Choice America, not to mention many less-prominent rank-and-file activists.

That the pro-choice movement is so conservative is a deep irony. While the Left has long argued that the personal is political, it turns largely to elite allies to protect its interests. And while the Right ultimately wants greater governmental intervention, it spends most of its time trying to change hearts and minds.

The pro-choice movement's opposition to public deliberation will likely be perpetuated by yet another political irony. Whereas many religious conservatives have comfortably embraced distinguished allies in the academy, abortion rights advocates cannot easily do so. In fact, pro-choice philosophers are badly at odds with the pro-choice movement. As Rosamund Rhodes, the pro-choice director of bio-ethics at Mt. Sinai School of Medicine, confessed more than three decades after *Roe*, abortion rights proponents are simply not prepared to explain "how or why the fetus is transformed into a franchised 'person' by moving from inside the womb to outside or by reaching a certain level of development."[39] Even Judith Jarvis Thompson's famous defense of abortion rights conceded that the "prospects for 'drawing a line' in the development of the fetus look dim."[40] Meanwhile, the pro-choice philosopher Peter Singer has been even more critical of the pro-choice movement. As Singer put it, "[L]iberals have failed to establish a morally significant dividing line between the newborn baby and fetus."[41]

Nonetheless such thinkers have articulated strong pro-choice arguments. They are not likely, however, to be embraced by the pro-choice movement because of their political liabilities. For instance, although Judith Jarvis Thompson found resting abortion rights on the notion of human nonpersons difficult, she nonetheless offered a creative defense of the right to abortion through an inventive thought experiment. Thompson invites us to imagine that we have been captured by a society of music lovers. We are then attached to a famous violinist because our kidneys are necessary to sustain his life. Thompson then asks, Is it legitimate to detach oneself from the violinist?[42] Despite this argument's success in philosophical circles, it concedes far too much moral ground for the pro-choice movement. After all, Thompson is willing to grant that the embryo is a person, which is a concession that the pro-choice movement has not been willing to make.

Alternatively, the abortion rights movement could turn to pro-choice bioethicists who do not grant so much ontological ground. Scholars such as Mary Anne Warren, Michael Tooley, and Peter Singer defend abortion rights by rooting personhood in self-consciousness. From this perspective, human organisms acquire rights only when they become willful, self-aware beings. The pro-choice movement, however, has been reluctant to accept this view of the human person because it also justifies infanticide. As Singer has starkly put it, there is no "intrinsic wrongness [in] killing an infant."[43]

These problems have left abortion rights advocates severely handicapped in the context of public debates. When pressed by pro-life activists, they have no ready explanation for why fetuses become persons at any point between conception and birth.[44] This fact may explain why an undercurrent of self-doubt runs through some refusals to debate pro-life opponents. The Pro-Choice Action Network gave this explanation for its no-debate policy: "Debates are public relations events, usually staged by the anti-choice. . . . Truth often becomes a casualty in such debates, because the 'winner' is the side with the slickest presentation and fanciest rhetoric."[45]

SOCIAL SCIENCE AND TOLERANCE

In many respects these findings appear inconsistent with what social scientists know (or think they know) about the political tolerance of Christians and of evangelicals in particular. Traditional measures of tolerance as pioneered by such political scientists as Samuel Stouffer and John Sullivan have revealed higher levels of intolerance among evangelicals.[46] Although Christian activists have proven to be more tolerant than the general public, they have also been shown to be less tolerant than activists on the Left. This finding suggests that pro-choice activists would be more willing to embrace deliberative norms than would pro-life advocates.

To untangle this paradox, it is important to say more about these studies. According to traditional studies on tolerance, Americans are a deeply intolerant nation even among the well educated.[47] The pervasive intolerance unearthed by these studies is partly an artifact of their research design. In these studies, respondents are asked whether they would extend basic civil liberties, such as the right to make public speeches or teach in public schools, to the group they like least. Typically, these groups include those whom Americans tend to hold in very low regard, such as racists, atheists, and communists. Indeed, many are hostile to liberal democracy itself.

Many criticisms have been made of these studies. John Sullivan and his colleagues anticipated one normative critique. They wondered whether a perfectly tolerant society was even an ideal end since it might undermine other democratic values.[48] Meanwhile, others have argued that the "least-liked" method is not a good measure of general intolerance. As Steve E. Finkel, Lee Sigelman, and Stan Humphries put it, "This measurement strategy cannot establish whether intolerance is focused (that is, restricted to a certain group or type of group) or diffuse (that is, directed against a wide range of groups)."[49] Meanwhile, other methodological approaches have led scholars to radically difference conclusions. Alan Wolfe's ethnographic research on middle-class Americans finds that Americans are "tolerant to a fault." Not only did Wolfe find Americans unprepared to deny civil liberties to other citizens, but he even found a pervasive unwillingness to cast a judgment of any kind. As he put it, "Above all moderate in their outlook on the world, they believe in the importance of living a virtuous life but are reluctant to impose values they understand as virtuous for themselves on others; strong believers in morality, they do not want to be considered moralists."[50]

Although activists in the Christian Right cannot be faulted for the tolerance that Wolfe describes, there is also very little evidence that many Americans, whether in or outside of the Christian Right, actively try to deny fellow citizens basic civil liberties. This fact has inspired this book's emphasis on deliberative norms. While most political science has feared that citizens' actual political ends are undemocratic, this work instead argues that citizens' ends tend to be contestable and therefore what really matters is how they are pursued. Thus, I have conceptualized deliberative norms quite differently from traditional measures of political tolerance, which are a better measure of civil libertarianism than public civility and reasoning.

More generally, the larger problem with using survey data is that the relationship between political attitudes (as reported to surveyors) and political behavior is unclear. Whatever influence political values, such as tolerance, might have on the political behavior of rank-and-file activists, it is probably overwhelmed by other influences. For example, recall the last chapter's discussion of the dramatic confrontation between pro-choice and pro-life activists in San Francisco. Pro-life advocates were peaceful and on message, while the pro-choice advocates were generally belligerent. If we could somehow have surveyed those activists, it is unlikely that we would uncover dramatic differences in their reported democratic values, such as their tolerance and willingness to compromise. It is even possible that the pro-choice activists would score better on these kinds of measures. Instead, what seemed to matter in San Francisco was the way these groups were organized. The pro-life march was carefully organized by leaders who labored to regulate and control their activists, while the pro-choice counter-demonstration was situated in a relatively undisciplined movement where elites are very reluctant to discipline their rank-and-file activists. At the very least, social scientists need to be more careful about making inferences about political behavior from reported attitudes.

• • •

This chapter is a modest inquiry into the conditions that promote and undermine deliberation in democratic life. If social scientists are to take that investigation seriously, then they should pay special attention to the contextual forces that shape movements' disparate interest in deliberative norms.

Since context matters, then perhaps the pro-life movement is more invested in deliberative dialogue than are other socially conservative campaigns in the Christian Right. For instance, opponents of gay marriage are defending the status quo. And like the pro-choice movement, those that oppose gay marriage are not deeply invested in a massive campaign of moral suasion. In other Christian Right issue domains, there is simply nothing comparable to the varied organizational universe that exists in the pro-life movement.

On the other hand, Christian opponents of gay marriage labor under a negative public image and resist the participatory egalitarianism that guide New Left inspired organizations. As chapter 1 demonstrated, deliberative norms are also taught in multi-issue groups like the Christian Coalition, Concerned Women for America, and Focus on the Family. These possibilities should underscore the need for more research into our public life.

CHAPTER FIVE

Reviving Participatory Democracy

HOWEVER ONE ASSESSES the Right's fidelity to deliberative ideals, there is no gainsaying its influence on participation. Among reports of rising apathy and withdrawal from American politics, Christian Right organizations have successfully mobilized one of the most politically alienated constituencies in twentieth-century America. In the space of just a few election cycles, conservative evangelicals went from being the least knowledgeable, partisan, and active citizens to among the most politically sophisticated. The mobilization of Christian conservatives is also one of the most surprising developments in the post–civil rights era because it was the New Left that emphasized the importance of opening up American democracy to alienated citizens.

In some respects, this account is a familiar one and certainly far less controversial than other findings in this book. The participatory exceptionalism of the Right has even been acknowledged in some surprising quarters. According to the director of the Virginia Democratic Party Caucus, "The Christian Coalition has done nothing sinister. They've taken tactics used by Democrats and Republicans for years, mastered them, put them to work; and now even Democratic professionals like myself get the Christian Coalition training manuals, read them and appropriate things that are good, and now we go back to our people and try to teach them the same things."[1] In his famously despairing account of Americans' civic involvement, even Robert Putnam conceded the point, without finding much solace in it: "It is, in short, among Evangelical conservatives, rather than among the ideological heirs of the 1960s, that we find the strongest evidence for an upwelling of civic engagement."[2]

The mobilization of Christian conservatives, however, has never been told in a systematic way. Scholars have yet to use survey data to trace the gradual assimilation of conservative evangelicals into American politics using a wide range of indicators, including partisanship, political knowledge, and other forms of participation beyond voting. When these developments are traced carefully, we find that the participatory revival among evangelical conservatives was more dramatic and happened later than many observers reported. The Reagan Revolution, for example, had almost no effect on evangelical turnout. As chapter 2 argued, this is because the Moral Majority was not really a grassroots organization and because its militancy alienated its natural base. It was not until the rise of the Christian Coalition in the 1990s that millions of new evangelical voters were brought into American politics. Now that it has collapsed, the big question is whether evangelical turnout can be sustained in 2008 and beyond.

Conservative Evangelicals and Participatory Democracy

Throughout the twentieth century, evangelical voters turned out at far lower rates than other citizens. One important reason for this discrepancy is that much evangelical theology teaches that the political world is inherently sinful and corrupting. It further tends to insist that political and social problems are symptoms of individuals' failure to accept Christ as their savior.

Christian Right organizations have worked to overcome these obstacles by telling evangelicals that the political world is corrupt precisely because they have stayed out of the political process. Christian leaders especially emphasize that citizens have a duty to participate. Of greater importance, though, Christian Right organizations departed from the example set by liberal public interest groups and the Moral Majority. Instead, the Right embraced an older tradition established by many religious movements, including the abolitionist, temperance, and civil rights campaigns, by mobilizing through church-based social networks.

Throughout the following analysis I draw upon National Election Studies (NES) surveys, which provides the very best and most comprehensive data on political participation since the 1950s. The principal problem with NES data for my purposes, however, is that they overestimate actual turnout. One reason why this routinely occurs is that some citizens claim to have voted when in fact they did not. Such misreporting is generally attributed to a social desirability basis. Another reason why NES surveys regularly overestimate turnout is that their samples contain a disproportionate percentage of citizens who are more likely to vote.

Although the following turnout data are likely to be somewhat distracting to the reader, given that they far exceed actual turnout, such overestimates will not affect the substance of my findings as long as evangelicals and other citizens are equally likely to be susceptible to social desirability bias. Put differently, although the absolute turnout totals are unreliable, *relative* changes in turnout among different groups and across time should be unaffected by these overestimates as long as social desirability bias is distributed equally.

Prior studies have tended to lump all evangelicals together. This chapter separates socially conservative evangelicals from liberal evangelicals, since the latter are not really the target of Christian Right mobilization and their turnout patterns look quite different. For example, lumping all evangelicals together overestimates conservative evangelical turnout in the 1970s and underestimates it in the 1990s.

But how does one distinguish liberal and conservative evangelicals? I rely on abortion opinion. Respondents who belong to an evangelical denomination and believe that abortion should either always be illegal or legal only in hard cases, such as rape and incest, were classified as conservative evangelicals.[3] There are a number of advantages to this measurement strategy. First, the NES has consistently asked a question on abortion since 1972.[4] Other prominent concerns of the evangelical conservatives, such as gay rights issues, have been addressed only by the NES in recent years. Second, pro-choice evangelicals are certainly not the targets of Christian Right mobilization and do not join movement organizations. Thus, they should not be classified as conservative evangelicals under any measurement scheme. Nonetheless perhaps the way I have classified conservative evangelicals is still too broad. Certainly some pro-life evangelicals do not regard themselves as conservative because they tend to emphasize the social justice concerns that preoccupy liberal evangelicals. Given the limitations of the NES, however, this method adequately distinguishes between conservative and liberal evangelicals.

Evangelical Alienation: 1920–1972

The alienation of evangelical Christians finds its origins at the turn of the century when Darwinism, liberal Protestant theology, and other modernist ideas dramatically influenced American culture and politics. These changes were so disorienting to orthodox believers that historian George Marsden concludes, "Respectable 'evangelicals' in the 1870s, by the 1920s had become a laughingstock, ideological strangers in their own land." In the 1920s, for example, Sinclair Lewis' *Main Street* and *Elmer Gantry* expressed many popular stereotypes of conservative evangelicals and their communities. Lewis depicted *Main Street* as a cultural backwater and Gantry as a charlatan who embraced fundamentalism partly because he was not smart enough to grasp secular knowledge.[5] Some eighty years later, even intellectuals who attempt to be fair-minded sometimes embrace Lewis's stereotypes. Peter Beinart of the *New Republic* grudgingly conceded after the 2004 elections that "occasionally liberals do treat evangelical Christians with derision and scorn." Yet, earlier that same year, Beinart himself described Pat Robertson as a "fundamentalist loon."[6]

An important theological consequence of this "collective uprooting," as Marsden called it, was the rise of premillennialism, which is the eschatological belief that the world must continue to fall deeper into sin before Christ returns and establishes his thousand-year reign on earth. According to Marsden, the "view that 'the world' would 'grow worse and worse' was an important departure from the dominant tradition of American evangelicalism that viewed God's redemptive work as manifested in the spiritual and moral progress of American society." In the nineteenth century, evangelicals tended to believe that the creation of a truly Christian civilization would usher in the return of Christ. Such a view, of course, demanded active participation in social and political life. But with the rise of premillennialism, true Christianity demanded that "one was separated from sin and worldliness." Marsden refers to this retreat from political and social concerns as "the great reversal." Many evangelicals found refuge in "the equivalent of an urban ghetto" with its own "institutions, mores, and social connections."[7]

Even the rise of premillennial eschatology, however, did not lead to the complete destruction of the nineteenth-century emphasis on social reform. According to Marsden, the "older tradition was in many ways culturally optimistic and reformist. When premillennialism was added on, this tradition was by no means obliterated. Rather the two were fused together despite the basic tension between them."[8]

This tension is so important and enduring that it was evident among the fundamentalists who would eventually embrace political action in the 1980s and 1990s. According to James Risen and Judy Thomas's account of the rescue movement, for example, "[M]any evangelicals sought to ignore the conflict for fear of alienating their core supports." Other Christian leaders, such as Randall Terry, concluded that premillennialism and political action were irreconcilable. Reflecting back on his activism, Terry reported, "I became a pro-life activist while I was a fierce premillennial dispensationalist, and for a time I lived an inconsistent life. But I eventually realized that this [dispensationalism] is utter nonsense. . . . It kept Evangelicals out of politics for fifty years, very successfully."[9]

Though we do not have any hard data on evangelicals prior to 1960, NES data suggest that they remained among the most politically alienated citizens in America in the 1960s and 1970s. Between 1960 and 1972, in fact, the turnout gap between white evangelicals and non-evangelicals never dipped bellow 14 percent. In 1972—the first year the NES queried attitudes on abortion—the turnout gap between white non-evangelicals and conservative evangelicals reached 19 percent (see table 5.1). Even African Americans turned out at a higher rate than conservative evangelicals, as did liberal evangelicals.

TABLE 5.1
Participation in the 1972 Election

	Conservative evangelicals	Liberal evangelicals	Non-evangelicals	African Americans
Turnout	59	68	78	65
Influence others to vote	23	34	34	31
Follow public affairs	65	78	76	64
Identify Reps. as conservative	47	64	67	79
Important party differences	45	47	50	74
Split ticket	44	31	29	14

Source: Virginia Sapiro, Steven J. Rosenstone, and National Election Studies, *American National Election Studies Cumulative Data File, 1948–2002* (Ann Arbor, MI: Inter-university Consortium for Political and Social Research, November 2004).

Other indicators in 1972 suggested that conservative evangelicals were relatively withdrawn from American politics. By significant margins, conservative evangelicals in 1972 were less likely than other Americans to influence other citizens to vote and less likely to follow politics. Their ties to the major political parties were also more attenuated. Some 44 percent of conservative evangelicals split their tickets in 1972, which continued a tradition of support for Republican presidents and Democratic candidates for local and state offices. In addition, only 47 percent of conservative evangelicals identified the Republicans as the conservative party compared to 67 percent of non-evangelicals and 79 percent of African Americans. Other groups, blacks in particular, were also more likely to see important differences between the two major parties.

As some of these comparisons suggest, African Americans were much more engaged in American politics than conservative evangelicals. Although African Americans followed politics to the same extent as conservative evangelicals, they were much more likely to influence their fellow citizens to vote, notice party differences, and identify the Republicans as the conservative party; and they were far less prone to split their ticket. For the first time in American history, African Americans were brought into politics on a mass scale and they were strongly loyal to the party that led the way in creating greater political equality.

Political Awakenings: 1976–1988

Throughout the 1970s and into the 1980s the participation rate of conservative evangelicals did improve moderately. In 1976, for instance, evangelicals—both liberal and conservative alike—were somewhat more en-

TABLE 5.2
Turnout, Various Groups, 1972–1988

	1972	1976	1980	1984	1988	Change
Conservative evangelicals	59	67	67	66	61	+2
Liberal evangelicals	68	71	72	69	64	–4
Non-evangelicals	78	76	76	79	76	–2
African Americans	65	66	67	66	60	–5
All Americans	73	73	71	74	70	–3

Source: Virginia Sapiro, Steven J. Rosenstone, and National Election Studies, *American National Election Studies Cumulative Data File, 1948–2002* (Ann Arbor, MI: Inter-university Consortium for Political and Social Research, November 2004).

gaged in politics due to the election of Jimmy Carter, an evangelical himself. Additionally, 1976 was the first election in which evangelicals were actively courted as a distinct voting bloc—a fact that encouraged George W. Gallup to declare the bicentennial the "year of the evangelical." Yet, conservative evangelicals remained relatively estranged from politics as their turnout rate improved only marginally and continued to trail far behind that of non-evangelicals (see table 5.2).

Contrary to popular belief, evangelical turnout did not continue to increase during the so-called Reagan Revolution that followed. In spite of all the reports of a new and powerful Right with the Moral Majority and conservative media leading the way, turnout among conservative evangelicals did not increase in 1980 and 1984, while the turnout gap between evangelicals and non-evangelicals continued to widen. By 1988, evangelical turnout was barely higher than in 1972, despite Pat Robertson's candidacy.

Although a majority of evangelicals supported Reagan in 1980 and 1984, a full party realignment did not take place. In fact, in 1984 Stuart Rothenberg and Frank Newport still wondered in *The Evangelical Voter* whether "evangelicals or fundamentalists could be mobilized to vote for specific candidates or positions." Much like Hispanics today, evangelicals were regarded as an undermobilized group that was up for grabs, and all candidates campaigned for their votes in 1980. To the extent that evangelicals had real party allegiances, they swung decidedly in favor of Democrats rather than Republicans. For example, Rothenberg and Newport's comprehensive 1983 survey of evangelicals revealed that a plurality of evangelicals claimed that they usually voted for the Democrats and even self-identified fundamentalists were a mere 3 percent more likely to have registered as Republicans than non-fundamentalists. Such findings led Rothenberg and Newport to conclude that evangelicals remained a "solidly

Democratic" voting bloc in spite of their social conservatism on some issues and that they would remain so unless the Republican Party "provide[d] them with a reason to cross over and vote Republican."[10]

In part, conservative evangelicals remained an undermobilized constituency because the emerging Christian Right organizations had done such a poor job at reaching them. As I argued in chapter 2, evangelicals hardly noticed Falwell and the Moral Majority, and those who did were not impressed. Like so many public interest groups, the radicalism and stridency of the Moral Majority alienated its natural constituency. And because the Moral Majority could not even command the respect of a majority of evangelicals, it never managed to build a truly grassroots organization. As with other public interest groups, most of its support came from a diffuse group of members whose donations were solicited through direct mail.[11]

Other indicators, however, pointed to a real and growing party realignment among conservative evangelicals in spite of the failed mobilization efforts of the Moral Majority. As the major parties became more cohesive and distinct ideologically, conservative evangelicals became far better at identifying important differences between them. For example, only 45 and 47 percent of conservative evangelicals agreed that important party differences existed in 1972 and 1976 respectively (see table 5.3). By 1984, however, fully 67 percent believed important differences existed. Likewise, conservative evangelicals were more likely to identify correctly the Republicans as the conservative party. In 1972, a mere 47 percent of conservative evangelicals could identify the Republicans as conservative compared to 64 percent of liberal evangelicals, 67 percent of non-evangelicals, and 79 percent of African Americans. With the election of Ronald Reagan in 1980, however, 73 percent of conservative evangelicals could place the Republicans in their appropriate ideological home.

Because it was easier for conservative evangelicals to identify a conservative party, they were far more likely to identify as a Republican. As table 5.3 reveals, the percentage of conservative evangelicals who identified as a Republican jumped from 30 percent in 1980 to 50 percent in 1984, a trend that would continue into the 1990s. In part, this movement represented a more general phenomenon since Republican identification increased among liberal evangelicals and non-evangelicals as well.

Conservative evangelicals were also more likely to identify as strong partisans. In 1972 only 23 percent of conservative evangelicals regarded themselves as strong partisans, but 34 percent did so by 1988. Evangelicals were also less prone to split their tickets. Fully 44 percent of conservative evangelicals split their tickets in 1972, but only 23 percent did so by 1984. This meant that they were increasingly less likely to support Democratic candidates in state and local races.

TABLE 5.3
Measures of Partisanship, 1972–1988

	1972	1976	1980	1984	1988	Change
Important party differences						
Conservative evangelicals	45	47	59	67	56	+11
Liberal evangelicals	47	47	61	66	50	+3
Non-evangelicals	50	51	64	69	65	+15
African Americans	74	72	70	73	66	−8
All Americans	51	53	63	68	63	+12
Identify Reps. as conservative						
Conservative evangelicals	47	56	73	64	67	+20
Liberal evangelicals	64	65	74	67	66	+2
Non-evangelicals	67	71	76	69	75	+8
African Americans	79	78	70	55	64	−15
All Americans	65	70	75	67	71	+6
Republican Party ID						
Conservative evangelicals	35	34	30	50	51	+16
Liberal evangelicals	36	37	41	48	43	+7
Non-evangelicals	38	39	38	43	48	+10
African Americans	11	6	8	11	12	+1
All Americans	34	34	33	39	41	+7
Strong partisans						
Conservative evangelicals	23	25	35	32	34	+11
Liberal evangelicals	19	17	18	25	28	+9
Non-evangelicals	24	23	22	29	29	+5
African Americans	40	37	48	34	41	+1
All Americans	25	24	26	29	31	+6
*Split ticket**						
Conservative evangelicals	44	34	29	23	26	−18
Liberal evangelicals	31	24	38	27	37	+6
Non-evangelicals	29	26	29	26	26	−3
African Americans	14	5	5	15	12	−2
All Americans	30	25	28	25	25	−5

* Between president and House
Source: Virginia Sapiro, Steven J. Rosenstone, and National Election Studies, *American National Election Studies Cumulative Data File, 1948–2002* (Ann Arbor, MI: Inter-university Consortium for Political and Social Research, November 2004).

TABLE 5.4
Turnout, Various Groups, 1972–2004

	1972	1976	1980	1984	1988	1992	1996	2000	2004	Change
Conservative evangelicals	59	67	67	66	61	70	80	74	77	+18
Liberal evangelicals	68	71	72	69	64	80	75	67	78	+10
Non-evangelicals	78	76	76	79	76	81	81	82	80	+2
African Americans	65	66	67	66	60	68	68	75	74	+9
All Americans	73	73	71	74	70	75	77	76	79	+6

Source: Virginia Sapiro, Steven J. Rosenstone, and National Election Studies, *American National Election Studies Cumulative Data File, 1948–2002* (Ann Arbor, MI: Inter-university Consortium for Political and Social Research, November 2004); Nancy Burns, Donald R. Kinder, Steven J. Rosenstone, Virginia Sapiro, and National Election Studies, *American National Election Study, 2000: Pre- and Post-Election Survey* (Ann Arbor, MI: Inter-university Consortium for Political and Social Research, February 2002); University of Michigan, Center for Political Studies, American National Election Study, *American National Election Study, 2004: Pre- and Post-Election Survey* (Ann Arbor, MI: Inter-university Consortium for Political and Social Research, February 2006).

This new political life among conservative evangelicals, however, was obscured by reports that the Christian Right was finished. At the close of the decade, many observers pointed to the collapse of the Moral Majority and Pat Robertson's weak showing in the 1988 presidential race as evidence of the Right's demise. Michael D'Antonio, formerly a religion writer for *Newsday*, even described the Right's decline as inevitable. According to D'Antonio, "Ultimately, any movement based on enchantment and unreason comes to face with reality. . . . Because the Christian Right resisted critical thinking . . . they were bound to be disappointed individually and defeated politically."[12]

Participatory Revival: 1992–2004

The political alienation of conservative evangelicals did not last. While turnout among other groups has been relatively stable since the 1970s, there has been a participatory revival among conservative evangelicals. In addition to turning out at higher rates, evangelicals are far more likely to engage in other forms of participation, know important facts about politics, as well as identify and behave in partisan terms. In fact, in all these cases, the once large participatory divide between evangelicals and other citizens has either been closed or opened anew in favor of evangelical citizens.

In the 1990s conservative evangelicals enjoyed sustained and dramatic increases in turnout for the first time since the NES had been collecting election data (see table 5.4). After a disappointing showing in 1988,

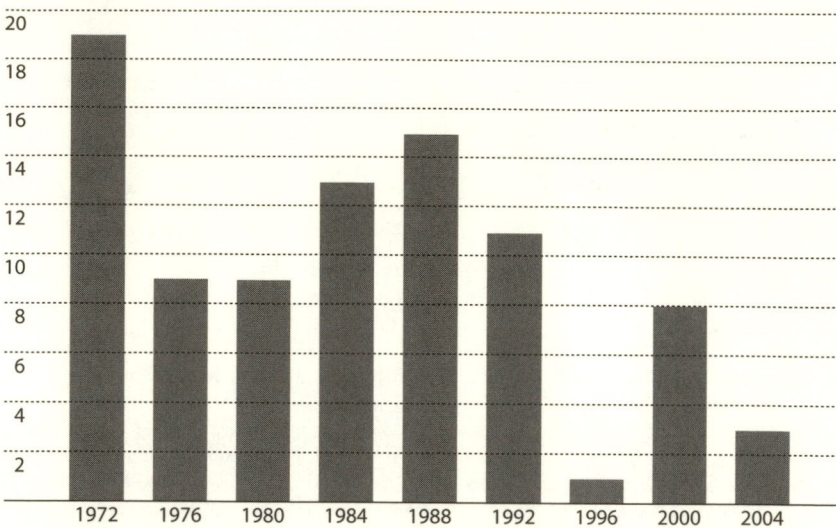

Figure 5.1. Turnout Gap between Conservative Evangelicals and Non-Evangelicals, 1972–2004

Source: Virginia Sapiro, Steven J. Rosenstone, and National Election Studies, *American National Election Studies Cumulative Data File, 1948–2002* (Ann Arbor, MI: Inter-university Consortium for Political and Social Research, November 2004); Nancy Burns, Donald R. Kinder, Steven J. Rosenstone, Virginia Sapiro, and National Election Studies, *American National Election Study, 2000: Pre- and Post-Election Survey* (Ann Arbor, MI: Inter-university Consortium for Political and Social Research, February 2002); University of Michigan, Center for Political Studies, American National Election Study, *American National Election Study, 2004: Pre- and Post-Election Survey* (Ann Arbor, MI: Inter-university Consortium for Political and Social Research, February 2006).

turnout among conservative evangelicals soared from 61 percent in 1988 to 70 percent in 1992—an increase of nearly 10 percent in a single election cycle. Building on these gains, the turnout of conservative evangelicals increased another 10 percent in 1996 and was fully 21 percent higher than it was in 1972. These gains, moreover, were largely sustained in 2000 and 2004 despite significant organizational decline in Christian Right organizations.

Of perhaps more significance, though, the decades-long participation gap between white conservative evangelicals and white non-evangelicals was bridged (see figure 5.1). It is important to note that this divide has been closing because of absolute gains in evangelical turnout rather than decline in non-evangelical turnout. In fact, non-evangelical turnout increased moderately in the 1990s. Therefore, in spite of turnout gains for non-evangelicals in the 1990s, the participation gap that once divided conservative evangelicals and non-evangelicals declined to a mere 1 and 3 percent in 1996 and 2004, respectively. A wider gap did return, however, in 2000 for reasons that will be discussed shortly.

Rising evangelical turnout is only part of this participatory revival. Many other indicators show that today conservative evangelicals are not only more engaged in politics than they were in earlier decades, they are also more engaged than other groups that they once lagged behind. For example, in most elections since 1988, evangelicals have been more likely than all other groups to report that they tried to encourage someone else to vote (see table 5.5). This is true in spite of evangelicals being less likely than other citizens to encourage others to vote in the 1970s. In 1972, only 23 percent of conservative evangelicals tried to influence another citizen to vote, but 49 percent did so by 2004—an increase of 26 percent.

Evangelicals also now display a campaign button, sign, or sticker just as often as other citizens. This, too, is a dramatic reversal, since all other groups were at least twice as likely to make such displays in 1972 as were conservative evangelicals. After 1992 conservative evangelicals also followed public affairs just as frequently as other citizen groups if not more so.

Meanwhile, other data suggest that conservative evangelicals have enjoyed greater gains in political knowledge than other citizens (see table 5.6). In 1972, only 52 percent of conservative evangelicals correctly identified the party that controls the House. This rate was lower than all other groups and hardly improved in the 1980s. By 2004, however, some 86 percent of conservative evangelicals correctly identified the majority party in the House and were more successful than other citizens at doing so. In recent elections, conservative evangelicals have also become much more successful at identifying the Democrats as the liberal party, the Republicans as the conservative party, and the Democrats as the party that favors a stronger government in Washington. On all these measures, they have either achieved parity with or outperformed citizens whom they once lagged far behind.

NES data not only suggest that conservative evangelicals are becoming more knowledgeable, they also reveal a stronger resurgence of partisanship (see table 5.7). By the 1990s, conservative evangelicals were less likely to split their tickets than non-evangelicals and liberal evangelicals. This is true despite their being the most likely group to do so in the 1970s. Declines in ticket splitting reflect a growing loyalty to the Republican Party. Conservative evangelicals are now about twice as likely to identify as Republicans as they were on the eve of the Reagan Revolution. With the exception of African Americans, conservative evangelicals have also been somewhat more likely to identify as strong partisans in recent years.

TABLE 5.5
Other Forms of Participation, 1972–2004

	1972	1976	1980	1984	1988	1992	1996	2000	2004	Change
Influence others to vote										
Cons. evangelicals	23	29	34	35	32	47	36	37	49	+26
Lib. evangelicals	34	38	42	32	23	42	29	36	54	+20
Non-evangelicals	34	39	38	35	29	38	30	37	51	+17
African Americans	31	32	29	26	26	27	23	28	36	+5
All Americans	32	37	36	32	29	38	29	35	49	+17
Display button, sign, or sticker										
Cons. evangelicals	6	5	6	5	10	11	9	13	20	+14
Lib. evangelicals	12	9	10	8	3	12	14	11	17	+5
Non-evangelicals	16	9	7	10	9	12	11	10	21	+5
African Americans	16	8	5	12	11	11	10	12	22	+6
All Americans	14	8	7	9	9	11	10	10	21	+7
Follows public affairs										
Cons. evangelicals	65	67	56	62	57	67	68	63	64	−1
Lib. evangelicals	78	73	61	62	52	71	59	52	57	−21
Non-evangelicals	76	72	64	67	64	70	65	64	72	−4
African Americans	64	65	55	52	53	66	65	47	68	+4
All Americans	73	70	61	63	59	68	63	59	68	−5
Attend meeting for a candidate										
Cons. evangelicals	3.0	3.2	4.1	3.3	3.0	5.5	5.6	3.3	5.4	+2.4
Lib. evangelicals	1.4	5.7	5.9	2.7	2.3	10.5	6.2	3.3	3.6	+2.2
Non-evangelicals	11.3	7.5	8.6	8.9	7.4	8.8	7.3	6.4	9.6	−1.7
African Americans	7.4	4.1	6.6	9.6	10.1	8.3	6.3	8.6	5.1	−2.3
All Americans	10.4	6.4	7.5	7.8	7.2	8.1	5.9	5.5	7.6	−2.8

Source: Virginia Sapiro, Steven J. Rosenstone, and National Election Studies, *American National Election Studies Cumulative Data File, 1948–2002* (Ann Arbor, MI: Inter-university Consortium for Political and Social Research, November 2004); Nancy Burns, Donald R. Kinder, Steven J. Rosenstone, Virginia Sapiro, and National Election Studies, *American National Election Study, 2000: Pre- and Post-Election Survey* (Ann Arbor, MI: Inter-university Consortium for Political and Social Research, February 2002); University of Michigan, Center for Political Studies, American National Election Study, *American National Election Study, 2004: Pre- and Post-Election Survey* (Ann Arbor, MI: Inter-university Consortium for Political and Social Research, February 2006).

Conservative evangelicals, therefore, have been most impacted by the partisan tide that swept American politics in the 1980s and 1990s.

Grassroots Mobilization

Although the continuing rise of partisanship among conservative evangelicals can be traced to trends that began in the 1980s, the Right's success at mobilization in the 1990s was altogether new. The Right succeeded

TABLE 5.6
Measures of Political Knowledge, 1972–2004

	1972	1976	1980	1984	1988	1992	1996	2000	2004	Change
Democrats favor strong government										
Cons. evangelicals	17	30	42	31	28	39	NA	52	NA	+35
Lib. evangelicals	27	25	40	41	13	25	NA	40	NA	+13
Non-evangelicals	24	26	37	29	26	26	NA	55	NA	+31
African Americans	41	47	27	24	41	27	NA	31	NA	−10
All Americans	24	28	36	29	26	28	NA	48	NA	+24
Democrats are liberal										
Cons. evangelicals	62	74	58	59	60	70	75	75	74	+12
Lib. evangelicals	66	66	57	59	61	61	68	72	75	+9
Non-evangelicals	66	71	63	61	67	68	69	75	73	+7
African Americans	69	75	45	42	36	49	37	53	36	−33
All Americans	66	71	60	58	59	64	64	72	67	+1
Republicans are conservative										
Cons. evangelicals	47	56	73	64	67	67	71	75	74	+27
Lib. evangelicals	64	65	74	67	66	68	75	69	75	+11
Non-evangelicals	67	71	76	69	75	73	77	80	79	+12
African Americans	79	78	70	55	64	62	57	60	49	−30
All Americans	65	70	75	67	71	70	73	76	73	+8
Identify party that controls the house										
Cons. evangelicals	52	50	62	47	56	63	63	82	86	+34
Lib. evangelicals	69	63	82	59	53	70	72	78	70	+1
Non-evangelicals	66	67	77	62	68	65	81	83	80	+14
African Americans	59	46	50	38	41	35	57	76	80	+21
All Americans	64	62	71	55	59	59	75	82	80	+16

Source: Virginia Sapiro, Steven J. Rosenstone, and National Election Studies, *American National Election Studies Cumulative Data File, 1948–2002* (Ann Arbor, MI: Inter-university Consortium for Political and Social Research, November 2004); Nancy Burns, Donald R. Kinder, Steven J. Rosenstone, Virginia Sapiro, and National Election Studies, *American National Election Study, 2000: Pre- and Post-Election Survey* (Ann Arbor, MI: Inter-university Consortium for Political and Social Research, February 2002); University of Michigan, Center for Political Studies, American National Election Study, *American National Election Study, 2004: Pre- and Post- Election Survey* (Ann Arbor, MI: Inter-university Consortium for Political and Social Research, February 2006).

because it departed from the example set by the Moral Majority and other public interest groups, which relied heavily on checkbook activism to sustain themselves. Instead, Christian Right organizations labored to build ecumenical chapter-based organizations that could be called on to lobby public officials and mobilize uninvolved evangelicals.

At the forefront of this effort was the Christian Coalition, which began in 1989 with the mission of recruiting ten committed activists in every political precinct in America. Such a task called for the mobilization of

TABLE 5.7
Measures of Partisanship, 1972–2004

	1972	1976	1980	1984	1988	1992	1996	2000	2004	Change
Important party differences										
Cons. evangelicals	45	47	59	67	56	68	67	70	84	+39
Lib. evangelicals	47	47	61	66	50	62	62	70	87	+40
Non-evangelicals	50	51	64	69	65	64	69	74	81	+31
African Americans	74	72	70	73	66	63	64	61	71	−3
All Americans	51	53	63	68	63	63	66	68	80	+29
Republican Party ID										
Cons. evangelicals	35	34	30	50	51	60	62	57	67	+32
Lib. evangelicals	36	37	41	48	43	39	40	42	52	+16
Non-evangelicals	38	39	38	43	48	40	41	42	41	+3
African Americans	11	6	8	11	12	8	9	7	7	−4
All Americans	34	34	33	39	41	38	38	38	40	+6
Strong partisans										
Cons. evangelicals	23	25	35	32	34	30	36	34	36	+13
Lib. evangelicals	19	17	18	25	28	31	24	29	25	+6
Non-evangelicals	24	23	22	29	29	30	30	33	35	+9
African Americans	40	37	48	34	41	43	45	46	31	−9
All Americans	25	24	26	29	31	29	32	32	33	+8
Split ticket*										
Cons. evangelicals	44	34	29	23	26	20	13	17	15	−29
Lib. evangelicals	31	24	38	27	37	28	21	20	16	−15
Non-evangelicals	29	26	29	26	26	24	20	23	21	−8
African Americans	14	5	5	15	12	16	11	12	11	−3
All Americans	30	25	28	25	25	22	18	20	18	−12

* Between president and House

Source: Virginia Sapiro, Steven J. Rosenstone, and National Election Studies, *American National Election Studies Cumulative Data File, 1948–2002* (Ann Arbor, MI: Inter-university Consortium for Political and Social Research, November 2004); Nancy Burns, Donald R. Kinder, Steven J. Rosenstone, Virginia Sapiro, and National Election Studies, *American National Election Study, 2000: Pre- and Post-Election Survey* (Ann Arbor, MI: Inter-university Consortium for Political and Social Research, February 2002); University of Michigan, Center for Political Studies, American National Election Study, *American National Election Study, 2004: Pre- and Post- Election Survey* (Ann Arbor, MI: Inter-university Consortium for Political and Social Research, February 2006).

1.75 million volunteers. To this end, the coalition took careful note of the Moral Majority's failures. As discussed in chapter 2, Jerry Falwell organized the Moral Majority around the Baptist Bible Fellowship clergy. But as Mary Bendyna and Clyde Wilcox have shown, this strategy proved to be a poor method of building a grassroots organization. Aside from the fierce independence and intolerance of these radical Baptists toward other Christians and Catholics in particular, Protestant clergy in general are much more concerned with building their own churches than political organizing.[13] Even today it is very common to hear Christian activists complain about the fear and inaction of evangelical clergy.

Because of these failures, the Christian Coalition built its chapters around strongly committed lay people within congregations. The Christian Coalition developed an extended network of "church liaisons" that organized voter registration drives and distributed voter guides within their own churches. It also recruited "neighborhood coordinators," who organized at the precinct level. Such coordinators conducted door-to-door canvassing in an effort to identify and mobilize like-minded citizens. Other activities included the circulation of voter guides to sympathetic neighbors, petition drives, and making phone calls on Election Day to help ensure that Christian got to the polls.[14] All of these activities required training for their success. By 1997 the coalition had trained some 55,000 citizens in its grassroots training seminars.[15]

Ralph Reed, then the director of the Christian Coalition, was widely criticized in 1991 when he described these various grassroots strategies as "guerilla welfare." As Reed put it, "It's better to move quickly, with stealth, under the cover of night."[16] Critics took this only to be further proof that the coalition's operations were not really a significant break with the tactics of the Moral Majority. Lost in all the hysteria surrounding Christian Right mobilization, however, was just how much Reed's comments signaled a radical departure from the tactics of both the Moral Majority and liberal public interest groups. In advocating "stealth," Reed rejected the mass media strategies that are so critical to the maintenance of traditional public interest groups. The Moral Majority, of course, was no exception. As Jeffrey Haden and his colleagues noted, it "was primarily an organization for grabbing media attention."[17] The quiet activism of the Christian Coalition in churches and neighborhoods could not have been more different.

In part, the Christian Coalition avoided media-driven campaigns because it recognized that the press was hostile to its cause. As the director of the Washington State Christian Coalition, Rick Forcier, explained to me, "We're not trying to drop headlines."[18] In California, the Christian Coalition was even less visible. When I tried to find the state office in Huntington Beach, I discovered that it displayed no signage. As John Fugatt, the director of the Christian Coalition of California explained with apparent understatement, "We like to keep a low profile."[19]

To look at just the Moral Majority and Christian Coalition, however, overemphasizes the change in Christian politics in the 1990s. After all, many other Christian Right organizations enjoyed an active grassroots base and could trace their origins to the 1980s and even earlier. Concerned Women for America (CWA), for instance, reported some 1,200 chapters in 1989 and certainly did not comprise classic checkbook activists. One 1990 survey of religious activists revealed, in fact, that over 90 percent of CWA members had signed or circulated a petition, some three quarters had contacted a public official, and approximately half had written a letter to the editor. Like the Christian Coalition, many CWA members were actively involved in grassroots mobilization. For example, a quarter of CWA members in the same survey reported that they had participated in door-to-door campaigning.[20] Likewise, the National Right to Life Committee (NRLC) has long had chapter-based affiliates in every state and has actually remained vital while the Christian Coalition and CWA have deteriorated. The NRLC also produces its own voter guides, which are often distributed in Catholic churches. A whole host of state-level and local pro-family organizations also competed with these larger organizations for members.

What did make the Christian Coalition distinct, however, was its devotion to mobilizing new voters over and above other activities, such as grassroots lobbying. The Christian Coalition even made voter mobilization a more central objective of fellow Christian Right organizations since it often enlisted their support in distributing voter guides. For example, CWA played an important role in distributing Christian Coalition voter guides in the state of Virginia.

As the foregoing discussion suggests, one of the principal means by which the Christian Coalition mobilized voters was through the distribution of voter guides that highlighted candidates' positions on issues of concern to religious conservatives. These guides were primarily distributed in evangelical churches, although some Catholic and mainline Protestant churches cooperated as well. By 1996 the Christian Coalition claimed that it had distributed some 66 million voter guides to 125,000 churches in the primary and general elections, up from 40 million in 1992.[21] Direct precinct-level organizing took place on a massive scale as well. In 1996 the Christian Coalition estimated that it had contacted about 5 million voters through phone calls and door-to-door canvassing.[22] That same year it also reported some 2,000 chapters and 1.9 million members.[23]

Skeptics have rightly questioned these numbers since they rest precariously on the estimates of the Christian Coalition, which has a vested interest in exaggerating its influence.[24] And because the distribution of voter guides is so decentralized, the leaders in the central offices of the Christian Coalition often do not know themselves just what percentage of voter guides actually reach citizens. In fact, it is not unusual to hear state directors complain that activists sometimes drop voter guides on church doorsteps or on car windshields.[25] And certainly no one within the central offices of Christian Right organizations is collecting data on voter guide distribution as a social scientist would. Instead the figures

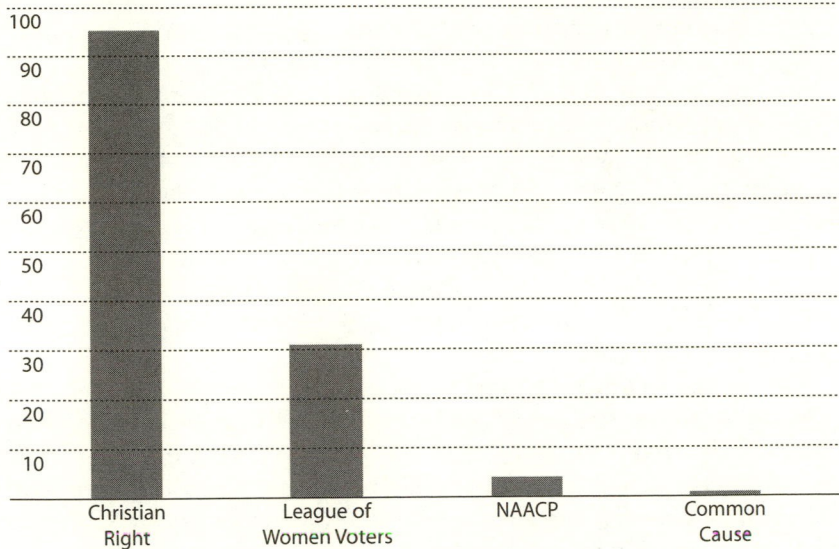

Figure 5.2. Voter Guide Distribution by Interest Group.
Source: Mark A. Chaves, *National Congregations Study, 1998* (Ann Arbor, MI: Inter-university Consortium for Political and Social Research, September 2002).

that Christian Right organizations tend to report is the number of guides that were printed—a figure that is far greater than the actual number of distributed guides.

The 1998 National Congregations Study (NCS), however, allows us to get a much better estimate of voter guide distribution. The NCS used a representative sample of U.S. congregations that was produced from a "hypernetwork sampling technique." In ordinary terms, congregations were selected from responses given from the General Social Survey, which asked respondents to name the congregation that they attended as well as an informed contact at their congregation. The entire list of congregations comprises the sample for the NCS. Of greater significance for the purpose of this study, congregation contacts were asked whether voter guides had been distributed in their church and, if so, by what organization.

The NCS suggests that voter guide distribution by Christian Right organizations has been substantial and has far outstripped rival efforts to mobilize religious voters. As figure 5.2 reveals, nearly one hundred churches reported that Christian Right interest groups had distributed voter guides in their church—a total that far outstrips similar efforts in liberal organizations such as the NAACP and Common Cause. In addition, Christian Right organizations reached 19 percent of all conservative evangelical churches in the sample.

Yet these data also suggest that Christian Right mobilization fell well short of the tens of millions of voter guides reported by groups like the Christian Coalition. If the NCS sample is accurate, for example, Christian Right organizations did not reach much more than about 15 percent of all Southern Baptist churches, or about 2.3 million members in some 6,000 congregations. And since Southern Baptists receive nearly one quarter of all Christian Right voter guides, it is likely that such information reached about 10 million Christians. Therefore, even accounting for the additional voter guides that were distributed in the primary campaign, the Christian Coalition did not distribute anything near the 66 million voter guides that it reported in 1996.

Of course, 10 million Christians is a lot of citizens, especially given that some 97 million voters turned out in the 1996 election. In addition, what is especially striking about NCS data is just how far the Christian Right reached beyond the Southern Baptist Convention into the diverse world of American evangelicalism. According to the NCS, some twenty-six other evangelical denominations participated as well, including Pentecostal churches (such as the Assemblies of God, Church of God in Cleveland, TN, and Pentecostal Assemblies of the World), Holiness churches (such as the Church of the Nazarene and Wesleyan Church), and other Baptists (such as Free Will Baptists and the Baptist Missionary Association).

Of greater significance, though, voter guide distribution appears to have had a significant effect on evangelical turnout. In 1992, the first presidential election in which voter guides were distributed in massive numbers, conservative evangelical turnout climbed 9 percent. It leaped another 10 percent in 1996. But however suggestive such comparisons are, it is hard to assess the actual effects of Christian Right mobilization by correlating aggregate level data, such as changing turnout and levels of reported voter guide distribution.

Fortunately, survey data allows us to move beyond such comparisons to individual-level evidence of citizen mobilization. Since 1996 the NES has asked two questions: (1) "Were there any groups concerned with moral or religious issues that tried to encourage you to vote in a particular way?" and (2) "Was information about candidates, parties, or political issues made available in your place of worship before the election?" Together these questions allow us to assess voter mobilization with more confidence and precision. They also suffer, however, from a common limitation since both overestimate Christian Right mobilization efforts. After all, other groups produce voter guides that are distributed in churches, such as local governments and even some liberal organizations. Likewise, "moral or religious" groups do not exist exclusively inside the Christian Right.

Nevertheless, nearly 80 percent of respondents who reported that they received information about political candidates were either evangelical or Catholic, while only 14 percent were mainline Protestants. Similarly, 74 percent of those who were contacted by a "moral or religious group" were also evangelical or Catholic, compared to some 17 percent who were from mainline Protestant denominations and 4 percent who were either atheists or agnostics. Therefore, in spite of these variables being far from perfect measures of Christian Right mobilization, they are certainly good ones.

In addition to these measures of mobilization, I controlled for several other influences on turnout. First, I used several variables to control for social conservatism, including one question that asked whether society would suffer fewer problems if more citizens adhered to "traditional family ties," another that assessed moral modernism by asking respondents whether people should adjust their morals to changing times, and a question on abortion. Second, I also accounted for religiosity with a question on church attendance. Combined, these variables allow us to determine the effect of Christian Right mobilization above and beyond individuals' social conservatism or religiosity. This is critically important since we know that religious conservatives are participating at higher rates in recent elections. Put differently, controlling for these variables allows us to assess the effects of Christian Right mobilization independent of the very attitudes and practices that are related to higher participation. I also controlled for other standard predictors of political participation, such as education, political interest, partisanship, age, and sense of efficacy.[26]

To assess turnout I conducted a probit regression, which is uniquely suited for models with dichotomous dependent variables. Such variables are simply those that can take only two values. In this case citizens either turned out to vote or they did not. Unlike standard OLS regressions, probit models allow us to determine the effects of any number of influences on the *probability* that one will vote. But although probit regressions are better suited for models with dichotomous dependent variables, they also introduce at least one important complication. Because the effect of each variable depends not only on its particular value but also on the level of all other variables, it is more difficult to assess each variable's influence. One common method is to hold all other variables at their mean while examining the effect of a single variable at its lowest and highest values. This will tell us the maximum effect of a given variable for an otherwise average individual. Using this method is especially well suited to dichotomous independent variables, since they have only two values.

When we turn to the mobilization variables, we find that they have strong effects on voter turnout. Table 5.8 reveals that an otherwise average individual who was contacted by a religious or moral group was 11

TABLE 5.8
Effects of Religious Mobilization on Voter Turnout, 1996, 1998, and 2000

Variables	Coefficients	Standardized bStdXY	Avg. min-max change	Avg. ± sd/2 change
Mobilization				
Candidate information at church	0.17*	0.04	0.05	–
Contact by religious or moral group	0.38***	0.10	0.11	–
Social conservatism				
Against traditional family	0.02	0.01	0.02	0.01
Moral traditionalism	0.03*	0.04	0.04	0.01
Abortion	0.11***	0.09	0.11	0.04
Church attendance	−0.13***	−0.17	−0.16	−0.07
Resources				
Education	0.16***	0.19	0.27	0.08
Income	0.17***	0.15	0.20	0.06
External efficacy	0.00	0.03	0.03	0.01
Internal efficacy	0.06	0.03	0.04	0.01
Interest in public affairs	0.24***	0.18	0.23	0.07
Partisanship	0.23	0.18	0.22	0.07
Demographics				
Age	0.20	0.27	0.36	0.11
Race	0.06	0.01	0.02	–
Sex	−0.02	−0.01	−0.01	–
Constant	−2.89	–	–	–
Observations	3254	–	–	–
Likelihood intercept	−1959.71	–	–	–
Likelihood full	−1522.62	–	–	–
Pseudo R-squared	0.22	–	–	–

* Significant at 10% ** significant at 5% *** significant at 1%

Source: Virginia Sapiro, Steven J. Rosenstone, and National Election Studies, *American National Election Studies Cumulative Data File, 1948–2002* (Ann Arbor, MI: Inter-university Consortium for Political and Social Research, November 2004).

percent more likely to turn out and vote. Similarly, an average citizen was 5 percent more likely to vote if having had received candidate information at his or her church. Both measures of Christian Right mobilization are statistically significant and compare favorably with other predictors of turnout. As we will see, however, such comparisons are more complicated in probit regressions. One reason is that many of the other independent variables, such as education or age, take on many values. And because such variables take on many values, assessing their maximum effect for an otherwise average person, as we just did for the mobilization variables, presents a problem. Put simply, it is not clear whether or not individuals are actually likely to have a single extreme characteristic while being average in every other respect. For instance, it is unlikely that someone has a graduate degree, but is average with respect to all other variables. Unlike our analysis of the dichotomous mobilization variables, then, treating other variables the same way may indicate a maximum theoretical effect but has little basis in empirical reality.

A better way to assess variables that take on many values is to set all variables at their mean and examine the effects of a half standard deviation change in their value on the dependent variable. For example, a half standard deviation increase in education increases by 8 percent the probability that one will vote (see table 5.8), holding all other variables at their mean. Likewise, a half standard deviation increase in church attendance raises the likelihood of voting by 7 percent. Therefore, the effects of Christian Right mobilization compare quite favorably to standard predictors of voter turnout.

When other measures of political participation are examined, only contact by a religious or moral group has a strong effect on participation. Voter guide distribution has no statistically significant effect on the probability that citizens will influence others to vote, engage in political discussions, or display campaign buttons or stickers (see tables 5.9, 5.10, and 5.11). This is hardly a surprising finding, however, given that voter guides are often distributed in the final days of the election. The Christian Coalition, in fact, has always distributed its guides on the Sunday before every election. Therefore, it is not surprising that having received a voter guide affects the probability that one will vote, but not one's engagement in the larger campaign.

Citizens who are contacted by moral or religious groups, however, are far more likely to participate in the campaign itself. Unlike those who receive voter guides in church, such individuals are much more likely to be situated in politicized social networks and therefore are ripe for political mobilization. Turning to table 5.9, we find that moral or religious group contact increases by 18 percent the probability that an otherwise average person will encourage others to vote—an effect that outstrips nearly all other variables. In fact, only political interest is comparable to the effect of group mobilization.

The effects of contact by a moral or religious group on the likelihood that citizens will engage in political discussions or display campaign buttons or stickers is somewhat less pronounced (see table 5.10). Group contact increases the probability that one participated in political discussions at least three times a week by 12 percent. Here again, Christian Right mobilization compares favorably with traditional predictors of political

TABLE 5.9
Effects of Religious Mobilization on Influencing Others to Vote, 1996, 1998, and 2000

Variables	Coefficients	Standardized bStdXY	Avg. min-max change	Avg. ± sd/2 change
Mobilization				
Candidate information at church	0.12	0.03	0.04	–
Contact by religious or moral group	0.49***	0.15	0.18	–
Social conservatism				
Against traditional family	−0.02	−0.02	−0.02	−0.01
Moral traditionalism	0.04**	0.05	0.06	0.02
Abortion	0.03	0.03	0.03	0.01
Church attendance	0.01	0.01	0.01	0.00
Resources				
Education	0.04**	0.05	0.06	0.02
Income	0.06**	0.06	0.07	0.02
External efficacy	−0.00	−0.01	−0.01	−0.00
Internal efficacy	0.09**	0.05	0.06	0.02
Interest in public affairs	0.34***	0.29	0.31	0.11
Partisanship	0.15***	0.13	0.15	0.05
Demographics				
Age	−0.01	−0.02	−0.03	−0.01
Race	0.10	0.03	0.03	–
Sex	0.14***	0.06	0.05	–
Constant	−2.88	–	–	–
Observations	3254	–	–	–
Likelihood intercept	−1950.68	–	–	–
Likelihood full	−1742.98	–	–	–
Pseudo R-squared	0.11	–	–	–

* Significant at 10%   ** significant at 5%   *** significant at 1%

Source: Virginia Sapiro, Steven J. Rosenstone, and National Election Studies, *American National Election Studies Cumulative Data File, 1948–2002* (Ann Arbor, MI: Inter-university Consortium for Political and Social Research, November 2004).

participation. A half standard deviation increase in education, for instance, makes frequent political discussion 6 percent more likely for an otherwise average person. Turning to table 5.11, we find that contact by a moral or religious group increases by 5 percent the likelihood that average citizens will display a campaign button or sticker. Christian Right mobilization once again performs well compared to other standard influences on participation.

Although voter guide distribution does not seem to affect participation in the campaign itself, it does influence *how* citizens vote. A couple of

TABLE 5.10
Effects of Religious Mobilization on Political Discussions, 1996, 1998, and 2000

Variables	Coefficients	Standardized bStdXY	Avg. Min-Max change	Avg. ±sd/2 change
Mobilization				
Candidate information at church	0.04	0.01	0.01	–
Contact by religious or moral group	0.29***	0.09	0.12	–
Social conservatism				
Against traditional family	0.05*	0.04	0.08	0.02
Moral traditionalism	0.01	0.01	0.02	0.01
Abortion	0.01	0.01	0.01	0.00
Church attendance	0.01	0.00	0.00	0.00
Resources				
Education	0.10***	0.14	0.20	0.06
Income	0.04	0.04	0.06	0.02
External efficacy	0.00***	0.06	0.07	0.03
Internal efficacy	0.02	0.01	0.01	0.00
Interest in public affairs	0.32***	0.28	0.36	0.12
Partisanship	0.12***	0.11	0.15	0.05
Demographics				
Age	0.01	0.01	0.01	0.00
Race	0.13*	0.04	0.05	–
Sex	–0.02	–0.01	–0.01	–
Constant	–13.88	–	–	–
Observations	3252	–	–	–
Likelihood intercept	–2234.81	–	–	–
Likelihood full	–2025.88	–	–	–
Pseudo R-squared	0.09	–	–	–

* Significant at 10%   ** significant at 5%   *** significant at 1%
Source: Virginia Sapiro, Steven J. Rosenstone, and National Election Studies, *American National Election Studies Cumulative Data File, 1948–2002* (Ann Arbor, MI: Inter-university Consortium for Political and Social Research, November 2004).

important features of the NES survey allow us to assess the influence of voter guide distribution on vote choice. Prior to each election the NES survey asks respondents which presidential candidate they intend to vote for. After the election, NES surveyors then ask those same respondents which candidate they voted for on Election Day. Table 5.12 reveals that those citizens who received candidate information at church prior to the 1996 election were much more likely to abandon the Democratic candidate than those who did not. Nearly 12 percent of those respondents who initially said they would vote for Bill Clinton and received a voter guide,

TABLE 5.11
Effects of Religious Mobilization on Displaying Campaign Buttons or Stickers, 1996, 1998, and 2000

Variables	Coefficients	Standardized bStdXY	Avg. min-max change	Avg. ± sd/2 change
Mobilization				
Candidate information at church	0.07	0.02	0.01	–
Contact by religious or moral group	0.31***	0.10	0.05	–
Social conservatism				
Against traditional family	0.01	0.01	0.01	0.00
Moral traditionalism	−0.06**	−0.07	−0.03	−0.01
Abortion	−0.05	−0.05	−0.02	−0.01
Church attendance	−0.03	−0.04	−0.02	−0.01
Resources				
Education	−0.00	−0.00	−0.00	−0.00
Income	0.07**	0.07	0.04	0.01
External efficacy	0.00	0.04	0.02	0.01
Internal efficacy	0.05	0.03	0.02	0.00
Interest in public affairs	0.18***	0.16	0.07	0.03
Partisanship	0.17***	0.16	0.07	0.03
Demographics				
Age	0.01	0.01	0.01	
Race	0.09	0.03	0.01	–
Sex	−0.03	−0.01	−0.00	–
Constant	−2.48	–	–	–
Observations	3254	–	–	–
Likelihood intercept	−987.09	–	–	–
Likelihood full	−930.28	–	–	–
Pseudo R-squared	0.06	–	–	–

* Significant at 10%   ** significant at 5%   *** significant at 1%

Source: Virginia Sapiro, Steven J. Rosenstone, and National Election Studies, *American National Election Studies Cumulative Data File, 1948–2002* (Ann Arbor, MI: Inter-university Consortium for Political and Social Research, November 2004).

ended up voting for another candidate on Election Day. Meanwhile, only 7 percent of such citizens defected when they did not receive a voter guide. The exact reverse pattern emerges for citizens who initially said that they would vote for Bob Dole—they were less likely to defect to another candidate if they received a voter guide.

The effects of moral and religious groups on voter decisions were even stronger. Nearly 17 percent of those voters who initially indicated support

TABLE 5.12
Effects of Religious Mobilization on Vote Decision, 1996 (percentages)

Party defections	Democratic defections	Republican defections
Candidate information at church	11.8	3.5
No information at church	7.2	6.3
Difference	+4.6	−2.8
Contact by religious or moral group	16.5	6.7
No contact by moral group	6.5	5.7
Difference	+10.0	+1.0

Republican gains	Democrats	Third party/ undecided
Candidate information at church	7.1	52.6
No Information at church	3.5	21.5
Difference	+3.6	+31.1
Contact by religious or moral group	6.3	53.8
No contact by moral group	3.6	29.9
Difference	+2.7	+23.9

Democratic gains	Republicans	Third party/ undecided
Candidate information at church	1.8	2.1
No information at church	3.0	21.5
Difference	−1.2	−19.4
Contact by religious or moral group	2.7	7.7
No contact by moral group	2.9	30.0
Difference	−0.2	−22.3

Source: Virginia Sapiro, Steven J. Rosenstone, and National Election Studies, *American National Election Studies Cumulative Data File, 1948–2002* (Ann Arbor, MI: Inter-university Consortium for Political and Social Research, November 2004).

for Clinton and were contacted by a moral or religious group voted for another candidate. However, less than 7 percent of those same voters defected if such a group did not contact them. The effects on Republicans are more ambiguous, since contact by a moral or religious group did not seem to affect rates of defection.

Voter guides and religious groups had an especially strong influence on the decisions of voters who indicated support for a third-party candidate, were undecided, or reported no preference. In fact, over 50 percent of such citizens ended up voting for the Republican candidate when they received a voter guide, but less than 22 percent supported Dole when they did not. Meanwhile, a mere 2 percent of these citizens voted for the Democrat when they received a voter guide, but nearly 22 percent supported Clinton when they did not acquire any candidate information at church. The effects of religious groups on such voters are equally strong.

It should be noted, however, that such effects are found in 1996 but not 2000. The reason is probably twofold. First, as table 5.12 suggests, the Christian Right enjoyed particular success drawing its natural base away from Ross Perot in 1996. But with no such candidate in 2000, the Right had a much better sense of where the major candidates stood on social issues well before the election. This finding indicates that voter guides probably have much more influence in local and state races where voter information is much lower. Second, by year 2000, Christian Right organizations and the Christian Coalition in particular had suffered significant decline. The Christian Coalition simply never recovered from the departure of Ralph Reed and has labored under poor leadership ever since.

The distribution of voter guides also had a strong influence on partisanship, which again suggests that those citizens who receive voter guides are far less politicized than those who are contacted by moral or religious groups. Receiving a voter guide increased the probability that an otherwise average person would identify important party differences by 11 percent (see table 5.13). Contact by moral or religious groups, on the other hand, increased average citizens' sense of party differences by 6 percent. Recipients of voter guides were also more likely to identify as strong partisans, while contact by a moral or religious group has no statistically significant influence on one's sense of partisanship (see table 5.14).

As crude and imprecise as these measures are, collectively they suggest that Christian Right mobilization has had a direct and significant influence on political participation. Voter guides, for instance, have had a strong influence on turnout, vote choice, identifying party differences, and partisanship, while contact by religious or moral groups enhanced turnout, campaign participation, vote choice, and identifying party differences.

Rights, Duties, and Evangelism

It was not merely church- and precinct-level grassroots mobilization that set the Christian Right apart from its opponents. The content of Christian Right mobilization differed as well. Christian leaders routinely claim that civic engagement is first and foremost a moral obligation rather than simply a right. For movement leaders, though, this emphasis is less a reaction to liberalism than a fight against evangelical theology itself. Christian

TABLE 5.13
Effects of Religious Mobilization on Identifying Party Differences, 1996, 1998, and 2000

Variables	Coefficients	Standardized bStdXY	Avg. min-max change	Avg.± sd/2 change
Mobilization				
Candidate information at church	0.31***	0.09	0.11	–
Contact by religious or moral group	0.18**	0.05	0.06	–
Social conservatism				
Against traditional family	0.05*	0.04	0.07	0.02
Moral traditionalism	0.07***	0.09	0.10	0.04
Abortion	0.03	0.03	0.04	0.01
Church attendance	0.01	0.02	0.02	0.01
Resources				
Education	0.15***	0.18	0.27	0.08
Income	0.09***	0.09	0.13	0.04
External efficacy	0.00	0.03	0.04	0.01
Internal efficacy	0.05	0.03	0.04	0.01
Interest in public affairs	0.27***	0.22	0.29	0.09
Partisanship	0.30***	0.25	0.33	0.11
Demographics				
Age	–0.04**	–0.06	–0.09	–0.03
Race	0.06	0.02	0.02	–
Sex	0.08	0.03	0.03	–
Constant	–2.65	–	–	–
Observations	2644	–	–	–
Likelihood intercept	–1724.83	–	–	–
Likelihood full	–1469.25	–	–	–
Pseudo R-squared	0.15	–	–	–

* Significant at 10%   ** significant at 5%   *** significant at 1%
Source: Virginia Sapiro, Steven J. Rosenstone, and National Election Studies, *American National Election Studies Cumulative Data File, 1948–2002* (Ann Arbor, MI: Inter-university Consortium for Political and Social Research, November 2004).

leaders have labored especially hard to challenge the assumption that Christians must retreat from an inherently corrupt political world to protect their souls and that politics distracts Christians from the more important work of soul saving. For all the concern on the Left that religion corrupts politics, many Christians have long held precisely the opposite position—it is politics that corrupts religion.

Thus, Christian leaders consistently argue that true Christian faith obligates believers to participate. This message is routinely found in Christian

TABLE 5.14
Effects of Religious Mobilization on Identifying as a Strong Partisan, 1996, 1998, and 2000

Variables	Coefficients	Standardized bStdXY	Avg min-max change	Avg ± sd/2 change
Mobilization				
Candidate information at church	0.16**	0.05	0.06	–
Contact by religious or moral group	0.04	0.01	0.01	–
Social conservatism				
Against traditional family	−0.04*	−0.04	−0.06	−0.02
Moral traditionalism	0.02	0.01	0.01	0.00
Abortion	−0.00	−0.00	−0.00	−0.00
Church attendance	−0.03*	−0.05	−0.05	−0.02
Resources				
Education	−0.00	−0.00	−0.01	−0.00
Income	0.07	0.01	0.01	0.00
External efficacy	0.02***	0.08	0.08	0.03
Internal efficacy	0.04	0.02	0.03	0.01
Interest in public affairs	0.33***	0.29	0.32	0.11
Demographics				
Age	0.08***	0.13	0.18	0.05
Race	−0.52***	−0.16	−0.19	–
Sex	−0.11**	−0.05	−0.04	–
Constant	−1.27	–	–	–
Observations	3254	–	–	–
Likelihood intercept	−2047.83	–	–	–
Likelihood full	−1877.34	–	–	–
Pseudo R-squared	0.08	–	–	–

* Significant at 10% ** significant at 5% *** significant at 1%

Source: Virginia Sapiro, Steven J. Rosenstone, and National Election Studies, *American National Election Studies Cumulative Data File, 1948–2002* (Ann Arbor, MI: Inter-university Consortium for Political and Social Research, November 2004).

media. Richard Land, host of nationally syndicated radio program *For Faith and Family*, which reaches about 1.5 million listeners every week, told his audience that "[o]bedient discipleship requires nothing less than active, principled involvement with society." Land continued, "Our Lord has commanded us to be the 'salt' and 'light' of the world."[27] Quoting Mark Twain, Ralph Reed, in his capacity as a Republican strategist, presented a similar argument in the pages of *Christianity Today*: "It will be conceded . . . that a Christian's first duty is to God. It then follows, as a matter of course, that it is his duty to carry his Christian code of morals to the polls and vote them."[28] Likewise, James Dobson has made shoring up Christian citizenship something of a crusade. On his Focus on the Family radio broadcast, which reaches about 4 million listeners every week, Dobson repeatedly has described voting as a "vital responsibility" as well as "a privilege *and* a duty!"[29] He even called the fact that so many Christians do not vote as nothing less than "a disgrace!"[30] and "an outrage."[31] Dobson also argued that Christians cannot be true to their faith and abstain from politics: "In our apparent unwillingness to bring our beliefs and values to bear on the world around us, we run the risk of losing our ability to act as salt and light." "Voting," Dobson continued, "is not only a privilege, but a responsibility to God, to our country, to our children and ourselves."[32]

James D. Kennedy, who, as noted earlier, also oversees an evangelical media empire, complements Dobson's efforts. On the website for one of his organizations, Center for Reclaiming America, we find these words: "For far too long many Christians have withdrawn into their churches and Christian subcultures and left society at large to fend for itself. This is not what we are called to do. We are called to be the 'salt and light of the world' (Matthew 5:13-14), living testimonies of Christ."[33]

Widely read evangelical authors have pushed similar messages. Ken Connor and John Revell describe evangelicals' withdrawal from politics as nothing less than a *Sinful Silence* in their new book.[34] Likewise, Tom Minnery discussed his new book, *Why You Can't Stay Silent*, on James Kennedy's radio broadcast, *Truths that Transform*. Echoing James Dobson's disgust with evangelicals' withdrawal from politics, Minnery told Kennedy's audience, "How sad it is that Christian people don't even cross the threshold of honoring that obligation [to express moral values] by casting a vote."[35] Finally, Chuck Colson, a best-selling evangelical author, routinely calls political participation a "sacred duty."[36]

Political organizations make similar arguments. One of the first Christian Coalition training manuals placed political action within Christians' larger responsibility to evangelize: "Christians, by example and by word, have a responsibility to teach the world in which we live the value of obeying the teachings of our Lord, even in the governing of a nation and the making of public policy."[37] State leaders routinely preach the same message to local activists. Bill Thompson, state chairman of the New Jersey Christian Coalition, reported that in his training seminars he always emphasizes that Christians have a duty to be involved in politics.[38] And John Fugatt, the executive director of the Christian Coalition of California, similarly told state pastors, "We have more than simply a right to vote here in the United States. It is our duty!!"[39] In pro-life circles, similar pleas are commonly heard. The National Pro-Life Religious Council made the following declaration: "Our identity as followers of Jesus Christ is not to be lived in the privacy of our hearts, homes, and churches. We are called to live the Gospel vigorously and publicly."[40]

Yet, anxieties about political action still linger even in the minds of Christian leaders themselves, which reveals a much deeper ambivalence about reconciling the Gospel with political activism. Cal Thomas, former vice president of communications at the Moral Majority, has now questioned the utility of political action. In the pages of *Christianity Today*, Thomas argued, "Real change comes heart by heart, not election by election, because our primary problems are not economic and political but moral and spiritual."[41] Thomas articulated a larger critique of the rising Christian devotion to politics in *Blinded by Might*.[42] Sandy Rios, the director of Concerned Women for America, admitted on a national radio broadcast that politically engaged Christians "can be guilty of losing sight of our goal, which is spiritual redemption."[43] Even the Christian Coalition discussed the dangers of political activism in one of its training seminars: "While Christians have a responsibility to be active participants in the world in which they live, they must avoid this pitfall prepared by Satan to lure them into his domain." The principal pitfall that coalition leaders have in mind is the temptation to "sell out" Christian values in "exchange for power."[44]

Christian activists themselves often succumb to the same ambivalence. A survey of religious activists asked whether the church should "change hearts," "change hearts and social institutions," or do both. Some 84 percent of CWA members reported that the church should focus on changing hearts. This figure was even higher for members of Focus on the Family as well as Americans for the Republic, which was the organizational base from which the Christian Coalition was created. In all these organizations, at least 7 out of 10 members also believed that "if people were converted, social ills would disappear."[45] Similarly, a 1997 survey of Christian Right activists found that fully 75 percent believed that "if enough people were brought to Christ, social ills would take care of themselves."[46]

Nonetheless these activists are not prepared to forsake politics. The same 1997 survey also revealed that Christian activists clearly believed that they should be involved in politics despite the belief that social problems are fundamentally rooted in a deeper spiritual crisis. Some 96 percent of activists reported that "Christians should be in politics to protest their values" and 89 percent agreed that "clergy and churches should be involved in politics."[47] This ambivalence suggests that the most contentious issue in the Christian Right is not *how* evangelicals should participate, since most embrace the kind of democratic education discussed in chapter 1, but *how much* they should participate.

Meanwhile, liberal elites and interest groups rarely scold their base for failing to meet their civic obligations. The contrast between the Left and Right is evident in their very different approaches to mobilizing young people. MTV's Rock the Vote, for example, appeals to young peoples' self-interest and rarely mentions anything approaching a civic duty much less a moral one. Instead young people should participate because of the "cost of education," "jobs and finances," and "healthcare."[48] Its evangelical counterpart Redeem the Vote is far more countercultural in its emphasis on moral obligation over and above self-interest or rights. Redeem the Vote tells young people that they should vote because "it is your responsibility as a Christian to participate in your community. It is a loving act to do so, and we are called to exhibit the love of Christ for our fellow man. Voting and caring is not a choice, it's your responsibility!"[49]

This distinction between the Right's emphasis on duty and the Left's on rights is sometimes obscured by the tendency of observers to claim that the Right has followed the Left by emphasizing its own victimhood. After the 2004 elections, Peter Bienart of the *New Republic* claimed that evangelicals were "playing victim politics with a gusto that would make campus radicals proud."[50] Although there is certainly something to Bienart's claim, Christian leaders also lay the responsibility of America's problems at the feet of evangelicals. Indeed, they often overturn the claim that politics corrupts faith by arguing instead that the world is so immoral precisely because the faithful have stayed out of politics. Charles Colson argued in *Christianity Today* as follows: "Don't tell me you don't want to get your hands dirty in the grimy world of politics and cultural debate. If Christians do not seize this moment and act on the cultural commission, there soon will be no culture left to save. But when we do our duty, we can change the world."[51] In his radio broadcast, James Kennedy argued that Christians' withdrawal from politics had this outcome: "The result was that presidents were nominated and elected that were very secularist in their attitudes and very uncommitted to the Christian world and life view."[52] This sense of Christian responsibility also creeps into the pulpits. David Hope told his congregation in Hernando Beach, Florida, "We can't blame the communists, and we can't even blame the ACLU for this nation's moral decay! We must blame ourselves, and the only way we can change things is to get out and vote." Hope continued, "Voting is not an option. It is a directive from Jesus."[53] Perhaps the greatest display of such blame shifting that I have witnessed came in a St. Louis church where a pro-life organizer with the Center for Bio-Ethical Reform was trying to recruit activists to drive large trailer trucks with paneled images of aborted embryos and fetuses into battleground states for the 2004 election. After only a few volunteers raised their hands, the organizer responded sharply, "Well don't complain about our lack of success then! Don't complain!"[54]

2008 and Beyond

Much like traditional religious revivals, it is not clear that the political interest cultivated by this remarkable participatory revival can be sustained. Political apathy may return for a number of reasons. As the last section underscored, evangelicals remain deeply ambivalent about politics. In addition, Christian Right organizations, and the Christian Coalition in particular, began to decline precipitously after the 1996 election. As a consequence, the turnout gap between evangelicals and non-evangelicals swelled once again in 2000.

Yet the Republican Party demonstrated in 2004 that it could effectively mobilize evangelicals directly. After losing the popular vote in 2000, Karl Rove and other elites in the Republican Party recognized that Christian Right organizations could no longer be counted on to turn out the evangelical vote. Thus, the Bush campaign did not rely on Christian Right organizations to mobilize evangelicals in 2004. Instead, the Bush team centralized its grassroots mobilization in its campaign headquarters in Arlington, Virginia. According to political scientists Sidney Milkis and Jesse H. Rhodes, this change in strategy was successful. As they put it, the Bush-Cheney campaign engineered a "tightly disciplined grassroots organization." The organization included over one million volunteers who organized rallies, canvassed neighborhoods, and registered 3.4 million new Republican voters between 2002 and 2004.[55]

To a large degree, the success of bypassing Christian Right organizations depended on the personal appeal of George W. Bush. Milkis and Rhodes emphasize just this point. According to one official in Ohio, the party's mobilization efforts in 2004 were fueled by "volunteers' admiration for and loyalty to George W. Bush" as well as frequent visits by the president to "fire up" the rank and file.[56] Therefore, the fate of evangelical participation may depend on whether or not the Bush-Cheney machine can be recreated in 2008 and beyond.

CHAPTER SIX

Participation, Deliberation, and Values Voters

A CAREFUL EVALUATION of the Christian Right is important not just because we have misunderstood one of the most important political movements of the twentieth century. The movement also contains important lessons for democratic theory. In particular, we should reevaluate two major prescriptions to cure American democracy of contentious moral conflict. One group believes that American democracy will become more participatory and deliberative if we can somehow push moral passions and issues to the margins of American politics. The other camp wants to retain moral issues while elevating debate over them by weakening our dogmatic commitments to them.

Both claims, however, fail to appreciate how the values of participation and deliberation play out in political practice. On the one hand, we must acknowledge the critical role that moral passions play in energizing civic participation. Liberal critics of the culture wars in particular would be well served to recall the New Left's insistence on a more contentious and ideological politics, while conservative critics need to acknowledge its appreciation of values voters. On the other hand, liberals and conservatives alike must also accept both the promise and limits of deliberation in public life. Social movements will never cultivate deliberation in the fullest sense because they are ultimately driven and maintained by strong moral convictions rather than moral skepticism. But, as previous chapters have demonstrated, they can foster important deliberative norms that at the very least contain the worst excesses of civic extremism and at best raise the level and tenor of political debate.

MARGINALIZING MORAL PASSIONS

In the 1960s liberal intellectuals and reformers longed for a more ideological politics. Greater moral controversy, in their view, would revitalize democratic life. Yet today many observers of the culture wars, particularly those on the Left, claim that our democracy would be more participatory, deliberative, and just if controversial moral issues were pushed to the margins of American politics. These thinkers use a variety of seemingly neutral, apolitical justifications for pushing our moral conflicts to the edges of American political life.

For some, economic issues should be central to American politics because they are somehow more fundamental to the public interest. The most polemical iteration of this thesis has come from Thomas Frank. As Frank describes his home state of Kansas, "In this land unassuageable cultural grievances are elevated inexplicably over solid material ones, and basic economic self-interest is eclipsed by juicy myths of national authenticity and righteousness wronged."[1] Sometimes a similar criticism has come from more sympathetic quarters, such as the liberal evangelical Jim Wallis, and in rare cases it has been directed to the Left.[2]

Others hope to remove controversial moral questions from politics by placing them in the hands of scientific experts. Chris Mooney's bestselling *The Republican War on Science* is a good example. Mooney criticizes what he regards as the excessive politicization of science by liberals and especially conservatives. In his view, scientific expertise and consensus should direct our political choices rather than our moral or ideological commitments.[3]

Most critics, however, hope that centrist public opinion directs policy-making and debate rather than ideological activists. In their view, vocal ideological activists have radicalized public debate and policy-making, leaving a relatively apolitical majority disaffected and disempowered. Brookings scholar E. J. Dionne argues that ideological battles have left a "restive majority" with the sense that politics does not address its real concerns, such as childcare, school reform, and healthcare.[4] Sidney Verba, Kay Schlozman, and Henry Brady likewise lament that American religious institutions have tended to "distort citizen activity" by mobilizing around social issues and abortion in particular rather than "an economic agenda focused on the less advantaged."[5] More recently, Jacob Hacker and Paul Pierson argued that American politics has moved "off center" as "most voters sit on the sidelines watching a political blood sport that plays out with little concern for what the moderate center of opinion thinks."[6] And Morris Fiorina even dedicated his book on the culture wars to "tens of millions of mainstream Americans."[7]

It is strange to hear these liberal critics celebrating "mainstream Americans." Certainly it represents a rejection of the more ideological politics that liberal academics and reformers promoted in the 1960s. These thinkers emphasized the relationship between a contentious, ideological politics and a more engaged citizenry.

Democratic Party activists advocated for a more ideological politics in the aftermath of World War II. In cities such as New York and Chicago, middle-class reformers struggled to take control of the local Democratic Party machinery from working-class ethnics. Above all, these reformers longed for a more issue-based party rather than one bent on holding power and distributing patronage. James Q. Wilson described the "essence of this reform ethic" in *The Amateur Democrat* as "a desire to moralize public life."[8]

Outside of these political trenches, professors and students in the ivory tower were full of the same ambitions. In 1950 the American Political Science Association convened a special committee on party reform. It concluded that American parties suffered from a near absence of ideological cohesion, an "ailment" that dangerously slowed "the heartbeat of American democracy."[9] By 1969 Theodore Lowi wrote darkly in *The End of Liberalism* of a politics deprived of conflict over larger moral principles. In Lowi's account, American governance was instead dominated by opaque interest-group bargaining, which left the public paralyzed by a "nightmare of administrative boredom."[10]

Meanwhile, New Left student activists agreed and hoped that American democracy would become divided over fundamental moral questions. Contrary to contemporary critics of the culture wars, the New Left argued that battles over economic self-interest had distorted the public agenda and depressed participation. According to the movement's manifesto, the *Port Huron Statement*, "[T]he focus of political attention is distorted by the enormous lobby force, composed predominately of economic interests."[11] Tom Hayden further described economic interests as poor vehicles for channeling and stirring public passions, a view he articulated inelegantly in a letter to the Students for a Democratic Society's executive committee: "Various interest groups . . . carry on public controversy to be sure, but theirs is economically motivated propaganda, hardly directed at creating an alive and curious public."[12]

The New Left further regarded the very complex and technical character of many public policy questions as another source of citizen alienation from politics. Complex, technical policy questions both demanded expertise and tended to obscure deeper value conflicts. As a result, they undermined a morally contentious politics and left enervated citizens with the sense that "nothing political is subject to mastery." The *Port Huron Statement* began with precisely this concern in mind: "Making values explicit—an initial task in establishing alternatives—is an activity that has been devalued and corrupted."[13]

The party system, like economic interest groups, embodied the "end of ideology politics,"[14] according to the New Left. The absence of clear ideological or moral differences between the two major parties alienated citizens from politics due to two reasons. First, without clear differences between the parties, Americans found it difficult to identify the party that best represented their values.[15] Second, without real ideological or moral controversy, there was little in politics to engage ordinary Americans. This concern is evident in the New Left's prescription for American parties: "What is desirable is sufficient party disagreement to dramatize major issues."[16] Thus, the *Port Huron Statement* called for the establishment of "two genuine parties, centered around issues and essential values, demanding allegiance to party principles."[17]

It was not long before American politics was transformed according to New Left hopes. After the 1968 election, Democratic reformers finally took control of their party's machinery from party bosses through the McGovern commission, creating primaries and caucuses accessible to issue advocates. And since state primary laws tended to cover both parties, the nominating process opened up in the Republican Party as well. Thus, both parties realigned along hardened ideological lines as a partial consequence. Meanwhile, with reformers such as Ralph Nader leading the charge, an advocacy explosion challenged the traditional power of classic economic interest groups. In fact, about half of all the current advocacy groups were formed sometime between the mid-1960s and early 1970s. Such changes were so dramatic that when describing them some political scientists now speak of a "new American political system."[18]

One might suppose that present-day conservatives would have declared war on a political system that was largely engineered by 1960s liberals. Yet it is liberals who are mounting a counterattack against this liberal revolution. What is more, their arguments often have a surprisingly conservative ring to them. For example, those who hope to enlist centrist voters against divisive moralists sound much more like Richard Nixon than Tom Hayden. In a strange political turn, they have embraced what Nixon called "the silent majority" as the source of their salvation from 1960s liberalism.

Was the New Left Wrong?

Why are so many contemporary liberals disenchanted with this new political system? One answer might be that ideological politics does not promote participation as the New Left believed. Certainly, many critics of the culture wars insist that it does just the opposite by fostering disaffection and alienation.

The problem with this view is that there is almost no evidence in its favor. It is true that American politics and parties have become more ideological in recent decades. But as Gary Jacobson has persuasively demonstrated, ordinary Americans have kept pace with rather than lagged behind the ideological tide that has swept Washington. For decades pollsters have asked respondents to locate themselves on a seven-point liberal-conservative scale. Since the 1970s, major party identifiers have moved 1.2 points further apart on this seven-point scale. Furthermore, the vast majority of these party identifiers report that their ideological position and that of their party are about the same. It is true that some

30 percent of respondents identify with an ideological position somewhere between that of the two parties, but this figure has not increased since the 1970s.[19]

Jacobson's findings are consistent with what we know more generally about the relationship between elite behavior and public opinion. According to John Zaller, "[W]hen elites divide, members of the public tend to *follow* the elites sharing their general ideological or partisan predisposition, with the most politically attentive members of the public mirroring most sharply the ideological divisions among the elite" (my emphasis).[20] Likewise, James Q. Wilson finds it difficult to accept the view that the culture wars exist in a political vacuum. As Wilson recently put it, "If we wish to think that the public is not polarized, we must imagine that the actions of Congress, the media, and certain interest groups have no effect on people."[21]

Meanwhile, turnout has not declined since the 1970s as many observers once believed. It is true that there seems to be a decline when turnout is calculated as a percentage of the voting-age population. But, as Michael McDonald and Samuel Popkin have shown, this method did not account for the growing number of people who are ineligible to vote, especially illegal immigrants and felons. When these ineligible people are excluded from turnout estimates, McDonald and Popkin find little evidence of growing political alienation.[22] In fact, McDonald has called the notion that growing apathy since the 1970s has led to a participation meltdown "the mother of all turnout myths."[23]

Other evidence shows that divisive and negative campaigns increase turnout and political knowledge. Mudslinging apparently has these civic virtues partly because it raises the stakes of campaigns and sharpens the contrast between the candidates.[24] And contrary to what critics would predict, the contentious presidential elections of 2004 produced a turnout of more than 60 percent, which was unusually high by twentieth-century standards.

Growing party polarization has improved civic life in other respects. Citizens are significantly less likely to split their tickets and far more likely to identify important party differences. They are also more likely to vote for the party that represents their values. According to Jacobson, the increasing coherence of the parties' ideologies has made "it easier for voters to recognize their appropriate ideological home" and provided citizens with "a much clearer idea of how their collective choices will translate into congressional action."[25]

Explosive moral issues also compare quite favorably to other public concerns as vehicles of political participation. For instance, when citizens actually try and grapple with complex administrative questions, they are often very deferential to experts. Mark Button and Kevin Mattson examined public debate in seven different associations and found that "the educative mode or frame to deliberation locked citizens into a deferential and sometimes passive role" and "that citizens find it difficult to move beyond the sense of deference they have toward the highly technical issues which frame modern politics," such as campaign finance reform and environmental policy.[26] Not surprisingly, even the press has a very difficult time understanding and explaining such issues to citizens.[27]

On the other hand, moral questions, whether they are over abortion, affirmative action, or gays in the military, constitute what Edward Carmines and James Stimson refer to as "easy issues." According to Carmines and Stimson, such issues "are readily communicated to mass publics. Technical issues are not. As prescriptions for public problems, technical policies require knowledge of important factual assumptions to be appreciated. Symbolic issues may be presented and *understood simplistically*."[28] Although Carmines and Stimson are no fans of "easy issues" and overlook their more complex moral dimensions, the virtue of such issues lies in their accessibility and ability to stir the public spirit. In fact, although many Americans' political opinions are shallow, ambivalent, and notoriously unstable, this is much less true of culture-war issues such as abortion, affirmative action, and the death penalty. Opinions on more technical and obscure issues are far less salient and stable.[29]

For these reasons, "easy issues" have the potential to connect Americans to larger public causes in our vast commercial and administrative republic. As Steven Rosenstone and John Mark Hansen explained in their study of political participation,

> [P]eople participate in politics when salient issues top the agenda. . . . Big moral issues such as prohibition and abortion, draw greater attention than more arcane issues, such as deregulation of natural gas pipelines and accounting rules for capital depreciation.[30]

Sidney Verba and his colleagues came to a similar conclusion in their classic study, *Voice and Equality*:

> The contrast between the influence of economic and abortion attitudes is quite clear. When other participatory factors—including a general interest in politics—are taken into account, having an extreme attitude . . . on government provision of jobs has no independent effect on activity, but having extreme positions on abortion does.[31]

What is more, with rising economic security since World War II, moral issues may be growing in salience and importance to the American public. As the political scientist Ronald Inglehart has emphasized, "[V]alue priorities" have "shift[ed] away from materialist concerns about economic and physical security toward greater emphasis on freedom, self-expression, and the quality of life, or postmaterialist values."[32] Inglehart's thesis finds some support in recent work on the culture wars. Edward L. Glaeser and Bryce A. Ward find that the "overall correlation between income and Republicanism among white males is essentially zero outside the extremes of income distribution," while "the relationship between religion and Republicanism is extremely strong throughout the distribution." Contrary to Inglehart, however, Glaeser and Ward conclude that the strong relationship between economics and voting that was so characteristics of the New Deal and its aftermath was something of an anomaly. As they explain, "Prior to 1930, the correlation between religion and party affiliation across states seems to have been at least as strong as it is today."[33]

Thus, it is not at all clear that the culture wars have undermined political participation. Indeed, the New Left may have been right all along. Moral conflict seems to invigorate American public life.

New Left Ideals and the Christian Right

So if civic disaffection cannot explain the new repudiation of an ideological politics, what does? Part of the answer is that liberals lost their enthusiasm for "values voters" because those voters turned out to have the wrong values. And if conservatives are far less critical of today's cultural activists, it is partly because the culture wars have driven the Republican ascendancy.

One of the great political ironies of the past few decades is that the Christian Right has been much more successful than its political rivals at fulfilling New Left hopes for American democracy. Far more than any movement since the early campaign for civil rights, the Christian Right has helped revive participatory democracy in America by overcoming citizens' alienation from politics.

This was a startling development. The New Left assumed that policy debates would swing somewhere between liberalism and socialism in a politicized America. Political scientists were not so sanguine. But they too rested their enthusiasm for a more ideological party system on the belief that it would advantage liberals within the Democratic Party. As Hacker and Pierson point out, "The committee implicitly assumed that liberal Democrats would benefit from the hardening of party differences. . . . But the rise of truly national parties," they lament, "has ultimately redounded to the benefit not of liberal Democrats but of conservative Republicans."[34]

The expectations of 1960s liberals were not altogether unreasonable. In the 1960s, ideological activists were overwhelmingly liberal, and political fights tended to take place within the Left. As E. J. Dionne concluded, "[T]he New Left saw itself in revolt not primarily against conservatism, since conservative thought seemed so marginal in the early sixties, but against 'establishment liberalism.' "[35] Even today, liberals are still more successful at creating well-funded public interest groups. According to Jeffrey Berry, civil rights advocates, feminists, and especially environmentalists are ascendant and enjoying rich institutional resources that far outstrip public interest groups on the Right.[36]

Despite this advantage, however, public interest groups on the Left have not helped to revitalize participatory democracy or mobilize the disaffected. Unlike the early civil rights movement, which birthed the 1960s movements, dense communal and social networks do not support the organizations that have continued liberal politics. Many contemporary civil rights, women's, consumer, and environmental organizations have members to be sure. Indeed, environmental organizations, such as the Environmental Defense Fund and Greenpeace, can boast hundreds of thousands of members. However, generally these members do little more than write checks.[37] Rising citizen group activity, then, has not meant the destruction of what the New Left described variously as "politics without publics," "democracy without publics," "collectivism from above," "corporate liberalism," and "new liberalism."[38]

As the last chapter emphasized, Christian conservatives did sometimes imitate liberal public interest groups. The Moral Majority, for example, was a large public interest group dominated by check-book activism. It even played an important role in pioneering direct mail. The Right, however, also built organizations through church-based social networks, including the National Right to Life Committee, Concerned Women for America, Christian Coalition, Operation Rescue, crisis pregnancy centers, and countless state and local Christian Right groups. Many of these organizations politicized alienated evangelicals. They were also a driving force behind the realignment of American parties along moral questions. In doing so, the Christian Right helped bring an end to the "end-of-ideology" politics that the New Left loathed.

Such affinities between the New Left and Christian Right have been missed by liberal critics. For instance, the liberal hysteria that surrounded the Right's distribution of voter guides obscured an odd truth: giving voter guides to nominally political citizens was consistent with the New Left goal of "making values explicit—an initial task in establishing alternatives."[39]

On the one hand, this political explanation is probably only a partial one. As the introduction to this book emphasized, political thinkers have long feared the power of explosive moral issues to undermine deliberative ideals and disorder the public agenda. They have also tended to regard economic interests as far more rational, calculating, and compromising. Viewed in this context, the New Left's emphasis on the virtues of moral conflict appears to be something of an exception. On the other hand, past anxiety about moral conflict in American life tended to be driven by conservative movements and anticommunism in particular.

Whatever drives contemporary assessments of moral conflict, liberal and conservative critics alike should rethink their analysis of the culture wars. Liberal observers who advocate for the marginalization of moral issues need to do a better job of demonstrating that the old liberal enthusiasm for moral conflict should be repudiated. Surprisingly, there has been remarkably little effort to do so. Meanwhile, if conservatives are inclined to regard the culture wars as good for democracy, then they need to acknowledge the wisdom of 1960s political thought. Whatever the excesses of the New Left, conservatives should appreciate its praise for values voters.

The Inescapability of Moral Conflict

Even if our democracy would benefit from pushing moral conflict to the edges of American politics, it is not easily done. In fact, those who call for the marginalization of moral issues hold hard positions on moral questions that they either conceal or fail to recognize. Nowhere is this clearer than in the debate over abortion.

Recall the claim by Sidney Verba, Kay Schlozman, and Henry Brady that religious groups have disordered the public agenda by emphasizing abortion instead of "the less advantaged." This argument assumes that human organisms prior to birth should not be regarded as human persons. If it is wrong, then the Right-to-Life movement is defending *the least advantaged*.

While critics like Verba, Schlozman, and Brady fault religious citizens for investing in the fate of embryos, not a single champion of mainstream Americans has criticized the Supreme Court for instituting an "off-center" abortion policy.[40] Some do, however, address this criticism by concluding that *Roe v. Wade* and its companion decisions are consistent with mainstream opinion. Morris Fiorina, for instance, commended the court for creating a national abortion policy that represents a "broadly acceptable compromise." According to Fiorina, most Americans oppose overturning *Roe* since they are generally in favor of abortion rights with some qualifications.[41]

It is true that a majority of Americans report that they do not want to see *Roe* overturned. The problem is that most of these same Americans believe that *Roe* created a restrictive abortion policy. According to James Hunter, this "mass legal illiteracy," explains why "Americans want to keep *Roe* intact, but . . . also favor proposals that would restrict (some severely) what it currently allows, if not undermine it altogether."[42] Few

Americans realize that *Roe* and its companion decisions, as Harvard law professor Mary Ann Glendon has emphasized, created the most liberalized abortion regime in the Western world.[43]

That the new advocates of centrist policy-making do not criticize liberal social policies that are badly "off center" should underscore just how difficult it is to marginalize moral issues. For better and for worse, we cannot push the very issues that divide us to the margins of American politics.

TRANSCENDING MORAL PASSIONS

Other critics of the culture wars want to keep moral positions at the center of American politics while loosening our dogmatic commitments to them. If only we held our moral commitments with some skeptical distance, these scholars argue, we might engage others in a more charitable way and even change our minds in light of new considerations. For example, the political theorist Stephen White advocates weak ontologies in democratic life. Contrasting such ontologies with their "strong" cousins, White argues that those who hold weak ontologies are necessarily uncertain of their own beliefs and therefore without "crystalline conviction." And because weak ontologists are skeptical of their own convictions and regard them as provisional, White believes that they are far less prone to the dogmatism and intolerance that plague strong ontologists, especially those who subscribe to a religious metaphysics. As he puts it, weak ontologies help citizens cultivate a "receptive ethos" that is "more generous in its attentiveness to others than tolerance and respect alone." This ethos, then, transcends even the ordinary liberal virtue of democratic tolerance.[44]

In a similar vein, Adam Seligman, a professor of religious studies and Jewish studies, calls for religious citizens to wed their faith to a "skeptical toleration" that he defines as an "epistemological modesty whose very uncertainty would prevent intolerance of the other." Therefore citizens would ideally engage in a public and moral reasoning that is "hesitant in its approach," "modest in its claims," and "continually subjected to rebuttal and counterfactual challenges."[45]

Elevating political discourse has been especially important to advocates of deliberative democracy. By far the most influential political work in this tradition is Amy Gutmann and Dennis Thompson's *Democracy and Disagreement*, which claims that we should strive for a democracy that transcends conflict among group interests. According to Gutmann and Thompson, deliberative democracy requires citizens to "recognize that they may be wrong, and that that their opponents may be right." Deliberative citizens, therefore, should ultimately be "uncertain about the truth or their own position" and should not even "try to get what they want." In short, they hope citizens will become rational skeptics who are committed to discerning the public good through deliberation.[46]

To a degree, this study should lend support to the optimism of deliberative democrats and undermine the pessimism of those who think that moral questions need to be marginal to American politics. After all, much of the Christian Right is laboring diligently to practice many deliberative norms. It even tries to abide by one of the most controversial deliberative requirements: the abandonment of religious arguments in public forums.

The view of a deliberative citizen that I've just sketched suffers, however, from a misguided enthusiasm for moral skepticism in public life. It does so partly because it assumes that civil and rational discourse can come about only if citizens hold moral truths provisionally and with critical distance. Yet, as previous chapters have demonstrated, some of the most dogmatic citizens are civil (sometimes remarkably so) and engage in a high level of moral reasoning. They do so partly because deliberative norms are grounded in the kind of metaphysics that many scholars consider incompatible with democratic ideals. The commitment to love one's neighbor even encourages Christians to transcend the thinner democratic requirements of toleration and civility. However short they certainly fall of this aim, the project itself is one that attempts to cultivate the kind of civic generosity that many find so admirable and wanting in public life.

Of course, Christian fundamentalism tends to vindicate and fuel the concerns of advocates of deliberation. Yet the stridency and public belligerency of groups such as Operation Rescue West comes out of a particular Christian tradition. This fact should demonstrate that common democratic ideals are not necessarily compromised by "strong religion" or "strong ontology." What matters is *how* orthodox believers understand and practice the fundamental truths that guide and give meaning to their lives. The content of citizens' metaphysics actually matters: some metaphysics or strong ontologies contain powerful resources internal to them that complement democratic ideals, while others do not.

Moreover, it is not clear that a world of citizens situated in paradigms, whether religious or secular, compromises the core of the deliberative project, which involves rational debate over the merits of public policy. Rather than build arguments from a position of skepticism, the most sophisticated Christian leaders and activists continue a long tradition of Christian apologetics. That is, working within a strong metaphysical paradigm or system, these thinkers defend their ethical views on secular ground accessible to all.

Consider the case of abortion. It is often assumed that the best pro-choice and pro-life arguments will come from more dispassionate minds. If this claim were true, one would expect to find stronger and more persuasive arguments from those scholars who have attempted to approach the subject with some emotional distance. This is decidedly not the case, however. Lawrence Tribe's *Abortion: The Clash of Absolutes* and Roger Rosenblatt's *Life Itself*, were billed as books that would elevate and even end the abortion debate.[47] Yet, as James Hunter has argued, these works "are really little more than pro-choice apologias for maintaining . . . a pro-choice resolution to the policy debate."[48] Amy Gutmann and Dennis Thompson similarly fail to make strong pro-life arguments.[49] In fact, they fail to articulate a case against abortion that is half as good as those routinely made by pro-life advocates. This shortcoming prompted Princeton professor Robert George to wonder "why they did not present and criticize arguments made by pro-life thinkers." George further found that "their presentation of the pro-life case suffers from inadequacies that obscure its rational strength."[50]

We should not be too surprised by this discrepancy. After all, pro-life leaders devote their lives to debating abortion and have the strongest incentive to make the best possible case for their position. Thus, passionate advocates who think of little else than the ethics of abortion and consume the best works on the subject, tend to make better arguments than even Ivy League intellectuals who attempt to apply dispassionately the principles of deliberative democracy to a wide range of moral questions.

In a world of moral skeptics, the moral positions of the Right and Left would be abandoned far more readily. But in the actual world of clashing paradigms, foundational beliefs are difficult to jettison and politics is more contentious. This seems true even in the academy, where the deliberative ideal of detached skepticism is most influential. Indeed, rare thinkers such as Ludwig Wittgenstein are so remarkable because they radically overturn their own theories and assumptions. Exceptions like him prove the rule. Nonetheless, deliberative progress exists in politics as well as in the academy as contending factions sharpen their arguments in light of counter-arguments and the merit of any particular claim affects its likely success. In addition, each respective paradigm is taken with the devotion and intellectual seriousness that it deserves. This struggle also raises the level of public debate for the benefit of the vast majority of more ambivalent Americans, most of whom tend to think about political questions far less than activists do. Perhaps the world of *deliberative partisans* is not such a bad one.

Whatever the limits of deliberative partisanship, there has simply never been a social movement of moral skeptics and doubters; only strong convictions have mobilized and sustained them. So, however desirable metaphysical doubt might be in theory, it collides with the democratic ideal of participation. To put the trade-off starkly, perhaps a degree of close-minded certainty is the price of a more participatory democracy.

Worse still for advocates of deliberation, the deliberative education of activists is only purchased at the price of mobilizing moral passions that are not always easy to control. In fact, the ongoing efforts of elites within the Christian Right to educate their activists attest to the persistence of moral passions rather than their demise. After all, if every activist were naturally disposed toward patient civility, there would be little need for the Right's massive investment in democratic education.

In important respects these findings and arguments parallel those found in Diana Mutz's work, which has emphasized the tension between participation and deliberation from a very different perspective. According to Mutz, different social contexts foster participation and deliberation: relatively closed, homogenous social contexts foster participation but not deliberation; while open, heterogeneous social network depress participation but do encourage deliberation.[51] This analysis is probably correct insofar as social networks are concerned.

My evidence, however, suggests that this tension is less stark in political organizations. Because citizens in Christian Right organizations receive their deliberative education only after, not before, they become involved in politics, there is simply no democratic education absent the mobilization of moral passions. Indeed, citizens have a strong incentive to deliberate only once they have been radicalized. In practice, then, citizens learn deliberative norms not primarily through public schools, as Amy Gutmann proposes,[52] but in some of the very interest groups that are regarded as corrosive to deliberative democracy.

Of course, the rancor of mobilization efforts is not simply a cost that must be borne for the sake of an imperfect deliberative education—it also contributes to the participatory character of American democracy. Therefore, proponents of deliberative democracy need to accept limits to the deliberative ideal if they also value participation. If deliberative democrats want a more participatory democracy, then they should be tolerant of the moral passions that are so important to mobilization efforts. Such tolerance is particularly needed when political organizations attempt to recruit and rally sympathetic citizens. On the other hand, if deliberative democrats ultimately decide their deliberative ideals are too compromised by undisciplined activists, then they should embrace the American Founders' more elitist version of deliberative democracy, which emphasized the tension between mass participation and deliberation. James Madison argued that deliberative decision-making was possible only in institutions that are insulated from public passions. Therefore, keeping the public weak and distant from their representatives was a necessary though insufficient condition for deliberative decision-making.[53]

Notes

INTRODUCTION

1. Thomas Friedman, "Two Nations Under God," *New York Times*, 4 November 2004.

2. Robert Kuttner, "An Attack on American Tolerance," *Boston Globe*, 17 November 2004.

3. Peter Beinart, "Morally Correct," *New Republic*, 29 November 2004.

4. For a sample of recent scholarly work, see James A. Morone, *Hellfire Nation: The Politics of Sin in American History* (New Haven: Yale University Press, 2004); Jason C. Bivins, *The Fracture of Good Order: Christian Antiliberalism and the Challenge to American Politics* (Chapel Hill, NC: University of North Carolina Press, 2003); Gabriel A. Almond, R. Scott Appleby, and Emmanuel Sivan, *Strong Religion: The Rise of Fundamentalisms around the World* (Chicago, IL: University of Chicago Press, 2003); William H. Simon, "Three Limitations of Deliberative Democracy: Identity Politics, Bad Faith, and Indeterminacy," in Stephen Macedo, ed., *Deliberative Politics: Essays on 'Democracy and Disagreement'* (New York: Oxford University Press, 1999); Ann Burlein, *Lift High the Cross: Where White Supremacy and the Christian Right Converge* (Durham, NC: Duke University Press, 2002); Herman Didi, *The Antigay Agenda: Orthodox Vision and the Christian Right* (Chicago, IL: University of Chicago Press, 1997); Fritz Detwiler, *Standing on the Premises of God: The Christian Right's Fight to Redefine America's Public Schools* (New York: New York University Press, 1996); Sara Diamond, *Roads to Dominion: Right-Wing Movements and Political Power in the United States* (New York: Guilford Press, 1995); Eugene F. Provenzo, Jr., *Religious Fundamentalism and American Education: The Battle for Public Schools* (Albany, NY: State University of New York Press, 1990).

5. Lawrence S. Rothenberg, *Linking Citizens to Government: Interest Group Politics at Common Cause* (New York: Cambridge University Press, 1992), 100.

6. This is partly because political scientists in particular have badly neglected the subject of religion. Kenneth Wald and Clyde Wilcox report that aside from "economics and geography, it is hard to find a social science that has given less attention to religion." Kenneth D. Wald and Clyde Wilcox, "Getting Religion: Has Political Science Rediscovered the Faith Factor?" *American Political Science Review* 10 (November 2006), 523–24.

7. Robert D. Putnam, "Bowling Alone," *Journal of Democracy* 6 (January 1995): 65–78.

8. Jed Dannenbaum, *Drink and Disorder: Temperance Reform in Cincinnati from the Washington Revival to the WCTU* (Chicago, IL: University of Illinois Press, 1984), xi.

9. See, for instance, Ruth Birgitta Anderson Bordin, *Women and Temperance: The Quest for Power and Liberty, 1873–1900* (New Brunswick, NJ: Rutgers Uni-

versity Press, 1990); Carol Mattingly, *Well-Tempered Women: Nineteenth-Century Temperance Rhetoric* (Carbondale, IL: Southern Illinois University, 1999); Janet Zollinger Giele, *Two Paths to Women's Equality: Temperance, Suffrage, and the Origins of Modern Feminism* (New York: Twayne Publishers, 1995).

10. Albert O. Hirschman, *The Passions and the Interests: Political Arguments for Capitalism before Its Triumph* (Princeton, NJ: Princeton University Press, 1977), 54, 32–33, 40–42, 50–52.

11. Thomas L. Pangle, "Commentary," in Robert A. Goldwin, Art Kaufman, and William A. Schambra, eds., *Forging Unity Out of Diversity: The Approaches of Eight Nations* (Washington, DC: AEI Press, 1989), 97.

12. Federalist 10 in Alexander Hamilton, James Madison, and John Jay, *The Federalist*, ed. Benjamin Fletcher Wright (New York: Barnes and Noble Books, 1996), 129–136.

13. Harold D. Lasswell, *Psychopathology and Politics* (Chicago, IL: Chicago University Press, 1930), 173, 184, 194–97, 78–79.

14. Joseph Gusfield, *Symbolic Crusade: Status Politics and the American Temperance Movement* (Chicago, IL: University of Illinois, Urbana, 1963), 177.

15. Seymour Martin Lipset, "Sources of the Radical Right (1955)," in Daniel Bell, ed., *The Radical Right*, 3rd ed. (New Brunswick, NJ: Transaction Publishers, 2002), 308–9; Seymour Martin Lipset and Earl Rabb, *The Politics of Unreason: Right-Wing Extremism in the United States, 1790–1977*, 2nd ed. (Chicago, IL: University of Chicago Press, 1978), 23.

16. Daniel Bell, *The End of Ideology: On the Exhaustion of Political Ideas in the Fifties*, with a new afterword (Cambridge, MA: Harvard University Press, 1988), 103–23.

17. Lipset, "Sources of the Radical Right (1955)," 308–9; Lipset and Rabb, *The Politics of Unreason*, 23.

18. Bell, *The End of Ideology*, 103–23.

19. Richard Hofstadter, "The Pseudo-Conservative Revolt (1955)," in Bell, ed., *The Radical Right*, 3rd ed., 81–84; Hofstadter, "Psuedo-Conservatism Revisited (1962)," in Bell, ed., *The Radical Right*, 3rd ed., 102–3; Hofstadter, *The Paranoid Style in American Politics and Other Essays* (Cambridge, MA: Harvard University Press, 1996), 87–88; Hofstadter, *Anti-Intellectualism in American Life* (New York: Vintage Books, 1962), 3, 125–31, 136–41.

20. Leo Lowenthal and Norbert Guterman, *Prophets of Deceit* (New York: Harper and Brothers, 1949), 91–92.

21. John H. Bunzel, *Anti-Politics in America* (Westport, CT: Greenwood Press, 1967), 68–69.

22. Mancur Olson, *The Logic of Collective Action: Public Goods and the Theory of Groups* (Cambridge, MA: Harvard University Press, 1965), 159–65.

23. Especially from Peter M. Blau, *Exchange and Power in Social Life* (New York: John Wiley and Sons, 1964).

24. Robert H. Salisbury, "An Exchange Theory of Interest Groups," *Midwest Journal of Political Science* 13 (February 1969): 1–32. See also Robert H. Salisbury and Lauretta Conklin, "Instrumental versus Expressive Group Politics: The National Endowment for the Arts," in Allan A. Ciglar and Burdett A. Loomis,

eds., *Interest Group Politics*, 5th ed. (Washington, DC: Congressional Quarterly Press, 1998): 283–302.

25. Morris P. Fiorina, "Extreme Voices: A Dark Side of Civic Engagement," in Theda Skocpol and Morris P. Fiorina, eds., *Civic Engagement in American Democracy* (Washington, DC: Brookings Institution Press, 1999): 395–426.

26. Salisbury, "An Exchange Theory of Interest Groups," 16.

27. Peter B. Clark and James Q. Wilson, "Incentive Systems: A Theory of Organizations," *Administrative Science Quarterly* 6 (September 1961): 129–66. See also James Q. Wilson, *Political Organizations* (Princeton, NJ: Princeton University Press, 1995), 34–35.

28. David C. King and Jack L. Walker, "Provision of Benefits by Interest Group in the United States," *Journal of Politics* 54 (May 1992): 397.

29. Salisbury, "An Exchange Theory of Interest Groups," 16.

30. Kristin Luker, *Abortion and the Politics of Motherhood* (Berkeley, CA: University of California Press, 1984), esp. chaps. 7 and 8.

31. See, for example, Louise J. Lorentzen, "Evangelical Life-Style Concerns Expressed in Political Action," *Sociological Analysis* 41 (Summer 1980): 144–54; Ann L. Page and Donald A. Clelland, "The Kanawha County Textbook Controversy: A Study of the Politics of Life Style Concern," *Social Forces* 57 (September 1978): 265–81; Louis A. Zucher, Jr., et al., "The Anti-pornography Campaign: A Symbolic Crusade," *Social Problems* 19 (Fall 1971): 217–37; James Davison Hunter, *Before the Shooting Begins: Searching for Democracy in America's Culture Wars* (New York: Free Press, 1994); E. J. Dionne, *Why Americans Hate Politics* (New York: Touchstone Books, 1992).

32. Sidney Verba, Kay Lehman Schlozman, and Henry E. Brady, *Voice and Equality: Civic Volunteerism in American Politics* (Cambridge, MA: Harvard University Press, 1995), 494–500, 518–21.

33. Thomas Frank, *What's the Matter with Kansas? How Conservatives Won the Heart of America* (New York: Owl Books, 2004), 1–10, 68–72, 122–30, 253–64.

34. Marsha Jones, "Fundamentalism Revisited," *Sociology Review* 10 (September 2000): 32.

35. R. Scott Appleby and Martin E. Marty, "Fundamentalism," *Foreign Policy* 6 (January–February 2002): 16.

36. Almond, Appleby, and Sivan, *Strong Religion*, 16–18

37. Martin E. Marty, "Our Religio-Secular World," *Daedalus* 132 (Summer 2003): 42–48.

38. Almond, Appleby, and Sivan, *Strong Religion*, 1–2, 16–18, 45–46, 156–157, 187, 198–199.

39. Ellen Willis, "Bringing the Holy War Home: There is a Link Between Our Own Cultural Conflicts and the Logic of Jihad," *Nation*, 17 December 2001, p. 15.

40. Barbara Ehrenreich, "Christian Wahhabists," *Progressive* 66 (January 2002): 12–13. See also Carla Power, "The Age of Fundamentalism," *Newsweek International*, 9 December 2002, 49.

41. Don Corrigan, "GOP Taliban: Gov. Blunt Tells Missouri Editors Sen. Danforth Is Wrong on Christian Right's Role in His Party," *St. Louis Journalism Re-*

view 35 (April 2005): 22–23; Sydney Tarrow, *Power in Movement: Social Movements and Contentious Politics* (Cambridge, UK: Cambridge University Press, 1998), 203–04.

42. "Vast Right-Wing Conspiracy," *American Prospect* 14 (June 2003): 9. See also E. L. Doctorow, "Why We Are Infidels," *Nation*, 26 May 2003, pp. 11–12.

43. Rebecca Beyer, "Journalist Aims to Expose 'Fascism' of the Christian Right," *National Catholic Reporter*, 1 April 2005. See also Chris Hedges, "Soldiers of Christ II: Feeling the Hate with the National Religious Broadcasters," *Harper's Magazine* 310, May 2005, pp. 55–61.

44. John M. Swomley, "Storm Troopers in the Culture War," *Humanist* 57 (September 1997): 13.

45. Sara Diamond, "The Christian Right's Anti-Gay Agenda," *Humanist* 54 (July–August 1994): 32. See also Sara Diamond, *Roads to Dominion: Right-Wing Movements and Political Power in the United States* (New York: Guilford Press, 1995); Diamond, *Facing the Wrath: Confronting the Right in Dangerous Times* (Monroe, ME: Common Courage Press, 1996).

46. Abby L. Ferber, ed., *Home-Grown Hate: Gender and Organized Racism* (New York: Routledge, 2003), 1.

47. Lewis H. Lapham, "The Wrath of the Lamb," *Harper's Magazine* 310, May 2005, p. 9.

48. Colbert I. King, "Hijacking Christianity," *Washington Post*, 23 April 2005.

49. Timothy M. Gray, "Intolerance Is Not a Value," *Washington Post*, 16 November 2004. See also Maureen Dowd, "Slapping the Other Check," *New York Times*, 14 November 2004.

50. Detwiler, *Standing on the Premises of God*, 10. See also Diamond, *Roads to Dominion*, 246–49; Diamond, *Facing the Wrath*, 47–56.

51. Bivins, *The Fracture of Good Order*, 180–81.

52. Mark E. Warren, *Democracy and Association* (Princeton, NJ: Princeton University Press, 2001), 15–16, 198; Simon, "Three Limitations of Deliberative Democracy," 50.

53. Hunter, *Before the Shooting Begins*, 46–47.

54. Dionne, *Why Americans Hate Politics*, 343.

55. Morris P. Fiorina, *Culture War? The Myth of a Polarized Culture* (New York: Pearson Education, 2005), 99–102.

56. Mathew Moen, *The Transformation of the Christian Right* (Tuscalossa, AL: University of Alabama Press, 1992); Mary E. Bendyna and Clyde Wilcox, "The Christian Right Old and New: A Comparison of the Moral Majority with the Christian Coalition," in Corwin E. Smidt and James M. Penning, eds., *Sojourners in the Wilderness: The Christian Right in Comparative Perspective* (New York: Rowman and Littlefield, 1997), 41–56; Mark J. Rozell, "Growing Up Politically: The New Politics of the New Christian Right," in Smidt and Penning, eds., *Sojourners in the Wilderness*; Mark J. Rozell and Clyde Wilcox, *Second Coming: The New Christian Right in Virginia Politics* (Baltimore, MD: Johns Hopkins University Press, 1996): 235–48.

57. Rozell, "Growing Up Politically," 238.

58. Michael Walzer, "Deliberation, and What Else?" in Stephen Macedo, ed., *Deliberative Politics: Essays on 'Democracy and Disagreement'* (New York: Oxford University Press, 1999), 60.

59. Reinhold Niebuhr, *Moral Man and Immoral Society* (New York: Charles Scribner's Sons, 1960), xv.

60. Fiorina, "Extreme Voices," 416.

61. Wilson, *Political Organizations*, 230, 226–28.

CHAPTER ONE
DEMOCRATIC EDUCATION IN THE CHRISTIAN RIGHT

1. Benjamin Barber, *Strong Democracy: Participatory Politics for a New Age* (Berkeley, CA: University of California Press, 1984), 267–73; James S. Fishkin, *Democracy and Deliberation: New Directions for Reform* (New Haven, CT: Yale University Press, 1991), 84; John Gastil, *By Popular Demand: Revitalizing Representative Democracy Through Deliberative Elections* (Berkeley, CA: University of California Press, 2000); Ethan Lieb, *Deliberative Democracy in America: A Proposal for a Popular Branch of Government* (University Park, PA: Pennsylvania State University Press, 2004).

2. Lawrence S. Rothenberg, *Linking Citizens to Government: Interest Group Politics at Common Cause* (New York: Cambridge University Press, 1992), 100.

3. Throughout the book I use the terms *elites* and *leaders* to refer to paid staff in Christian Right organizations and media; *activists* are volunteers.

4. James Davison Hunter, *Culture Wars: The Struggle to Define America* (New York: Basic Books, 1991); E. J. Dionne, Jr., *Why Americans Hate Politics* (New York: Touchstone Books, 1992); Morris P. Fiorina, "The Dark Side of Civic Engagement," in Theda Skocpol and Morris P. Fiorina, eds., *Civic Engagement in American Democracy* (Washington, DC: Brookings Institution Press, 1999), 395–426.

5. Lori Kehoe, interview by author, telephone, 13 July 2004.

6. Right to Life of Michigan, "President's Message: Working to Defend Life," newsletter, June/ July 2003.

7. Chuck Gosnell, "Raising the Standard," accessed on the website of the Christian Coalition of Colorado at www.ccco.org, 16 June 2002.

8. New Jersey Christian Coalition, "Christian Coalition—Mainstream?" accessed on the website of the New Jersey Christian Coalition at www .nychristiancoalition.org, 18 June 2002.

9. Beverly LaHaye, "Success Without Compromise," *Concerned Women for America Magazine*, May 1991, p. 7.

10. Participant observation, Albemarle County Board of Supervisors Meeting, Charlottesville, VA, 11 August 2004.

11. Email from Marnie Deaton, "CVFF Update for Week Ending 10–22–04," 22 October 2004.

12. Stand to Reason, "Ambassador's Creed," 2003.

13. Participant observation, Arvada Covenant Church, Arvada, CO, 10 April 2004.

14. Justice for All, "Volunteer Agreement," 1 August 2000.

15. Scott Klusendorf, interview by author, La Mirada, CA, 2 March 2004.

16. Focus on the Family radio broadcast, "Reaching Hearts on Abortion," 19 January 2004.

17. Stand to Reason instructor, interview by author, telephone, 23 July 2004.

18. Life Chain, *Code of Conduct*, accessed on the website of Life Chain at www.lifechain.net, 30 September 2004.

19. John W. Kennedy, "Mixing Politics and Piety: Christian Talk Radio," *Christianity Today*, 15 August 1994, pp. 42–46.

20. Focus on the Family radio broadcast, "A Call to Social Action," 4 March 2002.

21. Tom Minnery, "Moral Outrage Is Not Enough," *Citizen*, 15 April 1991, p. 1.

22. Charles Colson, "Don't Swing That Bible," *Citizen*, 21 April 1990, p. 2.

23. Center for Reclaiming America, "Writing Effective Letters," 1998.

24. Julie Parton, interview by author, Tyson's Corner, VA, 24 September 2004.

25. Care Net, *Serving with Care and Integrity: A Training Resource for Pregnancy Center Volunteers* (2003), 48–55.

26. Ralph Reed, "A Strategy for Evangelicals," *Christian American*, January 1993, p. 14.

27. Christian Coalition, *Training Seminar Manual, Level I1* (Chesapeake, VA: Christian Coalition, 1995), 52–54.

28. Mike Hanneschlager, interview by author, telephone, 9 July 2002; John Fuggat, interview by author, Huntington Beach, CA, 19 June 2002; Carolyn Kunkle, interview by author, telephone, 21 June 2002; Lou Beres, interview by author, telephone, 5 July 2002; and Bill Thompson, interview by author, telephone, 18 June 2002.

29. Carolyn Kunkle, interview by author, telephone, 21 June 2002.

30. Concerned Women for America, *Opportunities for Leadership in Concerned Women for America* (1995), 16, 18; Patricia Phillips, interview by author, telephone, 16 October 2001.

31. Christian Coalition, *Blueprint for Victory*, 12 September 1997, p. 6.

32. Concerned Women for America, *Opportunities for Leadership in Concerned Women for America*, 16, 18.

33. Lisa Andrusko, ed., *Infinite Possibilities: National Right to Life Committee Yearbook 2004* (Washington, DC: National Right to Life Committee, 2004), 148.

34. Arkansas Right to Life, "Citizen Guide for Contacting Elected Officials and Grassroots Lobbying," accessed on the website of the Arkansas Right to Life Committee at www.artl.org, 28 June 2004.

35. Future for Life, *The Future: Acting for Life in a New Age Handbook* (June 2004), 6–7.

36. Massachusetts Citizens for Life, "About MCFL," accessed on the website of Massachusetts Citizens for Life at www.masscitizensforlife.org, 28 June 2002.

37. Julie Watson, "Who We Are," *Life Lines*, September/October 2002, p. 7.

38. Human Life of Washington, "Writing Letters," accessed on the website of Human Life of Washington at www.humanlife.net, 29 June 2004.

39. Jane Grimm, *Life Times*, January/February 2002, p. 1–2.

40. Society for Truth and Justice, "Registration Form," accessed on the website of the Society for Truth and Justice at www.societyfortruthandjustice.com/registration.htm, 14 July 2004.

41. See OR Boston, "General Sidewalk Counseling Points," accessed on the website of OR Boston at http://www.orboston.org/SWC_seminar_1_30_01.htm, 3 August 2004.

42. Cheryl Sullenger, *Sidewalk Counseling: A Training Manual* (Sacramento, CA: Operation Rescue West), 17, 28.

43. Life and Liberty Ministries, "Sidewalk Counseling," accessed on the website of Life and Liberty Ministries at www.lifeandlibertyministries.com/sc_dialogue.thm, 14 July 2004.

44. Colson, "Don't Swing That Bible," 1–3. See also Minnery, "Moral Outrage Is Not Enough," 1; Tom Minnery, "How to Argue on Unfriendly Terrain," *Citizen*, 15 April 1991; and Tom Minnery and John Elredge, "Does Activism Seem Unloving (It Shouldn't)," *Citizen*, 18 December 1995.

45. Charles Glenn, "When Christians Speak Up in Public," *Christianity Today* 5 September 1986, pp. 26–28; Charles Colson, "How Pro-life Protest Has Backfired," *Christianity Today*, 15 December 1989, p. 72; Guy M. Condon, "You Say Choice, I Say Murder," *Christianity Today*, 24 June 1991, pp. 20–23; Paul Brenton, "Casualties of the Abortion Wars," *Christianity Today*, 16 October 1992, pp. 22–25; Charles Colson, "Sweet Reason and Holy Outrage," *Christianity Today* 19 July 1993, p. 64; John D. Woodbridge, "Culture War Casualties: How Warfare Rhetoric Is Hurting the Church," *Christianity Today*, 6 March 1995, pp. 20–26.

46. Woodbridge, "Culture War Casualties," 20.

47. Condon, "You Say Choice, I Say Murder," 22.

48. Andrew Walsh, "The Trouble with Missionaries," *Religion in the News*, Summer 2003, pp. 7–8, 27; Alan Cooperman, "Ministers Asked to Curb Remarks About Islam," *Washington Post*, 8 May 2003.

49. *Beverly LaHaye Live* radio broadcast, "The Culture War," 23 July 2003.

50. Included in Ohio Right to Life, "Coming Out of The Closet Kit" (n.d.).

51. Future for Life, *The Future*, 4.

52. Participant observation, Auraria Campus, Denver, CO, 12 April 2004.

53. Stand to Reason, "JFA Training Handout," (no date).

54. Sullenger, *Sidewalk Counseling*, 27.

55. Life and Liberty Ministries, "Sidewalk Counseling."

56. Care Net, *Serving with Care and Integrity*, 33, 50, 71, 87–89.

57. Barber, *Strong Democracy*; 173–78; Adolf G. Gunderson, *The Socratic Citizen: A Theory of Deliberative Democracy* (New York: Lexington Books, 2000).

58. Beverly LaHaye, "How to Communicate Your Convictions," *Concerned Women for America Magazine*, June 1991, p. 6.

59. Christian Coalition, *Training Seminar Manual*, 61.

60. Future for Life, *The Future*, 5–6.

61. Leadership Institute official, interview by author, Alexandria, VA, 13 August 2002.

62. Steve Wagner, interview by author, Denver, CO, 11 April 2004.

63. Center for Bio-Ethical Reform, "Genocide Awareness Project Video," accessed on the website of the Center for Bio-Ethical Reform at www .abortionno.org, 19 July 2004.

64. Participant observation, Arvada Covenant Church, Arvada, CO, 10 April 2004.

65. Stand to Reason, "JFA Training Handout," (no date).

66. See mission statement on the website of Patrick Henry College at www.phc.edu/about/mission.asp, 22 June 2006.

67. Michael Farris, "Training Christians to Be Politicians," a talk delivered at the Forum of the Miller Center of Public Affairs, University of Virginia, 16 November 2005.

68. Sullenger, *Sidewalk Counseling*, 26

69. Life and Liberty Ministries, "Sidewalk Counseling."

70. OR Boston, "General Sidewalk Counseling Points."

71. Cheryl Sullenger, interview by author, telephone, 21 September 2004.

72. Care Net, *Serving with Care and Integrity*, 76–86.

73. Excerpted from an email exchange between Scott Klusendorf of Stand to Reason and the director of Care Net.

74. Julie Parton, interview by author, Crystal City, VA, 24 September 2004.

75. Care Net, *Serving with Care and Integrity*, 53–55.

76. Amy Gutmann and Dennis Thompson, *Democracy and Disagreement* (Cambridge, MA: Harvard University Press, 1996), 52–57. For criticisms of this restriction on deliberative debate, see William A. Galston, "Diversity, Toleration, and Deliberative Democracy: Religious Minorities and Public Schooling," in Stephen Macedo, ed., *Deliberative Politics: Essays on Democracy and Disagreement* (New York: Oxford University Press, 1999); William Galston, "Democracy and Disagreement," *Ethics* 108 (April 1998); Robert M. Gordon, "Democracy and Disagreement," *Yale Law Journal* 106 (January 1997); Jeffrey Rosen, "In Search of Common Ground," *New York Times*, 29 December 1996.

77. On the movement away from religious argument in the Abolitionism movement see Gilbert Hobbs Barnes, *The Antislavery Impulse, 1844–1930* (New York: Harcourt, Brace, and World, 1964), 137–45; Eric Foner, *Free Soil, Free Labor, and Free Men: The Ideology of the Republican Party Before the Civil War* (New York: Oxford University Press, 1970), 43–44, 61–62. On the Temperance movement see Peter H. Odegard, *Pressure Politics: The Story of the Anti-Saloon League* (New York: Columbia University Press, 1928); Jonathan Zimmerman, *Distilling Democracy: Alcohol Education in America's Public Schools, 1880–1925* (Lawrence, KA: Kansas University Press, 1999). On the Catholic response to eugenics laws, see Sharon M. Leon, "'A Human Being, and Not a Mere Social Factor': Catholic Strategies for Dealing with Sterilization Statutes in the 1920s," *Church and History* 73 (June 2004): 383–411.

78. Adam Nagourney, "In Final Debate, Clash on Taxes and Health Care," *New York Times*, 14 October 2004.

79. Accessed on the website of the Religious Coalition for Reproductive Choice at http://www.rcrc.org/faith_choices/common_questions/answer3.htm, 2 January 2004.

80. Gary Weiand, "An Alternative Approach," *Arizona Right to Life Newsletter*, August 2000.

81. Dan Kennedy, "A Voice in the Wilderness: Raising Our Voices in the Public Square," *Human Life Newspaper*, July 2000.

82. Pat Chivers, interview by author, Crystal City, VA, 3 July 2004.

83. Georgia Right to Life, "Abortion Arguments No. 1," accessed on the website of Georgia Right to Life at www.grtl.org, 28 June 2004.

84. Lisa Roche, interview by author, telephone, 3 August 2004.

85. Greg Koukl, *Solid Ground* cover letter, 1 September 2004.

86. Scott Klusendorf, interview by author, La Mirada, CA, 2 March 2004.

87. Participant observation, Arvada Covenant Church, Arvada CO, 10 April 2004.

88. Participant observation, First Right meeting, University of Virginia, Charlottesville, VA, 7 September 2004.

89. First Right, "Human Rights for All," accessed on the website of First Right at www.student.virginia.edu/~1stright/ad.doc, 1 April 2005.

90. Concerned Women for America, "Pocket Guide on How to Lobby from Your Home," pamphlet, n.d. These messages are also emphasized in CWA's radio program *Beverly LaHaye Live*. Recent examples include the following broadcasts: "Grassroots Activism: Becoming an Effective Lobbyist," 8 February 2001; "Grassroots Activism: Becoming an Effective Lobbyist," 27 April 2001; "How to Lobby," 6 January 2004.

91. Colson, "Don't Swing That Bible," 1–3.

92. Minnery, "How to Argue on Unfriendly Terrain," 5–6.

93. Kerby Anderson, "Politics and Religion," accessed on website of LeadershipU at http://www.leaderu.com/orgs/probe/docs/pol-rel.html, 10 January 2008.

94. Thomas Grey, "How to Fight Gambling," *Christianity Today*, 18 May 1998, p. 39.

95. Woodbridge, "Culture War Casualties," 26.

96. Accessed on the website of Patrick Henry College at www.phc.edu/about/mission.asp, 22 June 2006.

97. Quoted in Hanna Rosin, "God and Country," *New Yorker*, accessed on the website of the *New Yorker* at http://www.newyorker.com/fact/content/articles/050627fa_fact, 27 June 2005.

98. Holly Gatling, interview by author, Crystal City, VA, 2 July 2004.

99. Barbara Listing, interview by author, Crystal City, VA, 2 July 2004.

100. Right to Life of Michigan, *Handbook for Affiliate President's* (updated March 1999), 43.

101. Michael Ciccocioppo, interview by author, Crystal City, VA, 1 July 2004.

102. Joseph Graham, interview by author, Crystal City, VA, 1 July 2004.

103. Mark J. Rozell, "Growing Up Politically: The New Politics of the New Christian Right," in Corwin E. Smidt and James M. Penning, eds., *Sojourners in the Wilderness: The Christian Right in Comparative Perspective* (New York: Rowman and Littlefield, 1997), 236–38.

104. Christian Coalition, *Citizen Action Seminar* (Chesapeake, VA: Christian Coalition, 1995), 14.

105. Care Net, *Serving with Care and Integrity*, 95–103.

106. "The President's Stem Cell Theology," *New York Times*, 26 May 2005; "Bush's Stem Cell Theology," *The International Herald*, 27 May 2005; Jerome Groopman, "Beware of Stem Cell Theology," *Washington Post*, 29 May 2005.

107. Groopman, "Beware of Stem Cell Theology."

108. Joseph M. Bessette, *The Mild Voice of Reason: Deliberative Democracy and American National Government* (Chicago, IL: University of Chicago Press, 1994), 46–47.

109. J.C. Willke, "Unity or Divisiveness?" *National Right to Life News*, 16 August 1990.

110. Andrusko, *Infinite Possibilities*, 148.

111. Mark Hartwig, "Check Your Facts Before You Act," *Citizen*, 17 May 1993, pp. 6–7.

112. Woodbridge, "Culture War Casualties," 25.

113. Center for Reclaiming America, "Working with Your School Board," 1997.

114. Chuck Cunningham, Pat Garland, and Rick Schencker, "Voter Guides: Educating Pro-Family Voters" (transcript of the Christian Coalition Conference and Strategy Briefing Workshop, Washington, DC, 17 September 1994).

115. Care Net, *Serving with Care and Integrity*, 121–147.

116. Julie Parton, interview by author, Arlington, VA, 24 September 2004.

117. Dauneen Dolce, "Commentary from the Editor, *Viva Life*, September 2003, p. 2.

118. Ohio Right to Life, "Tips for Successful Legislative Contacts," n.d.

119. Texas Right to Life, "Lobbying Guidelines for a Visit with Your Legislator or Congressional Candidate," accessed on the website of Texas Right to Life at www.texasrighttolife.com, 29 June 2004.

120. Pat Chivers, interview by author, Crystal City, VA, 3 July 2004.

121. Janice Shaw Crouse, *Strategies for Reclaiming America's Future* (Washington, DC: Beverly LaHaye Institute, 2000), 7.

122. Pamphlet titles include *The Facts About Existing State ERA Laws*; *A Painful Choice: Breast Cancer's Link to Abortion*; *RU-486: What You Need to Know*; *Sex Education in America's Schools: An Evaluation of Sex Information and Education Council of the United States*; and *Religion in Public Schools: Understanding Where the LineIs Drawn*.

123. Center for Reclaiming America, "Working with Your School Board," 1997.

124. Texas Christian Coalition, *Handbook for Grassroots Lobbying: 2001–2002 Edition* (2002), 4–8.

125. South Carolina Christian Coalition, "Keys to Effective Interaction with Lawmakers," accessed on the website of the South Carolina Christian Coalition at www.scchristiancoalition.org/resources.shtml#interact, 16 June 2002.

126. Christian Coalition of Oregon, "How to Be a Lobbyist: A Vestpocket Handbook for Citizen Lobbyists," accessed on the website of the Christian Coalition of Oregon at www.coalition.org, 16 June 2002.

127. Hanna Rosin, "God and Country," *New Yorker*, accessed on the website of the *New Yorker* at http://www.newyorker.com/fact/content/articles/050627fa_fact, 27 June 2005.

128. Michael Farris, "Training Christians to be Politicians," a talk delivered at the Forum of the Miller Center of Public Affairs, University of Virginia, 16 November 2005

129. Scott Klusendorf, interview by author, La Mirada, CA, 2 March 2004.

130. Scott Klusendorf, "What the Average Person Can Do to Stop Abortion," accessed on the website of Stand to Reason at www.str.org/free/bioethics/average.htm, 2 February 2004.

131. Focus on the Family radio broadcast, "Reaching Hearts on Abortion," 19 January 2004.

132. Hunter, *Before the Shooting Begins*, 61–67.

133. Center for Bio-Ethical Reform GAP Video.

134. David Lee, interview by author, Auraria Campus, Denver, CO, 12 April 2004.

135. Participant observation, Auraria Campus, Denver, CO, 12 April 2004.

136. Excerpted from email exchange between Klusendorf and Care Net director.

137. Gregg Cunningham, "Reproductive 'Choice' Trucks Have Pro-Aborts Running Scared," *In Perspective*, Winter 2001.

138. For the origins of this alienation, see George M. Marsden, *Fundamentalism and American Culture: The Shaping of Twentieth-Century Evangelism, 1870–1925* (New York: Oxford University Press, 1980).

139. Participant observation, Arvada Covenant Church, Arvada, CO, 10 April 2004.

CHAPTER TWO
CHRISTIAN RADICALISM

1. Paul E. Johnson, "Interest Group Recruiting: Finding Members and Keeping Them," in Allan J. Cigler and Burdett A. Loomis, eds., *Interest Group Politics*, 5th ed. (Washington, DC: Congressional Quarterly Press, 1998): 35–62.

2. Jane Mansbridge, "Everyday Talk in the Deliberative System," in Stephen Macedo, ed., *Deliberative Politics: Essays on Democracy and Disagreement* (New York: Oxford University Press, 1999): 211–42.

3. The following discussion draws on 144 pieces of direct mail distributed by the Christian Coalition and Concerned Women for America (CWA) between 1992 and 2001. This was all the mail from the Christian Coalition and CWA that was in the archives at the People for the American Way during this period.

4. CWA direct mailings: December 1992; 21 January 1993; January 1993; 20 February 1998; Christian Coalition direct mailings: July 1997; October 1997.

5. CWA direct mailings: March 1992; May 1992; July 1992; December 1992; October 1993; July 1994; 1 August 2001; 16 August 2001. Similar charges can be found in other CWA mailings: February 1993; April 1994; September 1996; November 1996; March 1997; February 1997; August 1997; 20 February 1998; 18 January 2000. Christian Coalition direct mailing: March 1997.

6. Christian Coalition direct mailings: October 1997; February 2000; May 2000.

7. CWA direct mailings: February 1992; 9 March 1998; August 1999. For similar claims, see March 1992; April 1992; April 1993; 9 December 1993; July 1997; March 1998; August 1998; September 1998; 18 September 2000.

8. CWA direct mailings: 4 June 1992; July 1992. For similar claims, see August 1993; January 1994; September 1994; 17 August 1998; May 1999; 4 January 2000; 16 November 2001.

9. Christian Coalition direct mailings: November 1993; July 1993; March 1994; September 1994; December 1994; March 1997; 3 July 1997; 2 September 1997; May 2000; five mailings had unknown dates. CWA direct mailings: May 1993; October 1994; February 1996; April 1999; August 1999; 21 February 2000.

10. Christian Coalition direct mailings: May 1993; July 1993; September 1993; November 1993; June 1994; July 1994; September 1994; December 1994; May 1995; January 1997; March 1997; 3 July 1997; 2 September 1997; October 1997; 26 November 1997; 3 March 1999; May 1999; 4 June 1999; February 2000; May 2000; five mailings, date unknown. CWA direct mailings: January 1992; February 1992; May 1992; April 1992; May 1992; 4 June 1992; July 1992; August 1992; September 1992; October 1992; December 1992; 21 January 1993; February 1993; March 1993; May 1993; June 1993; 18 June 1993; September 1993; October 1993; January 1994; February 1994; March 1994; April 1994; May 1994; July 1994; August 1994; September 1994; October 1994; November 1994; January 1996; February 1996; April 1996; May 1996; July 1996; August 1996; September 1996; November 1996; January 1997; February 1997; March 1997; 3 June 1997; 16 June 1997; July 1997; August 1997; September 1997; November 1997; 2 December 1997; 16 December 1997; January 1998; February 1998; 5 February 1998; March 1998; 9 March 1998; April 1998; 18 May 1998; August 1998; September 1998; 17 August 1998; 2 June 1998; October 1998; February 1999; March 1999; May 1999; June 1999; October 1999; 18 January 2000; 7 February 2000; 21 February 2000; 4 May 2001; 1 August 2001; 16 August 2001.

11. CWA direct mailings: December 1992; July 1997; January 1998.

12. Christian Coalition direct mailing, date unknown.

13. CWA direct mailing, February 1992.

14. CWA direct mailing, July 1992.

15. Christian Coalition direct mailing, 2 July 1998.

16. Christian Coalition direct mailing, date unknown.

17. Such references were far more prevalent in CWA mailings than in Christian Coalition mailings. See CWA direct mailings: July 1992; August 1992; October 1992; October 1993; February 1994; August 1994; July 1996; November 1996; January 1997; February 1997; June 1997; September 1997; November 1997; January 1998; 9 March 1998; 30 July 1998; October 1998; February 1999; April 1999; May 1999; October 1999; 4 January 2000; 18 January 2000; 21 February 2000; 4 May 2001; August 2001; 16 August 2001. Christian Coalition direct mailings: October 1997; February 2000; one with unknown date.

18. CWA direct mailings: March 1992; May 1992; October 1992; December 1992; April 1993; September 1993; April 1994; September 1994; February 1996; May 1996; July 1996; September 1996; July 1997; September 1997; October

1997; 30 July 1998; August 1998; April 1999; May 1999. Christian Coalition direct mailings: May 1993; September 1993; November 1993; March 1994; 2 October 1997; May 2000; two with unknown dates.

19. Amitai Etzioni, *The New Golden Rule: Community and Morality in a Democratic Society* (New York: Basic Books, 1996), 99–100.

20. James Davison Hunter, *Culture Wars: The Struggle to Define America* (New York: Basic Books, 1991), 165–66.

21. James Davison Hunter, *Before the Shooting Begins: Searching for Democracy in America's Culture Wars* (New York: Free Press, 1994), 61–66.

22. Keith Cassidy, "The Movement and Its Message: Pro-Life Educational Campaigns and Their Critiques," paper presented at annual meeting of University Faculty for Life, 1994.

23. Mark J. Rozell, "Growing Up Politically: The New Politics of the New Christian Right," in Corwin E. Smidt and James M. Penning, eds., *Sojourners in the Wilderness: The Christian Right in Comparative Perspective* (New York: Rowman and Littlefield, 1997), 236–38.

24. Mathew C. Moen, *The Christian Right and Congress* (Tuscaloosa, AL: University of Alabama Press, 1989), 153–56.

25. See, for example, Steve Bruce, *The Rise and Fall of the New Christian Right* (New York: Oxford University Press, 1988).

26. Stuart Rothenberg and Frank Newport, *The Evangelical Voter* (Washington, DC: Free Congress Research and Education Foundation, 1984), 140.

27. James Davison Hunter, *Evangelicalism: The Coming Generation* (Chicago, IL: University of Chicago Press, 1993), 143–150.

28. James L. Guth, "Southern Baptist Clergy: Vanguard of the Christian Right?" in Robert C. Liebman and Robert Wuthnow, eds., *The New Christian Right: Mobilization and Legitimation* (New York: Aldine, 1983), 118–22.

29. Christian Smith, *Christian America? What Christians Really Want* (Berkeley, CA: University of California Press, 2002), 122–24.

30. Laura Berkowitz and John C. Green, "Charting the Coalition: The Local Chapters of the Ohio Christian Coalition," in Corwin E. Smidt and James M. Penning, eds., *Sojourners in the Wilderness: The Christian Right in Comparative Perspective* (New York: Rowman and Littlefield, 1997): 57–72.

31. Jeffrey Hadden, Anson Shupe, James Howdin, and Kenneth Martin, "Why Jerry Falwell Killed the Moral Majority," in Marshall W. Fishwick and Ray B. Browne, eds., *The God Bumpers: Religion in the Electronic Age* (Bowling Green, OH: Bowling Green State University Popular Press, 1987), 102.

32. Clyde Wilcox, *Onward Christian Soldiers? The Religious Right in American Politics* (Boulder, CO: Westview Press, 2000), 36–37.

33. James M. Ault, Jr., *Spirit and Flesh: Life in a Fundamentalist Baptist Church* (New York: Vintage Books, 2004), 117–19.

34. Mark J. Rozell and Clyde Wilcox, "Second Coming: The Strategies of the New Christian Right," *Political Science Quarterly* 111 (Summer 1996): 271–72.

35. Wilcox, *Onward Christian Soldiers?* 113–14.

36. James Risen and Judy L. Thomas, *Wrath of Angels: The American Abortion War* (New York: Basic Books, 1998), 19–20.

37. John T. McGreevy, *Catholicism and American Freedom: A History* (New York: W.W. Norton, 2003), 273

38. Bill Peterson, "As New Right Gets Old, Strategists Recast It as New Populism," *Washington Post*, 12 March 1983.

39. Nicholas D. Kristof, "Aid for 'Victims' of Welfare Urged," *Washington Post*, 29 July 1982; Nicholas D. Kristof, "New Right Meeting Grumbles About Reagan," *Washington Post*, 28 July 1982; Colman McCarthy, "Enlightening the New Right," *Washington Post*, 14 August 1982.

40. Beverly LaHaye, "Success Without Compromise," *Concerned Women for America Newsletter*, May 1991, p. 7.

41. Jane J. Mansbridge, *Why We Lost the ERA* (Chicago, IL: University of Chicago Press, 1986), 134–35.

42. Leadership Institute official, interview by author, Alexandria, VA, 13 August 2002.

43. Paul Henry, *Politics for Evangelicals* (Valley Forge, PA: Judson Press, 1974); H. Edward Rowe, *Save America!* (Tappan, NJ: Spire Books, 1974); William Billings, *The Christian's Political Action Manual* (Washington, DC: National Christian Action Coalition, 1980); James Robison and Jim Cox, *Save America to Save the World: A Christian's Practical Guide for Stopping the Tidal Wave of Moral, Political and Economic Destruction in America* (Wheaton, IL: Tyndale House, 1980); John Eidsmore, *God and Caesar: Biblical Faith and Political Action* (Westchester, IL: Crossway Books, 1984); Vern McLellan, *Christians in the Political Arena: Positive Strategies for Concerned Twentieth-Century Patriots!* (Charlotte, NC: Associates Press, 1986); Colonel V. Doner, *The Samaritan Strategy: A New Agenda for Christian Activism* (Brentwood, TN: Wolgemuth and Hyatt, 1988).

44. Eidsmore, *God and Caesar: Biblical Faith and Political Action*, 65–66.

45. Robison and Cox, *Save America to Save the World*, 35–36.

46. Mathew Moen, *The Transformation of the Christian Right* (Tuscaloosa, AL: University of Alabama Press, 1992); Mark J. Rozell and Clyde Wilcox, *Second Coming: The New Christian Right in Virginia Politics* (Baltimore, MD: Johns Hopkins University Press, 1996), esp. chap. 3.

47. See Risen and Thomas, *Wrath of Angels*, esp. chaps. 3, 5, and 6.

48. National Abortion Federation, "NAF Violence and Disruption Statistics," accessed on the website of the National Abortion Federation at http://www .prochoice.org/pubs_research/publications/downloads/about_abortion/ violence_statistics.pdf, 13 December 2006.

49. "Note: Safety Valve Closed: The Removal of Non-violent Outlets for Dissent and the On-Set of Abortion Related Violence," *Harvard Law Review* 113 (March 2000), 1218–19. On police brutality, see also Hunter, *Before the Shooting Begins*, 161–62.

50. William Cotter, interview by author, Boston, MA, 27 July 2004. See also Risen and Thomas, *Wrath of Angels*, 298.

51. Ibid., chap. 12.

52. National Abortion Federation, "NAF Violence and Disruption Statistics," accessed on the website of the National Abortion Federation at http://www

.prochoice.org/pubs_research/publications/downloads/about_abortion/violence
_statistics.pdf, 13 December 2006.

53. Institute for First Amendment Studies and Bliss Institute of the University of Akron, "Survey of Christian Right Activists," accessed on the website of the Institute for First Amendment Studies at www.ifas.org/library/survey/index.html, 9 July 2002.

54. National Abortion Federation, "NAF Violence and Disruption Statistics," accessed on the website of the National Abortion Federation at http://www
.prochoice.org/pubs_research/publications/downloads/about_abortion/violence
_statistics.pdf, 13 December 2006.

55. Christopher P. Keleher, "Double Standards: The Suppression of Abortion Protesters' Free Speech Rights," *DePaul Law Review* 51 (Spring 2002), 844–46. See also Risen and Thomas, *Wrath of Angels*, 314.

56. "Note: Safety Valve Closed," 1209–20.

57. "In their Own Words: Tiller and Staff Speak Out," accessed on the website of Dr. Tiller at http://www.dr-tiller.com/their-own-words.htm, 15 December 2006.

58. For these and other details, see the website of Women's Health Care Services at www.drtiller.com.

59. Participant observation, Holiday Inn Express, St. Louis, MO, 12 June 2004.

60. Ibid.

61. Participant observation, Church of St. Louis, St. Louis, MO, 11 June 2004.

62. Troy Newman, interview by author, St. Louis, MO, 9 June 2004.

63. Troy Newman, interview by author, St. Louis, MO, 10 June 2004.

64. Risen and Thomas, *Wrath of Angels*, 78, 101–31, 217–23.

65. Romans 13; Mark 12:17.

66. Randall A. Terry, "Selling Out the Law of Heaven," *Washington Post*, 18 September 1994.

67. Operation Save America, "Incrementalism—A Lie from the Pit of Hell!" accessed on the website of Operation Rescue at www.operationsaveamerica.org/news/news/2001–04.thml, 19 June 2002.

68. Guy M. Condon, "You Say Choice, I Say Murder," *Christianity Today*, 24 June 1991, p. 22.

69. Paul Brenton, "Casualties of the Abortion Wars," *Christianity Today*, 16 October 1992, pp. 22–23.

70. David Shaw, "Abortion Bias Creeps into the News" *Los Angeles Times*, 1 July 1990.

71. Hunter, *Before the Shooting Begins*, 157–63.

72. Louis Bolce and Gerald De Maio, "A Prejudice for the Thinking Classes: Media Framing, Political Sophistication, and the Christian Fundamentalist," draft of paper to be presented at the annual meeting of the Southern Political Science Association Meeting, January 2007, 26–27. See also Louis Bolce and Gerald De Maio, "Religious Outlook, Culture War Politics, and Antipathy Toward Christian Fundamentalists," *Public Opinion Quarterly* 63 (Spring 1999): 29–61.

73. Bolce and De Maio, "A Prejudice for the Thinking Classes," 33–34.

74. Ibid., 42–45, 68.

75. Risen and Thomas, *Wrath of Angels*, 101–5.

76. Ibid.,139–40.

77. Michael Gerson, "A New Social Gospel," *Newsweek*, 13 November 2006.

78. E. J. Dionne, Jr., *Why Americans Hate Politics* (New York: Simon and Schuster, 1991), 42–45.

79. Quoted in David Cantor, *The Religious Right: The Assault on Tolerance and Pluralism in America* (New York: Anti-Defamation League, 1994), 23–26.

80. See Barbara Bradley Hagerty, "Christian Leaders Balk at Robertson's Remarks," *All Things Considered* radio broadcast, January 12, 2006, accessed on the website of National Public Radio at http://www.npr.org/templates/story/story.php?storyId=5151840, 12 February 2006.

81. On Focus on the Family's embrace of public reason see W. Bradford Wilcox, *Soft Patriarchs, New Men: How Christianity Shapes Fathers and Husbands* (Chicago, IL: University of Chicago Press, 2004), 34–35.

82. Clyde Wilcox, "Of Movements and Metaphors: The Co-Evolution of the Christian Right and the GOP," paper prepared for presentation at conference on the Christian Conservative Movement and American Democracy, April 2007, pp. 8–10.

83. Thomas Frank, *What's the Matter with Kansas? How Conservatives Won the Heart of America* (New York: Owl Books, 2004).

CHAPTER THREE
THE VARIETIES OF PRO-LIFE ACTIVISM

1. Richard Fenno, "U.S. House Members in Their Constituencies," *American Political Science Review* 71 (September 1977): 884.

2. Abortion also has a greater influence on other kinds of political activity compared to other social issues, including voting, campaign work, financial contributions, and contacting public officials. See Sidney Verba, Kay Lehman Schlozman, and Henry E. Brady, *Voice and Equality: Civic Volunteerism in American Politics* (Cambridge, MA: Harvard University Press, 1995), 84–89.

3. Dana Patton and Sara Zeigler, "Who's Winning and Why? A Comparative Study of a Feminist and Conservative Interest Group," paper presented at the annual meeting of the American Political Science Association, Philadelphia, PA, 31 August–3 September 2006, p. 24.

4. James Davison Hunter, *Before the Shooting Begins: Searching for Democracy in America's Culture War* (New York: Free Press, 1994), 13.

5. Amy Gutmann and Dennis Thompson, *Democracy and Disagreement* (Cambridge, MA: Harvard University Press, 1996), 74–77.

6. Shortly after each outreach, JFA administers a brief questionnaire that invites activists to reflect in an open-ended way on their experiences. In accordance with an agreement with Justice for All, I have changed the names of the volunteers.

7. Participant observation, Auraria Campus, Denver, CO, 12 April 2004.

8. David France, interview by author, Denver, CO, 12 April 2004.

9. Participant observation, Auraria Campus, Denver, CO, 12 April 2004.

10. All reflections were placed on a CD-ROM by Justice for All. See JFA Reflections, 1, 44–45, 162–63.

11. JFA Reflections, 6–7, 34–35, 68–69, 86–88.

12. JFA Reflections, 27–28, 103–7, 124–25, 130–32, 141–42.

13. Participant observation, Auraria Campus, Denver, CO, 12–14 April 2004.

14. Jeremy Alder, interview by author, Denver, CO, 14 April 2004.

15. See Andrew Webb, "Display Ignites Controversy: Responses to Graphic Exhibit Run Gamut from Horror to Support," *Daily Lobo*, 19 February 2002.

16. Amanda Hutchinson, "Pro-Life Display Draws Pro-Choice Opposition," *Daily Texan*, 21 February 2001.

17. Stephanie, interview by author, Denver, CO, 13 April 2004.

18. Interview by author, Denver, CO, 13 April 2004.

19. Michael, interview by author, Denver, CO, 13 April 2004.

20. Mishka, interview by author, Denver, CO, 13 April 2004.

21. Participant observation, Arvada Covenant Church, Arvada, CO, 12 April 2004.

22. JFA Reflections, 8–9.

23. JFA Reflections, 106–8, 130–32.

24. JFA Reflections, 130–32, 141–44.

25. Participant observation, Auraria Campus, Denver, CO, 14 April 2004.

26. Participant observation, Auraria Campus, Denver, CO, 12 April 2004.

27. Ibid.

28. Ibid.

29. Michael, interview by author, 13 April 2004.

30. Stephanie, interview by author, Denver, CO, 13 April 2004.

31. JFA Reflections, 124–25.

32. JFA Reflections, 15–16, 61, 66–67, 70–74, 77–78.

33. JFA Reflections, 17–18, 158–59, 118–19.

34. JFA Reflections, 46–48, 111–12, 133–35, 153–55.

35. JFA Reflections, 15–16, 21–23, 160–61.

36. Participant observation, Auraria Campus, Denver, CO, 12 April 2004.

37. Interview by author, Denver, CO, 13 April 2004.

38. Participant observation, Auraria Campus, Denver, CO, 14 April 2004.

39. Ibid.

40. David France, interview by author, Denver, CO, 14 April 2004.

41. Paul Troiani, interview by author, Boston, MA, 24 July 2004.

42. NARAL Pro-Choice America, *NARAL's Campus Kit For Pro-Choice Organizers* (Washington, DC: NARAL Foundation, Fall 2001), 42.

43. Email from Jamia Wilson, Campus Outreach Manager, Planned Parenthood, 24 November 2004.

44. See Pro-Choice Action Network, "Why We Don't Debate Anti-Choice Spokespersons," accessed on the website of the Pro-Choice Action Network at http://www.prochoiceactionnetwork-canada.org/articles/debate.shtml, 28 February 2006.

45. Serrin M. Foster, "The Feminist Case Against Abortion," *The American Feminist*, Summer/Fall 2004.

46. Nolen, interview by author, Granite City, IL, 10 June 2004.

47. Jessica, interview by author, Granite City, IL, 10 June 2004.

48. Participant observation, Hope Clinic for Women, Granite City, IL, 10 June 2004.

49. Jessica, interview by author, Granite City, IL, 10 June 2004.

50. Heather, interview by author, Granite City, IL, 11 June 2004.

51. Michaela, interview by author, Granite City, IL, 11 June 2004.

52. Chuck, interview by author, Granite City, IL, 12 June 2004.

53. Nolen, interview by author, Granite City, IL, 10 June 2004.

54. Participant observation, Hope Clinic for Women, Granite City, IL, 10 June 2004.

55. Angela Michaels, interview by author, St. Louis, MO, 9 June 2004.

56. Participant observation, Hope Clinic for Women, Granite City, IL, 10–11 June 2004.

57. Ibid.

58. Jessica, interview by author, Granite City, IL, 10 June 2004.

59. Participant observation, Planned Parenthood, St. Louis, MO, 12 June 2004.

60. Connie, interview by author, St. Louis, MO, 12 June 2004.

61. Participant observation, Planned Parenthood, St. Louis, MO, 12 June 2004.

62. Ibid.

63. Ibid.

64. Participant observation, Planned Parenthood, Boston, MA, 24 July 2004.

65. Tony, interview by author, Boston, MA, 24 July 2004.

66. Danny, interview by author, Boston, MA, 24 July 2004.

67. Phil, interview by author, Boston, MA, 24 July 2004.

68. Bill Cotter, interview by author, Boston, MA, 27 July 2004.

69. Participant observation, Planned Parenthood, Boston, MA, 23 July 2004.

70. Personal interview, Planned Parenthood, Boston, MA, 23 July 2004.

71. Participant observation, Planned Parenthood, Boston, MA, 23, 24, 27 July 2004.

72. Participant observation, Planned Parenthood, Boston, MA, 23 July 2004.

73. Theresa, interview by author, Boston, MA, 23 July 2004.

74. Courtney, interview by author, Washington, DC, 22 January 2005.

75. Participant observation, Planned Parenthood, Washington, DC, 22 January 2005.

76. "Remarks of President Bush via Telephone to March for Life Demonstration on the National Mall," *Federal News Service*, 24 January 2005.

77. Participant observation, Washington, DC, 24 January 2005.

78. In fact, the March for Women's Lives even made the Style Section of the *Washington Post*. See Hank Stuever, "Body Politics," *Washington Post*, 26 April 2004.

79. Participant observation, Washington, DC, 24 January 2005.

80. Ibid.

81. Ibid.

82. Bubba Garret, interview by author, Denver, CO, 14 April 2004.

83. Scott Klusendorf, interview by author, La Mirada, CA, 2 March 2004.

84. "Thousands Throng San Francisco Waterfront in Walk for Life," *America's Intelligence Wire*, 22 January 2005; Sara Steffens, "San Francisco Marchers Cover Both Sides of Abortion Issue," *Contra Costa Times*, 23 January 2005.

85. For video footage from a liberal group, see Jeff Patterson, "'Walk' for Life Meets Pro-Choice San Francisco," accessed on the website of Indybay at www.indybay.org/news/2005/01/1716850_comment.php, 8 February 2005; from Catholic sources see Eternal World Television Network, "Walk for Life: West Coast," *Life on the Rock*, aired 27 January 2005; Eternal World Television Network, "Walk for Life West Coast 2005," tapes 1 and 2.

86. Board of Supervisors, City and County of San Francisco, "San Francisco Supervisors Announce Official City Policy: San Francisco is Pro-Choice and Proud," Press Release, 11 January 2005.

87. Joe Garofoli, "Thousands Expected at Anti-abortion March," *San Francisco Chronicle*, 20 January 2005.

88. For video footage from a liberal group, see Jeff Patterson, "'Walk' for Life Meets Pro-Choice San Francisco," accessed on the website of Indybay at www.indybay.org/news/2005/01/1716850_comment.php, 8 February 2005; from Catholic sources see Eternal World Television Network, "Walk for Life: West Coast," *Life on the Rock*, aired 27 January 2005; Eternal World Television Network, "Walk for Life West Coast 2005," tapes 1 and 2.

89. Cicero A. Estrella and Henry K. Lee, "Protesters Face Off over Abortion Rights," *San Francisco Chronicle*, 23 January 2005.

90. Henry K. Lee, Wyatt Buchanan, and Michael Cabanatuan, "San Francisco Abortion Showdown," *San Francisco Chronicle*, 22 January 2006.

91. See "The 'Walk for Life' March and Counter-Demonstration," accessed on the website of Zombietime at http://www.zombietime.com/walk_for_life/, 14 June 2006; "Thousands Mark *Roe v. Wade* Anniversary," accessed on the website of the Fox News at http://www.foxnews.com/story/0,2933,182426,00.html, 14 June 2006.

92. Carol Morello and Yolanda Woodlee, "Anti-abortion Rally Confronts Huge March," *Washington Post*, 26 April 2004.

93. Toni Lacy, "Thousands March in DC to Protest 'War on Women,'" *USA Today*, 26 April 2004.

94. Danny, interview by author, Boston, MA, 24 July 2004.

95. Activist reflections can be found on the website of the Society for Truth and Justice at http://www.societyfortruthandjustice.com/letters_to_editor.htm, 10 November 2004.

96. Michael Ciccicioppo, interview by author, Alexandria, VA, 1 July 2004.

97. Participant observation of sermon delivered by Reverend Childress, Church of St. Louis, St. Louis, MO, 11 June 2004.

98. Participant observation, Boston, MA, 24–25 July 2004.

99. Paul Troiani, interview by author, Boston, MA, 25 July 2004.

100. Phil, interview by author, Boston, MA, 24 and 26 July 2004.

101. Melissa and Joy, interview by author, Boston, MA, 24 July 2005.

102. Participant observation, Boston, MA, 24–25 July 2004.

103. Participant observation, Boston, MA, 25 July 2004.

104. Participant observation, Boston, MA, 26 July 2004.

105. Ibid.

106. Ibid.

107. Ibid.

108. Ibid.

109. Gary McCullough, interview by author, Boston, MA, 26 July 2004.

110. Participant observation, Boston, MA, 26 July 2004.

111. Participant observation, Hope Clinic, Granite City, IL, 11 June 2004.

112. Troy Newman, interview by author, St. Louis, MO, 9 June 2004.

113. Participant observation, Granite City, IL, 11 June 2004.

114. See Kimberly Sevcik, "One Man's God Squad," accessed on the website of *Rolling Stone* at http://www.rollingstone.com/news/story/_/rnd/1091568353213/pageid/rs.Politics/has-player/true/id/6388324/version/6.0.11.847/page%20region/single6?rnd=1108067839843&has-player=true&version=6.0.8.1024, 12 February 2005.

115. Troy Newman, interview by author, St. Louis, MO, 9 July 2004.

116. These ideas are discussed at great length in Troy Newmnan, *Their Blood Cries Out* (Wichita, KS: Restoration Press, 2003), 184–86.

CHAPTER FOUR
DELIBERATION AND ABORTION POLITICS

1. Surveys have shown that the public regards pro-life activists as more "intolerant" and "extremist" than pro-choice activists. See James Davison Hunter, *Before the Shooting Begins: Searching for Democracy in America's Culture Wars* (New York: Free Press, 1994), 114–16.

2. David Shaw, "Abortion Bias Creeps into the News" *Los Angeles Times*, 1 July 1990.

3. Lori Kehoe, interview by author, telephone, 13 July 2004.

4. Hunter, *Before the Shooting Begins*, 163.

5. Eileen McDonagh, "Adding Consent to Choice in the Abortion Debate," *Society* 42 (July/August 2005): 19.

6. Dana Patton and Sara Zeigler, "Who's Winning and Why? A Comparative Study of a Feminist and Conservative Interest Group," paper presented at the annual meeting of the American Political Science Association, Philadelphia, PA, 31 August–3 September 2006, 24–26.

7. Kristin Luker, *Abortion and the Politics of Motherhood* (Berkeley, CA: University of California Press, 1984), esp. chaps. 7 and 8.

8. Cynthia Gorney, "Gambling with Abortion," *Harpers Magazine*, November 2004, p. 38.

9. Scott Klusendorf, interview by author, La Mirada, CA, 2 March 2004.

10. Cheryl Sullenger, interview by author, telephone, 21 September 2004.

11. Participant observation, Fredericksburg, VA, 19 October 2005.

12. Donna, interview by author, Boston, MA, 24 July 2004.

13. See Appleton's testimony on the website of the Pro-Life Action League at www307.pair.com/ejs/plal1/joan_appleton.htm, 13 December 2004.

14. See website of the Pro-Life Action League at www307.pair.com/ejs/plal1/Dr._Joseph_Randall.htm, 14 December 2004.

15. See website of the Pro-Life Action League at www307.pair.com/ejs/plal1/judithfetrow.htm, 13 December 2004.

16. See website of the Pro-Life Action League at www307.pair.com/ejs/plal1/kathy_spanks.htm, 13 December 2004.

17. Julia Duin, "Bernard Nathanson's Conversion," accessed on the website of the Eternal World Television Network at http://www.ewtn.com/library/prolife/bernconv.txt, 15 December 2004.

18. Robin Hoffman, interview by author, telephone, 13 July 2004.

19. Phil, interview by author, Boston, MA, 24 July 2004.

20. Hunter, *Before the Shooting Begins*, 116–17.

21. James Risen and Judy L. Thomas, *Wrath of Angels: The American Abortion War* (New York: Basic Books, 1998): 59.

22. National Abortion Federation, "NAF Violence and Disruption Statistics," accessed on the website of the National Abortion Federation at http://www.prochoice.org/pubs_research/publications/downloads/about_abortion/violence_statistics.pdf, 13 December 2006.

23. Focus on the Family radio broadcast, "Saving Babies Through Ultrasound," 26 April 2004.

24. Charles Taylor, *Sources of the Self: The Making of the Modern Identity* (Cambridge, MA: Harvard University Press, 1989), 393–401, 513–21.

25. Richard Sennett, *The Fall of Public Man* (New York: W. W. Norton, 1976), 3–6, 36–38, 259–68.

26. Jane J. Mansbridge, *Why We Lost the ERA* (Chicago, IL: University of Chicago Press, 1986), 133–35, 128–33.

27. Maryann Barakso, *Governing NOW: Grassroots Activism in the National Organization of Women* (Ithaca, NY: Cornell University Press, 2004), 64–68, 147, 151.

28. Interview with Anne Slater, WTO History Project, 12 December 2000.

29. Hank Stuever, "Body Politics," *Washington Post*, 26 April 2004.

30. David S. Broder, *Changing of the Guard: Power and Leadership in America* (New York: Simon and Schuster, 1980), 476.

31. Jon A. Shields, "Spiritual Politics on the Left," *Society* 43 (September/October 2006): 57–62.

32. Doug Rossinow, *The Politics of Authenticity: Liberalism, Christianity, and the New Left in America* (New York: Columbia University Press, 1998), 4–5.

33. Paul Berman, *A Tale of Two Utopias: The Political Journey of the Generation of 1968* (New York: W. W. Norton, 1997), 56.

34. E. J. Dionne, Jr., *Why Americans Hate Politics* (New York: Simon and Schuster, 1992), 37–38

35. Berman, *A Tale of Two Utopias*, 55–63, 83–90.

36. Sennett, *The Fall of Public Man*, 264–65.

37. NARAL Pro-Choice America, *NARAL's Campus Kit For Pro-Choice Organizers* (Washington, DC: NARAL Foundation, Fall 2001), 35.

38. Pro-Choice Action Network, "Why We Don't Debate Anti-Choice Spokespersons," accessed on the website of the Pro-Choice Action Network at

http://www.prochoiceactionnetwork-canada.org/articles/debate.shtml, 28 February 2006.

39. Rosamond Rhodes, "Reproduction, Abortion, and Rights," in David C. Thompson and Thomasine Kushner, eds., *Birth to Death: Science and Bioethics* (Cambridge, UK: Cambridge University Press, 1996), 59.

40. Judith Jarvis Thompson, "A Defense of Abortion," *Philosophy and Public Affairs* 1 (Fall 1971): 47.

41. Peter Singer, *Practical Ethics*, 2nd ed. (Cambridge, UK: Cambridge University Press, 1993), 149, 135–37.

42. Thompson, "A Defense of Abortion," 47–66.

43. Singer, *Practical Ethics*, 173, 169–74.

44. This is perhaps why Eileen McDonagh has recently insisted that pro-life advocates need to change the debate from what the fetus "is" to what it "does." See McDonagh, "Adding Consent to Choice in the Abortion Debate," 22–23.

45. Pro-Choice Action Network, "Why We Don't Debate Anti-Choice Spokespersons," accessed on the website of the Pro-Choice Action Network at http://www.prochoiceactionnetwork-canada.org/articles/debate.shtml, 28 February 2006.

46. Samuel Stouffer, *Communism, Conformity, and Civil Liberties* (New York: Doubleday, 1955); John L Sullivan, James E. Pierson, and George E. Marcus, "An Alternative Conceptualization of Political Tolerance," *American Political Science Review* 73 (September 1979): 233–49. On evangelicals, see Clyde Wilcox and Ted Jelen, "Evangelicals and Political Tolerance," *American Politics Quarterly* 18 (January 1990): 25–46; Clyde Wilcox, *Onward Christian Soldiers? The Religious Right in American Politics* (Boulder, CO: Westview Press, 2000), 110–11.

47. Some 40 percent of those with a college degree indicated that they would not allow a racist to teach in colleges or universities. Robert S. Erikson and Kent L. Tedin, *American Public Opinion*, 6th ed. (New York: Longman, 2001), 151.

48. John L. Sullivan, James Pierson, and George E. Marcus, *Political Tolerance and American Democracy* (Chicago, IL: University of Chicago Press, 1982), 2–3.

49. Steven E. Finkel, Lee Sigelman, and Stan Humphries, in John P. Robinson, Phillip R. Shaver, and Lawrence S. Wrightman, eds., *Measures of Political Attitudes* (San Diego, CA: Academic Press, 1999), 214–15.

50. Alan Wolfe, *One Nation, After All* (New York: Viking, 1998), 278.

CHAPTER FIVE
REVIVING PARTICIPATORY DEMOCRACY

1. Quotation from Mark J. Rozell and Clyde Wilcox, *Second Coming: The New Christian Right in Virginia Politics* (Baltimore, MD: Johns Hopkins University Press, 1996), 85.

2. Robert D. Putnam, *Bowling Alone: The Collapse and Revival of American Community* (New York: Simon and Schuster, 2000), 162.

3. African Americans were treated separately. Those who identified as members of nondenominational, community, interdenominational, and "just Christian" churches were counted as evangelicals.

4. However, there was a minor question wording change in 1980.

5. George M. Marsden, *Fundamentalism and American Culture: The Shaping of Twentieth-Century Evangelism, 1870–1925* (New York: Oxford University Press, 1980), vi, 185, 188–89.

6. Peter Beinart, "Morally Correct," *New Republic*, 29 November 2004, pp. 6–8; Peter Beinart, "Parlor Game," *New Republic*, 26 January 2004, p. 6.

7. Marsden, *Fundamentalism and American Culture*, vi, 35–39, 66–71, 85–93, 118–23, 204–5.

8. Ibid., 127–32, 142–45, 149–50, 160–61, 210–11.

9. James Risen and Judy T. Thomas, *Wrath of Angels: The American Abortion War* (New York: Basic Books, 1998), 218–19.

10. Stuart Rothenberg and Frank Newport, *The Evangelical Voter* (Washington, DC: Free Congress Research and Education Foundation, 1984), 10, 81–90, 103.

11. Jeffrey Hadden, Anson Shupe, James Howdin, and Kenneth Martin, "Why Jerry Falwell Killed the Moral Majority," in Marshall W. Fishwick and Ray B. Browne, eds., *The God Bumpers: Religion in the Electronic Age* (Bowling Green, OH: Bowling Green State University Popular Press, 1987), 102.

12. Michael D'Antonio, *Fall from Grace: The Failed Crusade of the Christian Right* (New York: Farrar, Straus, Giroux, 1989), 13.

13. Mary E. Bendyna and Clyde Wilcox, "The Christian Right Old and New: A Comparison of the Moral Majority with the Christian Coalition," in Corwin E. Smidt and James M. Penning, eds., *Sojourners in the Wilderness: The Christian Right in Comparative Perspective* (New York: Rowman and Littlefield, 1997), 42–45.

14. Christian Coalition, *Training Seminar Manual, Level 1* (Chesapeake, VA: Christian Coalition, 1995), 19–45.

15. Christian Coalition, *Blueprint for Victory*, 12 September 1997, 28–36.

16. Quoted in Mathew Continetti, "A Decade of Reed: One Republican's Long, Lucrative March Through the Institutions," *Weekly Standard*, 27 June 2005.

17. Hayden et al., "Why Jerry Falwell Killed the Moral Majority," 102.

18. Rick Forcier, interview by author, telephone, 17 June 2002.

19. John Fugatt, interview by author, Huntington Beach, CA, 19 June 2002.

20. James L Guth et al., "Onward Christian Soldiers: Religious Activist Groups in American Politics," in John C. Green et al., eds., *Religion and the Culture Wars: Dispatches from the Front* (New York: Rowman and Littlefield, 1996), 81.

21. Christian Coalition, *Annual Report*, 1996, p. 8.

22. Mark J. Rozell, "Growing Up Politically: The New Politics of the New Christian Right," in Corwin E. Smidt and James M. Penning, eds., *Sojourners in the Wilderness: The Christian Right in Comparative Perspective* (New York: Rowman and Littlefield, 1997), 243.

23. Justin Watson, *The Christian Coalition: Dreams of Restoration, Demands for Recognition* (New York: Palgrave Macmillan, 1997), 54.

24. Most academic accounts, for example, placed the Christian Coalition's actual membership at less than 1 million members. See Bendyna and Wilcox, "The Christian Right Old and New," 47.

25. John Dickey, interview by author, telephone, 24 June 2002; John Fugatt, interview by author, Huntington Beach, CA, 19 June 2004.

26. Collinearity is not a concern. The largest correlation was between education and income at .40.

27. Richard C. Land, "Why Christians Should Vote Their Values," accessed on website of the National Right to Life Committee at nrlc.org/news/2000/NRL10/land.html, 21 February 2004.

28. Ralph Reed, "We Can't Stop Now," *Christianity Today*, 6 September 1999.

29. Letter by James Dobson, 13 August 2004.

30. James Dobson, "Your Voice Matters," *Focus on the Family*, October/November 2004, pp. 8–9.

31. Bill Sammon, "Evangelicals Endeavor to Redeem the Vote, *Washington Times*, 19 October 2004.

32. James Dobson, "Family News Forum," October 2004.

33. Accessed on the website of the Center for Reclaiming American at http://www.reclaimamerica.org/PAGES/grassroots.asp, 14 June 2005.

34. Ken Connonr and John Revell, *Sinful Silence: When Christians Neglect their Civic Duty* (Nashville, TN: Ginosko Publishing, 2004).

35. Transcript of the radio broadcast was accessed on the website of Coral Ridge Presbyterian Church at http://www.coralridge.org/specialdocs/minnerytranscript.pdf, 14 June 2005.

36. Chuck Colson, "A Sacred Duty: Why Christians Must Vote," accessed on the website of Townhall at http://www.townhall.com/columnists/chuckcolson/cc20040514.shtml, 16 June 2005.

37. William L. Fisher, Ralph Reed, and Richard L. Weinhold, *Christian Coalition Leadership Manual*, 1990, p. 2.3.

38. Bill Thompson, interview by author, telephone, 18 June 2002.

39. Letter to pastors, 30 August 2002.

40. National Pro-Life Religious Council, "A Statement by the National Pro-Life Religious Council on the Urgent Necessity of Participation in Our National Elections," accessed on the website of the National Right to Life Committee at www.nrlc.org/news/2000/NRL10/nprc.html, 21 February 2004.

41. Cal Thomas, "Have We Settled for Caesar?" *Christianity Today*, 6 September 1999.

42. Cal Thomas and Ed Dobson, *Blinded by Might: Can the Christian Right Save America* (Grand Rapids, MI: Zondervan, 1999).

43. *Beverly LaHaye Live*, radio broadcast, "Go Out to Vote," 31 October 2002.

44. Fisher, Reed, and Wienhold, *Christian Coalition Leadership Manual*, p. 2.2.

45. Guth and others, "Onward Christian Soldiers," 72.

46. Institute for First Amendment Studies and Bliss Institute of the University of Akron, "Survey of Christian Right Activists," accessed at the website of the Institute for First Amendment Studies at www.ifas.org/library/survey/index.html, 9 July 2002.

47. Ibid.

48. Accessed on the website of Rock the Vote at http://www.rockthevote.com/ is_whyvote.php, downloaded 16 June 2005.

49. Accessed on the website of Redeem the Vote at http://www.capitolconnect .com/redeemthevote/, 16 June 2005.

50. Peter Beinart, "Morally Correct," *New Republic*, 29 November 2004.

51. Charles Colson and Anne Morse, "Reclaiming Occupied Territory: The Great Commission and Cultural Commission Are Not in Competition," accessed on the website of *Christianity Today* at http://www.christianitytoday.com/ct/ 2004/august/11.64.html, 15 June 2005.

52. Transcript of the radio broadcast was accessed on the website of Coral Ridge Presbyterian Church at http://www.coralridge.org/specialdocs/ minnerytranscript.pdf, 14 June 2005.

53. Tom Zucco, Tim Grant, and Jeffrey Gettleman, "Thou Shall Vote," *St. Petersburg Times*, 4 November 1996.

54. Participant observation, Church of St. Louis, St. Louis, Missouri, 11 June 2004.

55. Sidney M. Milkis and Jesse H. Rhodes, "George W. Bush, the Republican Party, and the 'New' American Party System," *Perspectives on Politics 5* (September 2007): 469, 471.

56. Milkis and Rhodes, "George W. Bush, the Republican Party, and the 'New' American Party System," 473

CHAPTER SIX
PARTICIPATION, DELIBERATION, AND VALUES VOTERS

1. Thomas Frank, *What's the Matter with Kansas? How Conservatives Won the Heart of America* (New York: Owl Books, 2004), 239.

2. Jim Wallis, *God's Politics: Why the Right Gets It Wrong, and the Left Doesn't Get It* (New York: HarperCollins, 2005). Richard Rorty argues that since the 1960s the Left has been obsessed with cultural politics at the expense of the material concerns that preoccupied earlier generations of leftists. Richard Rorty, *Achieving Our Country: Leftist Thought in Twentieth-Century America* (Cambridge, MA: Harvard University Press, 1998), 76–77.

3. Chris Mooney, *The Republican War on Science* (New York: Basic Books, 2006). For a similar enthusiasm for neutral expertise, see Jonathan Chait, *The Big Con: The True Story of How Washington Got Hoodwinked and Hijacked by Crackpot Economics* (New York: Houghton Mifflin, 2007).

4. E. J. Dionne, Jr., *Why Americans Hate Politics* (New York: Simon and Schuster, 1991), chap. 13.

5. Sidney Verba, Kay Lehman Schlozman, and Henry E. Brady, *Voice and Equality: Civic Volunteerism in American Politics* (Cambridge, MA: Harvard University Press, 1995), 494–500, 518–21.

6. Jacob S. Hacker and Paul Pierson, *Off Center: The Republican Revolution and the Erosion of American Democracy* (New Haven: Yale University Press), 9.

7. Morris P. Fiorina, *Culture War? The Myth of a Polarized America*, 2d ed. (New York: Pearson Longman 2006).

8. James Q. Wilson, *The Amateur Democrat: Club Politics in Three Cities* (Chicago, IL: University of Chicago Press, 1962), 2–16.

9. Report of the Committee on Political Parties, "Toward a More Responsible Two-Party System," *American Political Science Review* 3 (September 1950): suppl: v.

10. Theodore J. Lowi, *The End of Liberalism: The Second Republic of the United States*, 2nd ed. (New York: W.W. Norton, 1979), 313.

11. Excerpts from *The Port Huron Statement* are found in an appendix in James Miller, *Democracy is in the Streets: From Port Huron to the Siege of Chicago* (New York: Simon and Schuster, 1987), 337. Charles Capper and Kim Moody, "The Case for a Third Party: A Critique of American Liberalism," paper prepared for the 1964 National Convention of Students for a Democratic Society, June 1964, pp. 5, 10.

12. Tom Hayden to Students for Democratic Society Executive Committee, 5 April 1962, p. 6.

13. See appendix in Miller, *Democracy is in the Streets*, 331, 337.

14. Richard Flacks, "American Scene Document (Draft)," 7 June 1973, I-8.

15. See appendix in Miller, *Democracy is in the Streets*, 362.

16. Ibid.

17. Ibid., 331, 362.

18. Anthony King, ed., *The New American Political System* (Washington, DC: AEI Press, 1979).

19. Gary C. Jacobson, "Party Polarization in National Politics: The Electoral Connection," in Jon R. Bond and Richard Fleisher, eds., *Polarized Politics: Congress and the President in a Partisan Era* (Washington, DC: Congressional Quarterly Press, 2000): 9–30.

20. John R. Zaller, *The Nature and Origins of Mass Opinion* (New York: Cambridge University Press, 1992), 9.

21. James Q. Wilson, "Polarization in America: Politics and Polarization," Tanner lecture delivered at Harvard University, 3 November 2005, p, 16

22. Michael P. McDonald and Samuel L. Popkin, "The Myth of the Vanishing Voter," *American Political Science Review* 95 (December 2001): 963–74.

23. Michael McDonald, "5 Myths about Turning out the Vote," *Washington Post*, 29 October 2006.

24. John G. Geer, *In Defense of Negativity: Attach Ads in Presidential Campaigns* (Chicago, IL: University of Chicago Press, 2006); Paul Freedman and Kenneth Goldstein, "Measuring Media Exposure and the Effects of Negative Campaign Ads," *American Journal of Political Science* 43 (October 1999): 1189–208.

25. Jacobson, "Party Polarization in National Politics," 9–30.

26. Mark Button and Kevin Mattson, "Deliberative Democracy in Practice: Challenges and Prospects for Civic Deliberation," *Polity* 31 (Summer 1999): 609–37.

27. Thomas E. Patterson, *Out of Order* (New York: Vintage Books, 1994), 62–63; Doris A. Graber, *Mass Media and American Politics*, 6th ed. (Washington, DC: Congressional Quarterly Press, 2002), 178–79.

28. Edward G. Carmines and James A. Stimson, "The Two Faces of Issue Voting," in Richard G. Niemi and Herbert F. Weisberg, eds., *Classics in Voting Behavior* (Washington, DC: Congressional Quarterly Press, 1994), 115.

29. Robert S. Erikson and Kent L. Tedin, *American Public Opinion: Its Origins, Content, and Impact*, 6th ed. (New York: Longman, 2001), 58–61.

30. Steven J. Rosenstone and John Mark Hansen, *Mobilization, Participation, and Democracy in America* (New York: Macmillan, 1993), 34, 214–19.

31. Verba, Schlozman, and Brady, *Voice and Equality*, 398–415.

32. Ronald Inglehart and Paul R. Abramson, "Economic Security and Value Change," *American Political Science Review* 88 (June 1994): 336–54.

33. Edward L. Glaeser and Bryce A. Ward, "Myths and Realities of American Political Geography," Discussion Paper No. 2100, Harvard Institute of Economic Research, Cambridge, MA, 10–11 January 2006, pp. 22–28.

34. Hacker and Pierson, *Off Center*, 186–87.

35. Dionne, *Why Americans Hate Politics*, 35–37.

36. Jeffrey M. Berry, *The New Liberalism: The Rising Power of Citizen Groups* (Washington, DC: Brookings Institution Press, 1999).

37. Robert D. Putnam, *Bowling Alone: The Collapse and Revival of American Community* (New York: Simon and Schuster, 2000), 51.

38. Flacks, "American Scene Document (Draft)," II-1; Tom Hayden to SDS Executive Committee, 5; Capper and Moody, "The Case for a Third Party," 2.

39. See appendix in Miller, Democracy is in the Streets, 331-

40. The few liberal thinkers who advocate for a reversal of *Roe* do so because they believe that liberals will benefit. See, for example, Benjamin Wittes, "Letting Go of *Roe*," *Atlantic Monthly*, January/February 2005, pp. 48–53.

41. Morris P. Fiorina, "Extreme Voices: A Dark Side of Civic Engagement," in Theda Skocpol and Morris P. Fiorina, eds., *Civic Engagement in American Democracy* (Washington, DC: Brookings Institution Press, 1999), 411–13.

42. James Davison Hunter, *Before the Shooting Begins: Searching for Democracy in America's Culture War* (New York: Free Press, 1994), 86–90.

43. Mary Ann Glendon, *Abortion and Divorce in Western Law* (Cambridge, MA: Harvard University Press, 1987); Mary Ann Glendon, *Rights Talk: The Impoverishment of Political Discourse* (New York: Free Press, 1991), chap. 3.

44. Stephen K. White, *Sustaining Affirmation: The Strength of Weak Ontology in Political Theory* (Princeton, NJ: Princeton University Press, 2000), 6–11, 149–53.

45. Adam B. Seligman, *Modernity's Wager: Authority, the Self, and Transcendence* (Princeton, NJ: Princeton University Press, 2000), 128–30, 136–41.

46. Amy Gutmann and Dennis Thompson, *Democracy and Disagreement* (Cambridge, MA: Harvard University Press, 1996), 77–78, 41–44.

47. Lawrence Tribe, *Abortion: The Clash of Absolutes* (New York: W. W. Norton, 1990); Roger Rosenblatt, *Life Itself: Abortion in the American Mind* (New York: Random House, 1992).

48. See Hunter, *Before the Shooting Begins*, 23–27. See also Michael W. McConnell, "How Not to Promote Serious Deliberation about Abortion," *University of Chicago Law Review* 58 (Summer 1991): 1181–202.

49. Gutmann and Thompson, *Democracy and Disagreement*, 74–79.

50. Robert P. George, "Democracy and Moral Disagreement: Reciprocity, Slavery, and Abortion," in Stephen Macedo, ed., *Deliberative Politics: Essays on Democracy and Disagreement* (New York: Oxford University Press, 1999), 191.

51. Diana C. Mutz, *Hearing the Other Side: Deliberative Versus Participatory Democracy* (New York: Cambridge University Press, 2006).

52. Amy Gutmann, *Democratic Education* (Princeton, NJ: Princeton University Press, 1985).

53. See Joseph M. Bessette, *The Mild Voice of Reason: Deliberative Democracy and American National Government* (Chicago, IL: University of Chicago Press, 1997), 34–36.

Index

Note: Page references in italics refer to illustrations.

abolitionist movement, 3
Abortion: The Clash of Absolutes (Tribe), 158
Abortion and the Politics of Motherhood (Luker), 11, 68, 102–3, 105–7
abortion clinics: disruption/harassment/violence at, 54–58, 56 (table), 58 (table), 96–98, 106 (*see also under* rescue movement); sidewalk counselors at, 31–32, 58 (*see also* sidewalk counselors). *See also* Hope Clinic for Women
abortion debate: abortion decisions as religious, 34; culture's influence on, 100, 107–10; dispassionate vs. passionate approaches to, 157–58; and the fetus's ontological status, 44, 111–12; images of aborted fetuses used in, 43–44, 47, 103–4; influence of on political/protest activity, 68–69, 176n2; "the less advantaged" vs. abortion, emphasis on, 155; motherhood conceptions in, 11, 102–7; vs. other social issues, 69; Judith Jarvis Thompson's violinist analogy, 111. *See also* deliberation and abortion politics; pro-choice movement; pro-life activism; *Roe v. Wade*
Abortion Handbook (B. Willke), 103
accuracy as a deliberative norm, 19, 39–45
activists, Christian Right: democratic education of (*see* democratic education in the Christian Right). *See* Christian radicalism; Christian Right; pro-life activism
advocacy groups, 150
agape, 107
Alcorn, Randy: *Pro-Life Answers to Pro-Choice Arguments*, 44
Alder, Jeremy, 76–77
Almond, Gabriel: *Strong Religion*, 12–13
American Academy of Arts and Sciences (University of Chicago), 12
American Political Science Association, 149
American Prospect, 13
Ammiano, Tom, 91
Anderson, Kerby, 36
anticommunism, 7, 112, 155

anti-intellectualism, 42
Appelby, R. Scott: *Strong Religion*, 12–13
Appleton, Joan, 104
Arizona Right to Life, 26, 34
Arkansas Right to Life, 26
Ault, James, 51–52
authenticity, 107–10. *See also* participatory freedom

Banfield, Edward, 17
Baptists, 128, 132
Barakso, Maryann, 108
Barber, Benjamin, 29
Beinart, Peter, 117, 145
Bell, Daniel, 8, 11
Bendyna, Mary, 128
Berman, Paul, 109
Berry, Jeffrey, 154
Beverly LaHaye Live, 169n90
bioethics, 39, 81, 111. *See also* abortion debate
Birthright, 38, 43
Bivins, Jason, 14
Black Power, 3
Bolce, Louis, 61–62
"bowling alone" thesis, 2
Brady, Henry, 11, 148, 155
Broder, David, 109
Bunzel, John, 9
Burgess, Sally, 96
Bush, George W., 14, 39, 66, 88–89, 146
Button, Mark, 151–52

California Life Coalition, 57, 103
Calvinism, 3, 59
Care Net: Abortion Education Guidelines, 43; on confrontation, 29; deliberative norms promoted by, 24, 32, 40–41; evangelical mission of, 38–39; on images of aborted fetuses, 43; size of, 20
Carmines, Edward, 152
Carter, Jimmy, 119–20
Catholics: vs. Baptists, 128; conservative, 54, 107; counter-demonstrations by,

Catholics (*cont'd*)
94–95; fundamentalist, 8; lower-class, 7–8; moderate, 52–53; and philosophical/scientific vs. religious arguments, 37–38, 50; in the rescue movement, 27; sidewalk counseling by, 84–88; sit-ins by, 63–64; voter guides distributed to, 130. See also *Abortion and the Politics of Motherhood*

Cavanaugh-O'Keefe, John, 64, 105

Center for Bio-Ethical Reform (CBR): dialogue promoted by, 31; media coverage of, 62; moral passion stoked by, 43; political action by, 145–46; pro-life leaders' criticism/praise of, 60; size of, 20, 71

Center for Reclaiming America, 24, 40–42, 143

Central Valley Family Forum (CVFF), 21

Childress, Clenard, 90, 92

Chivers, Pat, 34, 41

Christian apologetics, 2, 36, 44, 157

Christian authenticity, 107–10

Christian Coalition: church liaisons of, 129, 154; decline of, 68, 116, 140, 146; deliberative norms promoted by, 30, 38, 54; on duty of political action, 143–44; grassroots-mobilization strategies of, 127–32; on liberals' tactics/bigotry/intolerance, 47–48; mailings by, 47–49; membership figures for, 55; neighborhood coordinators of, 129; Reed's leadership of, 65, 129, 140; rise of, 116; Robertson's leadership of, 65; size of, 19–20, 25, 183n24; training seminars by, 25, 129; voter guides distributed by, 40, 129–32, 135

Christian Coalition–California, 129, 143

Christian Coalition–Colorado, 21

Christian Coalition–Florida, 25

Christian Coalition–New Jersey, 21

Christian Coalition–Ohio, 51

Christian Coalition–Oregon, 42

Christian Coalition–South Carolina, 42

Christian Coalition–Texas, 42

Christian Coalition–Washington State, 129

Christian conservatives: alienation of, 1–2, 18, 115, 117–19, 119 (table); and Islamic terrorists, 12–13. See also Christian Right

Christian diplomacy (ambassadorship), 21–23, 35, 58

Christianity Today, 27, 36, 40

Christian love, 2–3, 20, 22–24, 27–28, 59, 70. See also civility

A Christian Manifesto (Schaffer), 53

Christian radicalism, 46–67; biblically based militancy of, 59; on compromise, 52; vs. deliberative moderation, 3–4; of Falwell, 22–23; international effects of, 27–28; media coverage of, 46, 60–67, 63–64 (tables); mobilizing the faithful, 46–49 (*see also* grassroots mobilization; participatory democracy's revival among evangelicals); overview of, 17, 46; in the rescue movement, 17; rise and fall of organized fundamentalism, 50–60, 56 (table), 58 (table); of Robertson, 22–23, 117; sources of, 46. See also rescue movement; sidewalk counselors

Christian Right: accused of threatening democratic values, 1; characterizations of opponents of, 47–48; conservative Christians mobilized by, 1–3, 18 (*see also* grassroots mobilization; participatory democracy's revival among evangelicals); criticism of, overview of, 10–15; deliberative norms promoted by, 2, 17–19 (*see also* democratic education in the Christian Right); demise of, presumed, 123; democracy reinvigorated by, 2–3; direct mail used by, 47–49, 121; as fundamentalist, 12; on gay rights and homosexuals, 14; as hate-driven, allegedly, 14; incentives to excite moral passions of activists, 15–16, 19 (*see also* Christian radicalism); media coverage of (*see under* Christian radicalism); and the New Left, 47–48, 153–55; organizational decline in, 124; philosophical arguments encouraged over scriptural arguments, 2, 157; and pluralism, fear of, 12; socially conservative campaigns, 114. See also *specific organizations*

Ciccocioppo, Michael, 37, 92

Citizen, 27, 36, 40

Citizens Participation Survey, 68–69

civility: and authenticity, 107–10; of Christian Right activists, 2; democratic education in, 19–29, 44–45; and the politics of motherhood, 102–7; and strategic incentives, 101–2

civil rights movement, 3

Clark, Peter, 10

"clash of civilizations" theory, 13

Clinton, Bill, 48, 137–40
Colorado University–Denver, 22
Colossians, 24
Colson, Charles, 23, 27, 36, 143, 145
"Coming Out of the Closet" campaign, 28
Common Cause, 131
Community College of Denver, 22
Concerned Women for America. See CWA
Condon, Guy M., 27
Connor, Ken, 143
converts, 103–5
Cook, Tammy, 76
Coral Ridge Presbyterian Church
    (Fort Lauderdale), 23–24
Cords, Corrine, 76
2 Corinthians, 22
Corrigan, Don, 13
Cotter, William, 55, 86
counter-demonstrations, 79–80, 91–96
Creative Resistance, 73–74
Cromartie, Michael, 66
Crossed, Carol, 90
culture wars, 9–11, 14, 27, 41, 43,
    102–3, 151. See also abortion debate;
    moral conflict
Culture Wars (Hunter), 49, 68
Cunningham, Greg, 31, 43–44
CVFF (Central Valley Family Forum), 21
CWA (Concerned Women for America):
    decline of, 68; deliberative norms
    promoted by, 21, 30, 36, 41–42, 53,
    169n90; Freedom of Choice Act op-
    posed by, 48; grassroots mobilization
    by, 129–30; on liberals' tactics/bigotry/
    intolerance, 47–48; mailings by, 47–48;
    membership figures for, 55; size of,
    19–20, 25, 129–30; voter guides distrib-
    uted by, 130

Dannenbaum, Jed, 5
D'Antonio, Michael, 123
Darwinism, 117
Deaton, Marnie, 21
DeLay, Tom, 39
deliberation: limits of, 147, 158–59; norms
    of, 2, 4–5, 16–19, 100–102, 107, 112–
    14, 157 (see also civility; democratic edu-
    cation in the Christian Right; dialogue);
    and participation, 3–5, 46, 159
deliberation and abortion politics, 100–
    114; civility and authenticity, 107–10;
    civility and strategic incentives, 101–2;

civility and the politics of motherhood,
    11, 102–7; dialogue and abortion, 110–
    12; overview of, 18, 100, 113–14; social
    science and tolerance, 112–13, 182n47.
    See also pro-choice movement; pro-life
    activism
deliberative democracy: and interests, 15–
    16; Madison on, 159; moral skepticism's
    role in, 2–3, 156–58; participation as
    good for, 5; scholarship on, 17
De Maio, Gerald, 61–62
democratic education in the Christian
    Right, 19–45; in accuracy/moral reason-
    ing, 19, 39–45; in avoiding religious
    arguments in public forums, 19, 33–39,
    44–45, 169n90; in civility/respect, 19–
    29, 44–45; confidence vs. moral skepti-
    cism fostered by, 2–3; and conservative
    activists vs. ordinary Americans, 30; in
    dialogue, 19, 29–33, 44–45; moral pas-
    sion's role in, 43–44, 159; overview of,
    17, 19–20, 44–45; in skepticism/open-
    ness to alternative viewpoints, 19
Democratic National Convention, 86,
    91–92, 95
Democratic Party, 120–21, 148–49
Democrats for Life, 90
Detwiler, Fritz, 14
Dewey, John, 15
dialogue: and abortion, 110–12; demo-
    cratic education in, 19, 29–33, 44–45;
    by pro-life activists, generally, 106, 114
Diamond, Sara, 14
Dionne, E. J., 14, 64–65, 109, 148,
    153–54
direct mail, 47–49, 51, 121
Dobson, James, 23, 43, 65–67, 106, 143
Dolce, Dauneen, 41
Dole, Bob, 138–40
Donahue, 35
Duffy, Bevan, 91

Eagle Forum, 53
economic (rational) vs. noneconomic
    (irrational) interests, 6–11, 148, 154
eco-terrorists, 4
Ehrenreich, Barbara, 13
Eidsmore, John, 54
Elmer Gantry (Lewis), 117
embryonic stem cell research, 35, 39
Environmental Defense Fund, 154
environmental movement, 4

Ephesians, 97
Equal Rights Amendment (ERA), 108
Etzioni, Amitai, 49
everyday talk, 47
expressive group action, 9–10

FACE (Federal Freedom of Clinics En-
trance Act; 1994), 55–56
The Fall of Public Man (Sennett), 107–8
false witness, 2, 40
Falwell, Jerry: criticism/unpopularity of, 4,
22–23, 51; on homosexuality, 35; on
Islam, 28; political militancy of, 50; vs.
Reed, 54; sensationalism of, 52. See also
Moral Majority
Family Forum II (1982), 53
Farris, Michael, 31, 42
Federal Freedom of Clinics Entrance Act
(FACE; 1994), 55–56
Feminist Alliance, 74, 79–80
Feminist Majority, 94
feminists: on abortion, 90, 94–95; and
participatory freedom, 100, 108–9 (see
also pro-choice movement); and pro-life
activism, 105; on the temperance
movement, 5
Feminists for Life, 81, 89–90
Fenno, Richard, 17, 68
Ferber, Abby, 14
Fetrow, Judith, 104
FFI (Focus on the Family Institute; Colo-
rado Springs), 71
Finkel, Steve E., 112
Fiorina, Morris, 6, 9–10, 14–15, 148, 155
First Right, 35
Focus on the Family, 23, 27, 33, 40–41,
55, 66–67, 106, 143–44
Focus on the Family Institute (FFI; Colo-
rado Springs), 71
Forcier, Rick, 129
Forney, Georgette, 90
Foster, Serrin, 81
France, David, 77, 80
Frank, Thomas, 6, 66–67; What's the
Matter with Kansas? 8, 11, 148
Free Congress Foundation, 53
Freedom of Choice Act, 48
Friedman, Thomas, 1
Fugatt, John, 143
fundamentalism: bias against, 61–62; Cath-
olic, 8; Christian and Islamic, 12–13;
definition of, 12; militant, 3, 46; orga-

nized, rise and fall of, 50–60, 56 (table),
58 (table); party affiliations of fundamentalists, 120–21
Fundamentalism Project, 12

Gallup, George W., 120
Gandhi, Mahatma, 50
Gandy, Kim, 108
Garret, Bubba, 90
Garrisonians, 3
gay marriage/rights, 14, 69, 102, 114
gender roles, 11, 102–7. See also feminists
Genesis, 59
George, Robert, 50, 66, 158
Georgetown University, 81
Gerson, Michael, 64
Gitlin, Todd, 64–65
Glaeser, Edward L., 153
Glendon, Mary Ann, 156
global justice movement, 109
God Hates Fags, 3
Gorney, Cynthia, 103
Gosnell, Chuck, 21
Gospels, 2, 21, 99
Graham, Joseph, 38
grassroots mobilization, 126–40; by the
Christian Coalition, 127–32; by the
CWA, 129–30; influences/variables af-
fecting voter turnout, 132–36, 134
(table), 136–39 (tables), 184n26; and the
Moral Majority's failures, 126–29; by
the NRLC, 130; via religious groups,
135, 136–39 (tables), 138–40, 141–42
(tables); via voter guides, 40, 129–32,
131, 135–40
Greenpeace, 154
Grey, Thomas, 36
Grimm, Jane, 26
Grisez, Germain, 50
Groopman, Jerome, 39
Gunderson, Adolf, 29
Gunn, David, 55
Gusfield, Joseph, 7
Guterman, Norbert, 8–9
Guth, James, 51
Gutmann, Amy, 33, 69, 156–59

Hacker, Jacob, 148, 153
Hadden, Jeffrey, 51, 129
Hansen, John, 152
Hard Truth, 103–4
Harper's, 14

Harrison, Dian, 91
Harvard Club, 94
Harvard Law Review, 56
Hayden, Tom, 109, 149–50
Hedges, Chris, 13
Hirschman, Albert, 7, 16
Hoffman, Robin, 105
Hofstadter, Richard, 8, 11, 42
honesty, 2
Hope, David, 145
Hope Clinic for Women (Granite City, Illinois), 83–86, 96–97
Human Life of Washington, 26, 34
Humphries, Stan, 112
Hunter, James: on the abortion debate, 69, 155, 158; on activist rhetoric, 14; *Culture Wars*, 49, 68; on direct mail, 49; on media bias, 61; on the Moral Majority, 51
Huntington, Samuel, 13

Inglehart, Ronald, 152–53
interest-group theory, 9, 16
interviewing methods, 70
Iraq War, 92–93
Islam, 28

Jacobson, Gary, 150–51
Jesus Christ, 2; command not to judge others, 31; command to love one's neighbor, 3, 20; conditions for return of, 118; on respect for authority, 59; as vengeful, 58–59
JFA. *See* Justice for All
Johnson, Paul, 47
Jones, Marsha, 12
Justice for All (JFA): Auraria campus outreach (Denver), 22, 28, 71–80; deliberative norms promoted by, 31, 35, 72–79; media coverage of, 62; moral passion stoked by, 43; pro-choice counter-demonstrations against, 79–80; on the pro-choice response to images of aborted fetuses, 43; size of, 20, 71; supernatural orientation in, 75; volunteers trained in, 22, 28, 71–72, 76–77, 176n6

Kehoe, Lori, 20, 101
Keleher, Christopher, 56
Kennedy, Dan, 34
Kennedy, James D., 23–24, 143, 145
Kerry, John, 34, 92–93

King, David, 10
King, Martin Luther, Jr., 50
Klusendorf, Scott, 22–23, 35, 42–43, 80–81, 90, 103
Koukl, Greg, 35
Kuttner, Robert, 1

LaHaye, Beverly, 21, 53, 169n90
Land, Richard, 142
Lasswell, Harold, 7, 11
leaderless politics, 109
Leadership Institute, 30, 53
LEARN (Life Educational and Resource Network), 90
Lee, Patrick, 50
Left vs. Right, 106–7. *See also* Christian Right; New Left
Lerner, Michael, 53
Lewis, Sinclair: *Elmer Gantry*, 117; *Main Street*, 117
liberals. *See* New Left
Life Advocate, 88
Life and Liberty Ministries (Virginia), 27, 29, 32
Life Chain, 23
Life Educational and Resource Network (LEARN), 90
Life Itself (Rosenblatt), 158
Life Training Institute, 103
Lincoln, Abraham, 41, 66
Lipset, Seymour Martin, 6–8, 11
listening and asking questions. *See* dialogue
Listing, Barbara, 21, 37
The Logic of Collective Action (Olson), 9
Los Angeles Times, 60–61, 101
love, Christian. *See* Christian love
loving one's neighbor, 2–3, 20
Lowenthal, Leo, 8–9
Lowi, Theodore, 149
Luker, Kristen, 6; *Abortion and the Politics of Motherhood*, 11, 68, 102–3, 105–7

Madison, James, 6–7, 159
magazines. *See* media; *and specific magazines*
Mahoney, Pat, 92–94
Main Street (Lewis), 117
Mansbridge, Jane, 47, 108
marches, 29, 47, 90, 92, 99; March for Life, 88–89; March for Women's Lives, 89, 91, 101, 109

Marsden, George, 117–18

Marty, Martin E., 12

masks, 108, 110

Massachusetts Citizens for Life, 26

Mattson, Kevin, 151–52

McCarthyism, 7–8

McCullough, Gary, 95

McDonagh, Eileen, 101

McDonald, Michael, 151

McGreevy, John, 52

media: Christian radicalism covered by, 46, 60–67, 63–64 (tables), 101; of the Christian Right, 65–67 (*see also* Dobson, James; Robertson, Pat)

Merton, Thomas, 50

Metropolitan State College of Denver, 22

Michaels, Angela, 84

Michaels, Susan, 28

Miers, Harriet, 66

Milkis, Sidney, 146

Minnery, Tom, 23, 36, 143

missionaries, 27–28

mobilization of activists, 3, 16. *See also* grassroots mobilization; participatory democracy's revival among evangelicals

Moen, Mathew, 15, 50

Mooney, Chris: *The Republican War on Science*, 148

moral conflict: culture's/values' role in, 102, 106–7 (*see also* abortion debate); vs. economic interests, 7–9, 148–49, 154; inescapability of, 155–56; marginalization vs. transcendence of, 4, 18, 147–49, 155–59; New Left on, 2, 147–55, 185n2; participation vs. disaffection/alienation fostered by, 147, 150–53; and party identification/polarization, 150–51; vs. technical issues, 151–52; and tolerance, 4, 156; and value priorities, 152–53; as war, 48 (*see also* culture wars)

Moral Majority: Baptist Bible Fellowship at the core of, 128; checkbook activism of, 126–27, 154; collapse of, 123; failures/unpopularity of, 4, 38, 50–52, 54, 115–16, 121, 126–29; militancy of, 3, 46, 115–16, 121; moderates in, 53; rise of, 120

moral reasoning, 19, 39–45

moral skepticism, 2–4, 156–58

motherhood, politics of, 11, 102–7

Mutz, Diana, 159

NAACP, 131

Nader, Ralph, 150

NARAL Pro-Choice America, 34, 80, 95, 110

Nathanson, Bernard, 104–5

National Abortion Federation, 54–55, 56 (table), 57–58, 58 (table)

National Association of Evangelicals, 27–28

National Conference of Catholic Bishops (NCCB), 52

National Congregations Study (NCS), *131*, 131–32

National Election Studies. *See* NES

National Organization for Women (NOW), 34, 108

National Pro-Life Religious Council, 143–44

National Public Radio, 66

National Right to Life Committee (NRLC): on the Center for Bio-Ethical Reform, 60; deliberative norms promoted by, 25–26, 40, 50, 53; founding of, 50, 52; grassroots mobilization by, 130; membership figures for, 55; moderation in, 52–53; as nonsectarian, 37; size of, 19–20, 62, 67–68; voter guides distributed by, 130

natural law, 50

NCCB (National Conference of Catholic Bishops), 52

NCS (National Congregations Study), *131*, 131–32

NES (National Election Studies): accuracy of data from, 116, 132–33; displaying campaign buttons/stickers (1996, 1998, and 2000), 135–36, 138 (table); evangelical denomination of respondents in, 117, 182n3; identifying as a strong partisan (1996, 1998, and 2000), 140, 142 (table); identifying party differences (1996, 1998, and 2000), 140, 141 (table); influencing others to vote (1996, 1998, and 2000), 135–36, 136 (table); issues addressed by, 117; other forms of participation (1972–2004), 125, 126 (table); partisanship measures (1972–1988), 121, 122 (table); partisanship measures (1972–2004), 125–26, 128 (table); political discussions (1996, 1998, and 2000), 135, 137 (table); political-knowledge measures (1972–2004),

125, 127 (table); vote decisions (1996), 137–40, 139 (table); voter turnout (1972 election), 118, 119 (table); voter turnout of various groups (1972–1988), 120, 120 (table); voter turnout of various groups (1972–2004), 123–24, 123 (table), *124*

New Deal, 153

New Left: and authenticity, 109; and the Christian Right, 47–48, 153–55; commitment to participatory egalitarianism, 100, 109, 114; on democratic access by alienated citizens, 1–2, 115; vs. establishment liberalism, 153–54; media coverage of, 64–65; on moral conflict/ideological politics, 2, 147–55, 185n2; violent radicalist fringe of, 3–4

Newman, Troy, 56–58, 96–98

New Mexico Right to Life Committee, 41

Newport, Frank, 51, 120

New Republic, 1

newspapers. *See* media; *and specific newspapers*

New Testament, 59. *See also individual books*

New York Times, 39, 61

Niehbuhr, Reinhold, 15

Nixon, Richard, 150

NOW (National Organization for Women), 34, 108

NRLC. *See* National Right to Life Committee

Ohio Right to Life Society, 26, 28, 30, 41

O'Keefe, John (*later named* Cavanaugh-O'Keefe), 64, 105

Old Testament, 59. *See also individual books*

Olson, Mancur: *The Logic of Collective Action*, 9

OLS regressions, 133

ontologies, weak vs. strong, 156–57

Operation Rescue: collapse of, 55–56, 62–63; fines/prison sentences imposed on, 55; founding of, 26, 58; infighting in/mismanagement of, 55; media coverage of, 62–63; militant fundamentalists in, 3, 46

Operation Rescue Boston, 27, 32, 55, 86

Operation Rescue Dallas, 55

Operation Rescue Los Angeles, 55

Operation Rescue San Diego, 55

Operation Rescue West (ORW), 55, 60; abortion providers exposed/harassed by, 97–98, 106; aggressiveness promoted by, 28–29; clinics harassed/shut down by, 56–57, 96–97; deliberative norms promoted by, 27, 31–32; vs. feminists, 95; militancy of, 3, 100, 157; weaknesses of, 57–58

Operation Save America, 3, 55, 59

Opportunities for Leadership (CWA), 25

ORW. *See* Operation Rescue West

Pangle, Thomas, 7

partial-birth abortion, 35

participation: and deliberation, 3–5, 46, 159; forms of, 125, 126 (table); and moral conflict, 147, 150–53

participatory democracy's revival among evangelicals: African American participation, 118–19 (*see also* NES); alienation of evangelicals (1920–1972), 1–2, 18, 115, 117–19, 119 (table); anxieties about/withdrawal from politics by evangelicals, 116, 140–41, 144, 146; conservative vs. liberal evangelical participation, 117–19, 121 (*see also* NES); overview of, 18, 115–16; participatory revival (1992–2004), 123–26, 123 (table), *124*, 126 (table); party affiliations of evangelicals, 120–21; political action as a duty vs. a right, 140–46; political awakenings (1976–1988), 119–23, 120 (table), 122–23 (tables). *See also* grassroots mobilization

participatory freedom, 100, 108–9

parties. *See* Democratic Party; political parties; Republican Party

Parton, Julie, 24, 33

passions, moral. *See* culture wars; moral conflict

Patrick Henry College, 31, 36–37, 42

Patton, Dana, 69, 101–2

Paul (biblical figure), 2, 59

Pennsylvania Pro-Life Action League, 37, 92

Pentecostals, 66, 132

Perot, Ross, 140

1 Peter, 43

Phares, Sara, 97

Pierson, Paul, 148, 153

Planned Parenthood, 34, 49, 80, 85–88

political attitudes vs. political behavior, 113

political movements. *See* pro-choice
  movement; pro-life activism; social
  movements
political parties, 120–21, 140, 141 (table),
  150–51, 153. *See also* Democratic Party;
  Republican Party
Popkin, Samuel, 151
pornography, 36
Port Huron Statement, 109, 149
pregnancy centers: assertiveness/confronta-
  tion/acceptance by volunteers at, 29; deliberative norms promoted by, 24, 32,
  40–41; evangelical mission of, 38; media
  coverage of, 62; resources provided at,
  24; woman- vs. baby-centered, 33. *See
  also* Birthright; Care Net
Pregnancy Resource Forum (Georgetown
  University Right to Life), 81
Pregnancy Resource Ministry (Focus on
  the Family), 24, 41
premillennialism, 118
Price, Bill, 38
Probe Ministries, 36
probit regressions, 133–35
Pro-Choice Action Network, 81, 110, 112
pro-choice movement: abortion framed as
  religious issue by, 33–35; activism of,
  101; commitment to participatory freedom, 100, 108; conservatism of, 101,
  110; debate eschewed by, 80–81, 110–
  12; deliberative norms in, generally,
  100–101; dispassionate arguments of,
  vs. passionate pro-life arguments, 157–
  58; legislation favoring, 101–2; media
  bias toward, 61, 101; philosophers of,
  111; as reactionary, 101–2; response to
  images of aborted fetuses, 43; status quo
  defended by, 100–101, 110
pro-life activism, 68–99; Christian love,
  70; as the civil rights movement of
  today, 106; converts to, 103–5; counter-
  demonstrations, 91–96; deliberative
  norms encouraged in, 27, 100, 102,
  106–7, 114 (*see also under* democratic
  education in the Christian Right; sidewalk counselors); deliberative politics of,
  70–81 (*see also* Justice for All); direct action, 57–58, 70, 96–99, 103; disjointed
  politics of, 70, 81–96; on duty of political action, 143–44; and feminism, 105;
  and the fetus's ontological status, 44, 77;
  images of aborted fetuses used in, 43–

44, 47, 103–4; intellectual sophistication
  of, 44; legislation favoring, 101–2;
  marches, 88–92, 99; media coverage of,
  60–61, 63–64 (tables), 101; negative ste-
  reotypes/public image of, 26; vs. other social issues, 68–69; overview of, 17–18,
  68–70, 98–99; passionate arguments of,
  vs. dispassionate pro-choice arguments,
  157–58; pro-choice counter-demonstrations against, 91–92; pro-choice resistance to debate with, 80–81; public
  image of as negative, 100–101, 180n1;
  radical politics of, 70, 96–98 (*see also*
  rescue movement); religious arguments
  avoided in, 34–36; sidewalk counseling,
  82–88 (*see also* sidewalk counselors);
  woman- vs. baby-centered approach in,
  32–33. *See also* abortion debate
*Pro-Life Answers to Pro-Choice
  Arguments* (Alcorn), 44
Promise Keepers, 13
Protestant theology, liberal, 117
Proverbs, 27, 32, 59, 98
psychological expressivism, 7
public interest groups: checkbook activism
  of, 126–27, 154; direct mail used by, 47,
  51. *See also* New Left
public life, 108, 110
public opinion, 100, 102, 148, 151
purposive incentives, 10
Putnam, Robert, 2, 115

radicalism, Christian. *See* Christian
  radicalism
Randall, Joseph, 104
rational-choice theory, 9–10
Reagan, Ronald, 88, 120–21
Reagan Revolution, 115, 120, 125
Redeem the Vote, 145
Reed, Ralph: as Christian Coalition leader,
  65, 129, 140; on Christian duty, 142–43;
  on effective communication, 24; vs. Falwell, 54; pragmatism of, 24–25, 52; on
  stealthy grassroots mobilization, 129
religion, social scientific neglect of, 161n6
religious arguments in public forums,
  avoiding, 19, 33–39, 44–45, 169n90
Religious Coalition for Reproductive
  Choice, 34
Republican Party, 48, 120–21, 125, 146
The Republican War on Science (Mooney),
  148

rescue movement: blockades/violence against abortion clinics by, 17, 54–56, 56 (table), 58, 70; Christian radicalism in, 17, 58–59; as a cultural cause, 105–6; murder of clinic staff members, 54–55, 59; peaceful vs. violent faction of, 50, 52–56, 58–59, 64; and the politics of motherhood, 105–6; remnants of, 55–56, 70 (*see also* Operation Rescue West; sidewalk counselors)

Revell, John, 143

Rhodes, Jesse H., 146

Rhodes, Rosamund, 111

Rice, Charles, 50

Right to Life–Arizona, 34

Right to Life–Georgia, 34–35, 41

Right to Life–Michigan, 21, 37

right-to-life movement. *See* pro-life activism

Right to Life–New Mexico, 41

Right to Life–New York State, 20

Right to Life–Texas, 38, 41

Right vs. Left, 106–7. *See also* Christian Right; New Left

Rios, Sandy, 28, 144

Risen, James, 59, 64, 118

Robertson, Pat: as Christian Coalition president, 65; on Islam, 28; as a media personality, 65, 67; offensiveness/radicalism of, 22–23, 52, 65–66, 117; presidential candidacy of, 120, 123

Robison, James, 54

Roche, Lisa, 35

Rock for Life, 86–87, 90, 92–93, 105

Rock the Vote, 145

Roe v. Wade: and the fetus's ontological status, 44; moderates vs. radicals on, 82; and morality of abortion, 34; politics of, 68; protection/reversal of, 102, 155, 187n40; as restrictive vs. liberal, 155–56

Rorty, Richard, 185n2

Rosenblatt, Roger: *Life Itself*, 158

Rosenstone, Steven, 152

Rosin, Hanna, 42

Rossinow, Doug, 109

Rothenberg, Lawrence, 1

Rothenberg, Stuart, 51, 120

Rove, Karl, 146

Rozell, Mark, 15, 38, 50, 52

Salisbury, Robert, 9–10

sampling methods for research, 69–70

San Francisco, 90–91

San Francisco Chronicle, 91

Sanger, Margaret, 85

Saving Arrows, 87

Schaffer, Francis: *A Christian Manifesto*, 53

Scheidler, Joseph, 54, 56–57, 64

Schlafly, Phyllis, 53

Schlozman, Kay, 11, 148, 155

science, politicization of, 148

SDS (Students for a Democratic Society), 109

Seligman, Adam, 156

Sennett, Richard, 110; *The Fall of Public Man*, 107–8

700 Club, 65–66

Sharman, Mike, 21

Shaw, David, 61

sidewalk counselors, 82–88; African American, 85–86; boldness promoted among, 28; on Christian love, 83–84; deliberative norms promoted by, 27, 31–32; at Hope Clinic for Women, 83–86; origins of, 82; at Planned Parenthood, 85–88; public professions of faith by, 99; training/organization of, 82–83, 86, 88

Sigelman, Lee, 112

silent majority, 150

Silent No More, 90

Silent Scream, 103

Simon, William, 14

Singer, Peter, 111

Sivan, Emmanuel: *Strong Religion*, 12–13

Slater, Anne, 108–9

Smith, Christian, 51

social movements: convictions vs. moral skepticism as driving, 3–4, 158; deliberative moderation vs. violent radicalism in, 3–4; deliberative norms promoted by, 4–5, 16 (*see also* democratic education in the Christian Right); difficulties of studying, 16–17; evaluating, 4–6; nineteenth-century, 118; pragmatism of, 52

Society for Truth and Justice, 26, 95–96

sociologists: on economic interests vs. moral passions, 7–9, 148–49; on noneconomic interests as compromising deliberative ideals, 15, 154; on tolerance, 112–13, 182n47

Socratic method, 31, 60, 70, 78

Southern Baptists, 51, 132

Sparks, Kathy, 104

Stand to Reason: on avoiding religious arguments, 35; on being "normal," 30;

Stand to Reason (*cont'd*)
boldness/courage emphasized by, 28; on
Christian love and political success, 22–
23; emotionalism opposed by, 42; *Hard
Truth* shown by, 104; on images of
aborted fetuses, 43; importance of, 20;
volunteers trained by, 21–23, 71–72
status-movement theory, 7–8, 10
status quo, defense of, 100–102, 110, 114
stem cell research, 35, 39
Stimson, James, 152
Stouffer, Samuel, 112
Strong Religion (Almond, Appelby, and
Sivan), 12–13
Students for a Democratic Society
(SDS), 109
Sullenger, Cheryl, 32, 96, 103
Sullivan, John, 112
Survivors, 31, 43, 60, 94–95
Swindell, Brandi, 93–94
Swomley, John, 13–14

Tarrow, Sidney, 13
Taylor, Charles, 107
temperance movement, 3, 5–6
Terry, Randall: on civility, 26–27; on compromise, 59; at the Democratic National
Convention demonstration, 95–96; vs.
moderates in the Christian Right, 4, 59–
60; Operation Rescue founded/led by,
26, 55, 58; on premillennialism, 118;
rescue movement transformed by, 54;
Society for Truth and Justice founded
by, 26, 95. *See also* Operation Rescue
Texans United for Life, 38
theological appeals. *See* religious argu-
ments in public forums, avoiding
Thomas, Cal, 53, 144
Thomas, Judy, 59, 64, 118
Thompson, Bill, 143
Thompson, Dennis, 33, 69, 156–58
Thompson, Judith Jarvis, 111
Thoreau, David, 50
Tiller, George, 57, 96–98
tolerance: by Christians, 28–29, 47–48, 76,
128; by liberals, 47–48; religious, 8,

12–13, 26; social scientific approach to,
112–13, 182n47
Tooley, Michael, 111
Tribe, Lawrence: *Abortion: The Clash of
Absolutes*, 158

ultrasound technology, 104, 106
University of Virginia, 35, 81
USA Today, 91

values voters, 153, 155
Verba, Sidney, 11, 148, 152, 155
Virginia Democratic Party Caucus, 115
voter guides, 40, 129–32, *131*, 135–40

Wagner, Steve, 22, 30–31, 35, 44
Walker, Jack, 10
Walk for Life West Coast (San Francisco),
90–92, 113
Wallis, Jim, 148
Walzer, Michael, 15
Ward, Bryce A., 153
Warren, Mark E., 14
Warren, Mary Anne, 111
Washington Post, 14, 39, 61, 91, 109
Weathermen, 3–4
Wesley Medical Center, 98
What's the Matter with Kansas? (Frank),
8, 11, 148
White, Jeff, 94
White, Stephen, 156
Wilcox, Clyde, 15, 51–52, 66, 128
Willis, Ellen, 13
Willke, Barbara: *Abortion Handbook*, 103
Willke, J. C., 40
Wilson, James Q., 10, 16–17, 148–49, 151
Wilson, Jamia, 80
Winn, Sally, 90
Wittgenstein, Ludwig, 158
Wolfe, Alan, 112–13
Women's Health Care Services, 57, 96
women's movement. *See* feminists
Woodbridge, John D., 27

Zaller, John, 151
Zeigler, Sara, 69, 101–2